Education and theory:
strangers in paradigms

Education and theory:
strangers in paradigms

Gary Thomas

Open University Press

Open University Press
McGraw-Hill Education
McGraw-Hill House
Shoppenhangers Road
Maidenhead
Berkshire
England
SL6 2QL

email: enquiries@openup.co.uk
world wide web: www.openup.co.uk

and Two Penn Plaza, New York, NY 10121-2289, USA

First published 2007

© Gary Thomas 2007

A catalogue record of this book is available from the British Library

ISBN-13: 978 0 335 21179 1 (pb) 978 0 335 21180 7 (hb)
ISBN-10: 0 335 21179 8 (pb) 0 335 21180 1 (hb)

Library of Congress Cataloging-in-Publication Data
CIP data applied for

Typeset by YHT Ltd
Printed in Poland by OZ Graf. S.A.
www.polskabook.pl

The **McGraw·Hill** Companies

Contents

Preface

When I entered higher education as a lecturer about 20 years ago I was confused and slightly mistrustful about education academics' obsession with theory, paradigm and the 'ologies', half-thinking that this pre-occupation with the vocabulary of the philosophy of science had not a little to do with Maureen Lipman's *'You get an ology, you're a scientist!'* For those who didn't see the advertisement, a grandma (actress Maureen Lipman) is on the phone to her grandson Anthony, who has just received his GCSE results. Desultorily, he recalls two or three mediocre passes – in vocational rather than academic subjects. For Anthony this all amounts to abject failure and he confesses this to his worried-looking grandma. Then, almost worse than the performance in the vocational subjects, he pleads guilty to a pass in sociology. But grandma, suddenly delighted with this, calls to grandpa, 'An *ology*. He gets an ology and he says he's failed'. Turning back to her conversation with her grandson, she declares, 'You get an ology, you're a scientist!'

The germ of my interest lay in confusion which had strayed into mistrust and I wish I could say that I finished this book by having seen the sunlit path to understanding. But in fact I have finished more confused, albeit that my confusion is now more comprehensive and better organized. I hope that my reflections on the topic of theory will help others who have also suffered in silence on the topic and give them confidence to express their own uncertainties and doubts. Only thus will more clarity emerge about theory's meaning in education, and only thus will the use of the word – or at least the meanings to which the word is put – become more transparent. I hope that the book may be a small contribution to better understanding and richer kinds of inquiry.

I am indebted to the Leverhulme Trust and its anonymous referees for the award to me of a Leverhulme Research Fellowship on the subject of theory in education – a Fellowship that has helped considerably in my work for this book. Not many Leverhulme Fellowships are given to the field of education, and I'm deeply grateful for the support for what was ostensibly such an esoteric investigation. I am grateful also for having had the opportunity to lead an ESRC Teaching and Learning Research Programme's (TLRP) seminar series on quality in educational research, which has given the opportunity to debate and reflect on many of the issues that have arisen in this book.

I have many people to thank in putting this book together. I joined forces with David James on the work that led to Chapter 6 and it is unlikely that that work would ever have come to fruition without the synergy of our collaboration. I've never told him this, but I wish to thank Peter Vass, whose comments after reading a draft of an embryonic paper on theory gave me such confidence in it that I sent it to the most prestigious British journal in educational research, the *British Educational Research Journal (BERJ)*. In retrospect, I'm grateful to the Editors of that journal for rejecting it with such strange and contradictory comments that I was impelled to send it to an arguably equally good journal, the *Harvard Educational Review*, where it was accepted. One of the two *BERJ* reviewers was very positive, but the other said that the article was 'opinionated', as though this were in itself a satisfactory reason for rejection. The judgemental and deprecating use of 'opinionated' (as though to have opinions is in some way suspect) reminded me of the philosopher A.C. Grayling's (1997) comment that contemporary academic life has become industrialized, with an increasing tendency to produce Casaubons – 'scholarly and uninspired, ambitious and timid, scrupulous and dim-sighted'. The result is an intellectual environment in which considered dissent is increasingly rare. (The alternative take, of course – not entirely unwarranted – is in Flannery O'Connor's comment, 'Everywhere I go I'm asked if I think the university stifles writers. My opinion is that they don't stifle enough of them'). The use of 'opinionated' in one's critique as a term of censure betrays a view of knowledge as in some way separable from the unpleasant taint of the subjective. Mercifully, such naïvety is becoming rarer as research methodology is more widely discussed in educational discourse.

In fact, the peer review process conducted by *BERJ* had strange outcomes. The Editor (who happened to be a guest editor), unable to reconcile huge differences between the two reviewers' comments, took the highly unusual step of telephoning me to discuss what to do. Her first idea was that I reconsider entirely my submission of the manuscript, since, she suggested, its publication would be bad for my reputation. When I told her that I wasn't concerned about my reputation, for I felt I had to say what I had to say, her second suggestion was that I should split the article into two (which would only have made two incomprehensible articles). The peer review process engendered such frustration in me that peer review, as a discrete subject of academic interest, has stayed with me to this day.

Whenever I am writing for a journal I have two demons, one on each shoulder. The one on my right shoulder is the worst kind of peer reviewer, disagreeing with assertions that aren't supported by 100 references (and with those that are), taking offence at any narrative that is not squarely in the middle lane of orthodoxy – like Casaubon, scholarly and uninspired, ambitious and timid. The demon on my left shoulder is a faceless panel of a Research Assessment Exercise (RAE). Will they, in my worst nightmares, tut-tut at levity and come at me in their academic regalia and chanting in Latin – as a hybrid of Casaubon and McCarthy – and ask, 'Are you, or have you ever been, a contributor to a professional journal?' Fortunately, writing in a book liberates one from the fantasy fears about the imaginary peer reviewer (imaginary, since one's fears conjure up the incubus of the worst kind of reviewer, and most, fortunately, are not like this) and I have in this volume felt free to try to write accessibly (possibly succeeding less than I would have liked) and to include material that might provoke discussion. I have felt freer also at the close of the book to include material that makes suggestions for practice.

Moving back to thanks, I owe a great debt to Kanavillil Rajagopalan of the State University at Campinas, Brazil, who wrote a detailed reply to my article in the *Harvard Educational Review*, which was published in that journal and which encouraged me to think more deeply about some of the assertions that I was making. I feel much gratitude to the Editors of that journal for allowing me opportunity for a full reply to Professor Rajagopalan's response. I am indebted also to Martyn Hammersley, who, though he disagrees with me on much of what I say, provided invaluable comments on a draft of some work and has stayed remarkably friendly and helpful despite our areas of difference. Richard Pring kindly sent me a postcard from Prague on reading a review article of mine about a book on theory in special education. Receiving it reassured me that my views weren't complete nonsense (as at least one retired professor of education has told me my views are) and I'd like to thank Richard for his wit and intelligence during the friendship that has followed that postcard. Thanks also to all of those who have agreed or graciously disagreed with me informally or in seminars or correspondence and who have, whether they know it or not, helped me to shape my ideas, especially Hilary Cremin, Paul Croll, Ian Davison, Jim Donnelly, Gail Edwards, Georgina Glenny, Stephen Gorard, Ian Grosvenor, Joe Harkin, John Leach, John Lee, Ann Lewis, Andrew Loxley, Birgit Pepin, Andrew Pollard, Steve Rayner, Caroline Roaf, Ian Stronach, Jane Tarr and Peter Tomlinson. Thanks are due to all those who attended the excellent ESRC TLRP seminar series (at which many varying views were expressed), and especially those who contributed so invaluably with papers or other contributions: Steve Fuller, John Furlong, Mary James, Natasha MacNab, Terezinha Nunes, Alis Oancea, Helen Simons, Stephen Steadman, Kathy Sylva and Joe Tobin.

Parts of my articles first appearing in 67(1) and 69(1) of the *Harvard Educational Review*, and 24(2), 28(3) and 32(6) of the *British Educational Research Journal* have been adapted for inclusion in this book. I am grateful to the Editors and editorial boards of those journals for their original publication.

I'd like to thank my daughters, Kate and Emily, for occasionally asking questions about my interest in theory and forcing me to try, not very successfully, to explain it – an aim that led ultimately to the project of this book.

I am grateful to Harry Torrance, the Editor of the excellent series of which this book is a part, and Fiona Richman at the Open University Press for their confidence in the project of the book and their continual encouragement to finish it. Thanks to my partner Hilary for her insights and creativity on discussing elements of the book, for her patience and her unending support.

At various points I have – to try to self-censor any impulse to take myself too seriously – attempted humour, often in allusion to film lines. To those who don't find these funny, or who find their inclusion irreverent or off-putting, apologies.

Last, I am grateful to all of those whose ideas I have borrowed and used, always bearing in mind playwright Wilson Mizner's comment, 'Copy from one, it's plagiarism; copy from two, it's research'.

Journeys to understanding theory

If you want to get ahead, get a theory.
Karmiloff-Smith and Inhelder, 1974: 195, (without a trace of irony)

My journey to understanding theory in education began when I entered higher education as a lecturer in the mid-1980s. My new colleagues talked, often animated by what seemed to be genuine excitement and manifest sincerity, about the importance of theory. I soon appreciated that theory was central to the academic enterprise in education. At examination meetings, students' work would be discussed and marked down for not being 'located in theory'. August research councils and funding bodies would insist that research proposals engaged significantly with theory. People would talk about others' work as good or bad according to its development or use of theory.

Theory must be pretty important, I realized. In fact, it seemed almost to be the *sine qua non* of academic life in the field of education. But I didn't really understand what was meant when people used the word, though I kept my confusion to myself since I had a feeling that to speak out about my bewilderment would make me the subject of whispered derision. The concept appeared, after all, to be as clear as spring-water to my colleagues. What would my perplexity about theory say about me? So I set off to find out what theory meant and why it was thought to be so significant; my career will obviously depend on it, I thought. (That has turned out to be the case, but not quite in the way that I had anticipated.) In my previous work as a teacher and an educational psychologist I had only bumped up against the idea of theory in my academic training, as various commentators had noted its use in their writings. For example, the renowned personal construct theory psychologists, Bannister and Fransella (1971), had railed against the promiscuous use of the word 'theory' in their explication of construct theory. They said that people used the term theory to mean any mental construction around the level of an idea – and an idea is not a theory, they insisted. That revelation has stayed with me, and forms the basis of much of my position in this book: theory has to be more than mere mental organization.

Then there was the formidable psychologist Kurt Lewin (1951), who had said that there is nothing as practical as a good theory. Well, he should be right, but I've always had doubts about that rather-too-simple aphorism. Theory is certainly practical in physics, medicine, biology – it gives rise to useful practice, explanations and predictions. But in education? Theories abounded (and continue to abound) in education, and people got (and continue to get) very excited about them, but the more I looked and thought about these theories the more that it occurred to me that they weren't really theories in the sense that natural scientists talked about theory, or rather they were bounded by different kinds of constraints in the different arenas and were treated differently in each. And they weren't practical at all. Or at least they were practical in the most blatant sense – they led to practice – but that practice in the classroom or with individual children could be unhelpful or even damaging.

This is a conclusion that I still hold to, having looked at theory more and more in the intervening years since my transition from practitioner to academic (not that an academic is not a practitioner, but you know what I mean). I had already worried as an educational psychologist that Piagetian theory had led to all kinds of practical spin-offs such as 'reading readiness' (about which I heard a lot when I was an educational psychologist: 'Oh, she's not *ready* for reading yet, Mr Thomas') – spin-offs that did no service at all to children in my opinion. And there was the learning theory of B.F. Skinner, important to me as an educational psychologist, being so floriferous in practical spin-offs – from teaching machines to behaviour modification. Of course, each of these practical spin-offs has now experienced terminal decline as its unforeseen consequences have made themselves known.

Actually, I say 'unforeseen consequences', but one can't say that those consequences were unforeseen in the way that the word 'unforeseen' is usually used. Anyone with their eyes open should have been able to foresee the consequences of using this etiolated 'theory' as a basis for practice. In fact, the use of behavioural theory forms a clear example of one of the dangers of theory in education: the danger of its epistemological allure, which seems to blinker from its developers and users the almost palpable likelihood of its fallibility in practice. It was the allure of a theory that gave the silly and damaging methods that followed from behavioural 'science' their academic respectability. And what an impressive 'theoretical' pedigree behavioural 'science' had! Skinner's behaviourism had developed as a scion of logical positivism – such a sexy new theoretical domain in the modernism of the 1920s and 1930s, given added romantic caché from its provenance in the intellectual melting pot of middle-Europe. Logical positivism crystallized in the ferment of highbrow culture in Vienna at the time: one can almost imagine Rudolf Carnap, leader of the logical positivists' Vienna Circle, sipping his morning coffee to the distant strains of *Willkommen*. The logical positivists had insisted on the verification of meaningfulness through observation – not a bad idea philosophically, in fact quite exciting for a philosopher. It had all stemmed from Hume's principle of verification. We should ask of any learned work, said Hume (1748/1910), '*Does it contain any abstract reasoning concerning quantity or number?* No. *Does it contain any experimental reasoning concerning matter of fact and existence?* No. Commit it then to the flames: for it can contain nothing but sophistry and illusion'. Stirring stuff.

The trouble was that when psychologists tried to translate the latter-day philosophers' theoretical perspective on Humean verification into practice it meant that they insisted on some potty rules, for example that a child be seen to *do* something, rather than merely be noted vaguely to *enjoy* it.[1] Carnap, as an intelligent man, would no doubt turn in his grave at the knowledge that the philosophical school that he helped to pioneer had, 50 years later, provided the intellectual lead for a system of teaching that involved breaking down learning into dozens of sterile 'behavioural objectives'. That absurd system, with the idea of control unthinkingly at its centre, has of course since been readily expropriated by government and its agencies to produce a culture of aims, objectives and targets. As Onora O'Neill pointed out in her 2002 Reith Lectures (O'Neill, 2002: 46), 'Central planning may have failed in the former Soviet Union but it is alive and well in Britain today'.

So my phrase, 'anyone with their eyes open should have been able to foresee the consequences of this theory' is the key to my problem with theory (or at least one of my problems). For theory, it seems to me, closes one's eyes, or – perhaps less than this – in some way occludes one's view of the environment around. There has been a taken-for-granted assumption in education that the pursuance of theory ultimately confers improvements on practice. The consequences of the pursuance, discovery and refinement of theory by academics and by students are assumed to be in benefits for the conduct of education and for children's learning and well-being. I was coming to a different conclusion: that educational theory has nearly always led educational practice into wild goose chases and culs-de-sac.

And yet I was forced in my daily contacts with colleagues and in my reading of the academic literature of education to confront the fact that theory was universally regarded as a Good Thing and worth pursuing. Giants in the field such as Wilf Carr (1995) gave it approval, albeit in terms that emphasized its embeddedness in practice, and I somehow had to reconcile my own growing mistrust of theory with my respect for their authority. Would that I could have foreseen Carr's (2006) assertively anti-theory comments 11 years after his book *For Education*. Would that I could, in other words, been able to see that he would ultimately say,

> educational theory is nothing other than the name we give to the various futile attempts that have been made over the last hundred years to stand outside our educational practices in order to explain and justify them. And what I am going to propose on the basis of this argument is that the time has now come to admit that we cannot occupy a position outside practice and that we should now bring the whole educational theory enterprise to a dignified end.
>
> (2006: 137)

Had I been able to look into the future and know that Carr was going to revise his views so comprehensively, it would have saved me trouble, for there would have been less reconciling for me to do. Having said this, though, there is much left open following Carr's analysis, particularly surrounding his conception of theory, which to my mind is narrow – building an historical analysis of its place around its provenance mainly in the philosophy of education, yet largely uncoupling that history from a range of influences from sociology, from psychology and from inside education itself.

The King is dead. Long live the King!

'The King is dead. Long live the King!' seems essentially to be Carr's (2006) conclusion about the position of theory in education. Educators, especially academic educators, simply can't do without it and must always, like the Royal Council, have plans for the accession. The throne shall never be empty. Carr maps a distinct route of transmutations of theory from this to that, and his argument is persuasive. However, it seems to me that the journey has been more anarchic than his clean history implies, with myriad influences each contributing to the ultimate junk-sculpture.

It is worth looking in some detail at the history Carr provides for it gives an excellent narrative about the logic of educators' attachment to theory – or at least to the vocabulary of theory – during the twentieth century. In the article from which I have just quoted, Carr puts the very first spark of desire for educational theory down to a post-Enlightenment wish for social progress, which would depend on less dogma and on more rationality. He suggests that 'theory' was, at the time, the name given to the latter. Nineteenth-century educational reformers, he says, noted theory's absence from teacher education and in good post-

Enlightenment spirit set to filling the lacuna. As one of those reformers put it in 1884, 'I say boldly that what English Schoolmasters now stand in need of is *theory*; and further that the universities have special advantages for meeting this need' (Tibble, 1966: 4–5, cited in Carr, 2006). At that time, Carr says, the 'pupil–teacher method' lay at the heart of teacher education, resting in a process of apprenticeship (a process to which we have now ironically returned). As teacher education began to take place in universities at the turn of the century, this apprenticeship made way for courses in educational theory, which would – with a degree of ingenuity – find their core in historically influential philosophical texts: Socrates, Plato, Aristotle. Carr refers to the way in which Sir John Adams, the first professor of education at London University, cemented in place a rationale for such 'theory' with his books *The Evolution of Educational Theory* and *Educational Theories* (1912, 1927). The decline in the view that the 'Greats' of philosophy should provide the backbone of teacher education theory came, Carr suggests, with the advent of logical positivism mid-way through the twentieth century and the attempt of education to be more scientific. He quotes O'Connor's (1957: 7, 8) comment that 'the standards and criteria used to determine what is to count as a genuine theory in science can and should be used to judge the value of the various (and often conflicting) theories that are put forward by writers of education'. O'Connor suggested that the term theory in education was merely a 'courtesy title'. Carr notes the shift away from this restrictive view with Hirst's (1966) insistence that theory in education was a kind of 'practical theory' drawing on a range of disciplines for rational principles to guide educational activity. During the 1960s and 70s, teacher education curricula came thus to be dominated with these 'foundation disciplines' – the psychology, sociology, philosophy and history of education. That which was called 'educational theory' came to comprise the contribution of these disciplines to education. By the 1980s concerns about the lack of relevance to practice of this foundations-disciplines view of theory came to the fore – interest in practice came to supersede the foundations-disciplines view, and 'theory' came to mean various analyses of practice based on the ideas of figures such as Ryle, Gadamer, Polanyi and Oakeshott (ideas that are drawn on in the rest of this book).[2] Thus was 'personal' theory born – a term referring to these analyses of practice – developing via Stenhouse (1975) and Schön (1991) more or less to today's position: reflective practitioners employing and developing their own 'tacit theories' 'personal theories' or 'theories-in-use'.

Carr makes the point that during all of this time, essentially the twentieth century – over which 'theory' changed its meaning and its intellectual provenance and allegiance – there was no serious challenge to the idea that the practice of education should be based on theory, though he does make the point, in a footnote, that others have preceded him in his current questioning of theory, mentioning Mitchell (1985) in the humanities and my own musings (Thomas, 1997, 2002) in education. Generally, though, he notes, it is taken as received wisdom – or, rather, more than this, as too obvious for words – that theory is necessary.

The Dr Who view of theory

Before moving on in the rest of this book to outline why I feel Carr's current position to be correct (at least in relation to his views on 'personal theory'), it is worth pausing to look at where his description of theory may be taken to be limited. His mistrust of theory at this point, in 2007, based essentially on a what he calls a post-foundationalist position, finds its roots in an understanding of theory that takes the 'personal theory' form. This is all very well, and I support him in this mistrust. But it assumes that the contemporary understanding of theory is traceable in a clear lineage from first, obeisance to the Greek Greats, then to science, then to foundation disciplines, thence to 'personal theory': *a* gave way to *b*, which gave way to *c*, and so on. This is the Dr Who view of theory in education. In other words, a completely new face and body emerge at critical moments in history; only the name stays the same.

It isn't that clean, though. Theory in contemporary discourse means much more than personal theory and I shall touch on these meanings and the intellectual stables from which they have bolted as I progress through the book. Theory is *still* seen in some quarters, many quarters, as 'scientific theory' or a diluted version of such. I was talking recently to the Editor of a major journal, who told me that we need educational theory because it 'generates hypotheses' – I agree on the need for something that generates ideas, but 'theory' and 'hypothesis' set our journeying off on some less than helpful trajectories. It is *still* interpreted, often in the same paragraph, to mean wide bodies of knowledge, and more. I try to unpack some of the meanings in the following chapters. What is interesting is why this plethora of meanings should not only have survived but also prospered.

A conclusion that I have come to is that theory's pull is psychological as well as (or perhaps rather than) rational. In a field that has always had something of an inferiority complex about its academic status, theory has enormous cachet – as the cream of intellectual endeavour, the distillation of very clever people's thoughts. Its presence acts as a magnet. Carr's (2006) analysis ends with the inappropriateness of calling for theory in its current manifestation, personal theory, as if the intellectual incon- sistency involved in calling for personal theory were the only issue that 'theoriphiles' had to face. It seems to me that the sequelae of seeking and developing theory are wider.

Theory, in a broad variety of forms – that is to say, not just personal theory – seems somehow to have the power to curtain reality and the likely practical consequences of 'implementation' from the eyes of academics and practitioners who otherwise seem quite sensible. Could it not have been anticipated, returning to my earlier example, that the gross over-simplification involved in the reduction of complex learning to the 'behavioural objectives' that emerged from Skinnerian learning theory would not result in a kind of curricular desertification across education, not only in the curricula of special schools, but more widely?

Theory: intoxicant, hypnotic or hallucinogen?

When I was working as a teacher and as a psychologist, what concerned me was the distortion of thoughtful, reflective practice that theory seemed to enable. To my eyes, theory seemed to act as a kind of drug – a hybrid of intoxicant, hypnotic and hallucinogen – to otherwise sensible people in education, offering delusions about practical intervention. It didn't enable the 'reliable knowledge' that philosopher of science John Ziman (1991) suggested that theory enabled in natural scientific endeavour. In science, a model or theory may be mistaken – it may be a 'wrong' way of framing the world – but its test is in the kinds of consequence or practical knowledge that it produces, and it always produces reliable practical knowledge, or it would be dismissed. For example, Newtonian physics is now taken to be inadequate as a model for explaining the way the physical world works, having been superseded by Einsteinian physics. But the important point about it as a working theory is that for centuries it (Newtonian physics) provided a perfectly good way of producing 'reliable knowledge'. As Popper (1968: 252) notes, 'The old theory, even when it is superseded, often retains its validity as a kind of limiting case of the new theory; it still applies, at least with a high degree of approximation, in those cases in which it was successful before'.

In other words, for most practical purposes it still provides reliable knowledge, even though we now know Newtonian theory, as a way of explaining the world, to be inadequate (see also Feyerabend, 1993, for a discussion of the move from Newtonian to Einsteinian physics). No doubt the same fate awaits Einsteinian physics, but it will still produce reliable knowledge. And this is the important thing: that it produces reliable knowledge.

With education, that's not the story at all. In education, people come up with theory (or 'generate' it or 'discover' it in the aggrandizement popular among social scientists) all over the place – practical theories, personal theories, grounded theories, grand theories. These aren't measured against experience in the way that they are in the natural sciences and they go on to be used in quite unjustified ways. To make this point is not new, or at least it's not new in discussion about the social sciences: the search for theory – in the shape of the search for regularity and order – characterizes much social research and Alasdair MacIntyre has pointed eloquently to the futility of that search. In his classic *After Virtue* he says, 'the record of social scientists as predictors is very bad indeed, insofar as the record can be pieced together ... the salient fact about those [social] sciences is the absence of the discovery of any law-like generalizations whatsoever' (1985: 88). This is a point made also by Carr and Kemmis (1986: 79) in relation to the record of theory and its generation of laws specifically in education, which has, they say, been 'not very impressive'. Haack (2003) suggests gently that social scientific discoveries are hard to think of, and that one cannot really be sure that any real progress has been made. MacIntyre is less gentle in his critical vocabulary about theory in the social sciences generally, noting that in a study of 62 social science achievements presumed by leading social scientists to be 'major' (Deutsch et al., 1971), in not a single case is the predictive power of the theories in fact assessed in any way – a wise precaution, suggests MacIntyre.[3] I haven't done a systematic review, but I'd venture to suggest that the situation MacIntyre noted is very similar today, as Haack indicates. In fact, Butz and Torrey (2006: 1898), citing the earlier paper, still, 35 years on, talk about 'the fundamental challenge' of moving to useful prediction in social science.

Bateson, in his *Steps to an Ecology of Mind*, says something similar to MacIntyre:

> About fifty years of work [in the social sciences] ... have, in fact, produced ... alas, scarcely a single principle worthy of a place in the list of fundamentals. It is all too clear that the vast majority of the concepts of contemporary psychology, psychiatry, anthropology, sociology, and economics are totally detached from the network of scientific fundamentals.
>
> (1972/2000: xxvii)

One of the problems with these 'scientific fundamentals' in the human sciences is that 'theories' go from idea to application without any testing. And even when they have gone through a process of testing-in-practice and the evidence shows that they are not working, they are still believed in. This, aside from being barmy, seems to me to countermand one of the main principles of post-Popperian science: Popper suggested that theory is such a powerful and potentially volatile tool that it should be constructed in such a way that it can be falsified, and this process of falsification should be the aim of the scientific community. That's not what happens in education at all. Rarely, if ever, are there serious attempts at (a) setting up theory so that it can be falsified, or (b) falsification. In fact, the opposite is the case. Investment is made in theory as theory; the existence of theory – as theory – is satisfactory in itself to legitimize action. Not only this, but people's identity is constructed around theory – people see themselves as Piagetians, behaviourists, Marxists, critical theorists, constructors of personal theory, and so on – positions that are then defended. MacIntyre (1985: 88) had noted this also, suggesting that some of the nostrums of social science are '... so unquestionably false that no one but a professional social scientist dominated by the conventional philosophy of science would ever have been tempted to believe them'. I look into MacIntyre's critique more closely in Chapter 3.

Crude attacks on theory

So my initial confusions as to theory's meaning became more serious: they became doubts as to theory's integrity as a notion in education. And in the same way that I initially kept my confusions to myself, I now kept my doubts to myself. I kept this up for about ten years, realising that to talk about my uncertainties about theory would mark me out as a fool, a philistine or a *Daily Mail* reader (if indeed the three phenomena can be disaggregated), such was the strength and ubiquity of feeling about the importance of theory in education. Unwillingness to articulate my thoughts on the subject was compounded when there was a wave of attack in the 1990s from the press, from right-wing think-tanks and from the much disliked chief inspector of schools at the time, Chris Woodhead, on the teacher education community and its research (summarized well by Oancea, 2005). Teacher educators were taken in their research to be obsessed with theory and unconcerned with practice. I had no sympathy with these commentators, for their uninformed invective was directed, it seemed to me, at any kind of thinking about or problematization of the matters we concerned ourselves with in education. They called any of this problematizing discourse 'theory'. It seemed to me that the main concern of these commentators was to return to the halcyon days of boys in worsted shorts, girls in gingham frocks, and masters who wore leather-patched sports jackets. For them, the curriculum needed to comprise little more than the three Rs and competitive sports with lashings of ginger beer at close of play. For them – these people who had never read Harold Benjamin's allegorical tale of the dangers in education of tradition and ossification (Peddiwell, 1939) – 'theory' represented challenge to traditional values and practices, and they had no time for challenge.

It was not difficult for me to justify to myself and explain to others the difference between the criticisms of the New Right's commentators and my own. The new attacks, on closer analysis, were about more than a wish for a return to traditional values, although the latter certainly figured large in their polemic. But it was much more complicated than just this. Closer analysis revealed to me that the New Right in fact comprised two broad elements for whom theory comprised different kinds of threat. There were the neo-conservatives, who looked for traditional values and the order and authority that emerged from them, and neo-liberals who saw economic regeneration in dynamism and fluidity (see Levitas, 1986; Kavanagh, 1987; Newman and Clarke, 1994 for discussions). For both wings of the New Right, the intervention of a thoughtful academy, fomenting dissent in schools and instilling seditious thoughts in the minds of teachers was to be resisted since such stirring, such thought – such 'theory' – managed the simultaneous feat of threatening tradition (for the neo-conservatives) while also suggesting the horrors of regulation and control (for the neo-liberals). This unlikely alliance made for regular and coordinated attacks on what was assumed to be educational theory during the high days of the New Right's influence in the 1980s and 90s.

The origins of theory's kudos

I knew that my own worries about theory had nothing to do with the Right's. The origins of theory's high place and prestige in education were more complex, I felt. As I have already noted, I at first assumed, perhaps ungenerously, that the desire for theory came from a need among academic educators to associate themselves with that which seemed epistemologically secure (with a corollary concern that the epistemological cachet attaching to theory in other disciplines offered no grounds for theory's elevation in education). It seemed to me that educators, and social scientists more generally, wanted to associate with the big boys and girls in the natural sciences, who enjoyed such kudos in the knowledge stakes. Natural scientists had shown such real advances that educators and social scientists wanted to borrow their epistemological tools, and theory held pride of place in the natural scientists' tool-shed.

Natural scientists not only found things out that made a difference, but they enjoyed almost shamanic status. Stephen Hawking's *Brief History of Time*, with its incomprehensible stuff about gluons and bosons, sold a million even though it was unreadable. In the absence of belief in a deity, people appeared to have succumbed to believing in science. In place of the Bible, books like Hawking's had become what has been called 'scibles': a new form of scientism had emerged based not on science's rigour but on its magic and mystique. Science – from being during most of the twentieth century the repository of an optimistic hybrid of

Enlightenment hope and the Whig view of history (i.e. everything is getting better and better) – had changed position to become a new object of worship. This phenomenon, far from stimulating study among social scientists into the phenomenon itself, instead invigorated attempts to associate with the allure and prestige of science and its methods. There came a resurgence in calls for education and other social sciences to become more 'scientific' in their methods, with an accompanying rhetorical subscription from government for more 'evidence-based practice' (see Thomas and Pring, 2004).

In fact, though, the essence of science is not in a method or set of methods, as I try to make clear in Chapters 2 and 3. It is in the inter-rogative disposition, uncertainty and doubt. Whether this is expressed, as the great biologist J.B.S. Haldane (1965) expressed it, as 'the duty of doubt' or whether it takes the Popperian form of constructing one's theories in such a way that they are 'falsifiable' is relatively unimportant. What is important is the questioning attitude in moving forward one's ideas and the taken for given that one's knowledge is tentative. It is the taking of the new, the unexpected, the anomalous and using it to challenge existing schemata. The setting-up of theory in education seemed to me to represent the epistemological opposite: the desire for a security blanket for one's knowledge, and of course security blankets are difficult to relinquish. Contrary to its proper use in natural sciences, theory seemed to me to be set up more as intellectual stockade than tentative thinking tool. Haldane called for 'a little more thought and a little less belief' and theory's use in education seemed to me to be going against this helpful maxim.[4]

So, I felt that the century-long wish to be more like the natural sciences had not been entirely supplanted by new theory-forms in 'practical theory' or 'personal theory' as Carr (2006) suggested. In fact, the desire to be scientific represented a powerful undertow in the continuing desire for theory (a theme addressed in Chapters 2, 3 and 4) but one that was nevertheless misrepresented. I now feel that the repeated call for theory has more faces to it than this alone, and this complexity is, in part, what this book addresses.

The core of theory: from generalization to conceptual hop-scotch

The celebrated sociologist Howard Becker (1998: 3), in mentioning his university tutor, Everett C. Hughes, talks about Hughes's difficulty with the notion of theory and theorizing, suggesting that 'theorizing' for Hughes consisted of 'a collection of generalizing tricks he used to think about society, tricks that helped him interpret and make general sense of data'. (The extent to which one can use such 'tricks' or rules of thumb is explored in Chapter 7.) The question for the researcher in education is whether the generalizations manufactured out of educational research (and educational theory based on it) are better than those that emerge from, for example, 'common interpretive acts' (see Schatzman, 1991), or whether such generalizations in fact deserve the epistemological medal of 'theory'.

This theme of generalization arises frequently in the discussion of theory. Look at what the philosopher of education, Scheffler says,

> Theory is a creative and individualistic enterprise that goes beyond the data in distinctive ways, involving not only generalization, but postulation of entities, deployment of analogies, evaluation of relative simplicity, and, indeed, invention of new languages. Experience is relevant to knowledge through providing tests of our theories; it does not automatically generate these theories, even when processed by the human mind. That we have the theories we do is, therefore, a fact, not simply about the human mind, but about our history and our intellectual heritage.
>
> (1967: 122)

Generalization is at the knub of this definition. But the key words for me in this passage are the 'not only' appearing just before the 'generalization', for Scheffler does what most in education and the social sciences do: he immediately wants to broaden the ambit of theory. Theory becomes a conceptual poltergeist, jumping unpredictably all over the furniture – not only generalizing but postulating, analogizing, evaluating, but even inventing new languages. Whether it is useful for one word to encapsulate such a lot of different kinds of conceptual endeavour is one of the principal questions I shall ask in this book.

Unusually for anyone discussing theory, the psychologists Hall and Lindzey proffer some quite detailed discussion of what is meant by theory in their textbook *Theories of Personality* (1978). They clearly feel it is valuable to discuss the meaning and uses of theory before they begin on the substantive matter of their volume. They start by saying, 'There is by no means complete agreement concerning all of the issues' (p.10) concerning the meaning of theory. Well, you can say that again. In fact you can say that there is no agreement *at all* concerning *any* of the issues, or even agreement on what the issues (p. 10) are. In fact, there is little discussion about the need for agreement, since there are rarely identified any issues about which agreement is needed. They do, however, go on to make some important points concerning theory in the social sciences and particularly in their field, psychology. They start by saying that

> theories are not 'given' or predetermined by nature, the data, or any other determinant process. Just as the same experiences or observations may lead a poet or novelist to create any one of a multitude of different

art forms, so the data of investigation may be incorporated in any of countless different theoretical schemes. The theorist in choosing one particular option to represent the events in which he or she is interested is exercising a free creative choice that is different from the artist's only in the kinds of evidence upon which it focuses and the grounds upon which its fruitfulness will be judged. We are emphasizing here the creative and yet arbitrary manner in which theories are constructed and this leads naturally to the observation that we can specify how a theory should be evaluated or appraised but we cannot specify how a theory should be constructed. There is no formula for fruitful theory construction any more than there is a formula for making enduring literary contributions.

(1978: 1–11)

This is a valuable observation. They go on to note that theory is not inevitable or prescribed by known empirical relations. A theory emerges from a choice made by the theory maker. This quality, they say, 'emphasizes the lack of appropriateness of truth or falsity as attributes to be ascribed to a theory. A theory is only useful or not useful' with usefulness defined by how well the theory generates 'predictions or propositions concerning relevant events that turn out to be verified' (1978: 10–11).

Their discussion represents a scientific model of theory construction and use, a model that has been comprehensively critiqued in the human sciences by MacIntyre, whose criticisms I have touched on already, and will go into in more detail in Chapter 3. But let us stay for a while on the discussion of Hall and Lindzey, for they do what so many do when they lift the lid on theory discourse, or what Stanley Fish (1989) has called 'theory-talk' (of which more later). They say,

It is important to distinguish between what may be called the systematic and the heuristic generation of research. It is clear that in the ideal case the theory permits the derivation of specific testable propositions and these in turn lead to specific empirical studies. However, it is also manifest that many theories, for example, Freud's and Darwin's, have had a great effect upon investigative paths without the mediation of explicit propositions. This capacity of a theory to generate research by suggesting ideas or even by arousing disbelief and resistance may be referred to as the heuristic influence of the theory. Both types of influence are of great importance ...

A second function that a theory should serve is that of permitting the incorporation of known empirical findings within a logically consistent and reasonably simple framework. A theory is a means of organizing and integrating all that is known concerning a related set of events. An adequate theory of psychotic behavior should be able to arrange all that is known concerning schizophrenia and other psychoses in an understandable and logical framework. A satisfactory learning theory must embrace in a consistent manner all the dependable findings dealing with the learning process. Theories always commence with that which has thus far been observed and reported and in this sense begin in an inductive phase and are guided and to some extent controlled by what is known. However, if the theories did nothing more than make consonant and orderly what was presently known they would serve only a very minor function. Under such circumstances the dogged investigator would be justified in the conviction that theories are mere verbal fluff floating in the wake of the experimenter who has done the real business of science. The empiricist who insists that theories are mere after-the-fact rationalizations of what the investigator has already reported fails to appreciate the main function of the theory – which is to point out new and, as yet, unobserved relations. The productiveness of the theory is tested before the fact not after the fact.

(1978: 13)

In these two paragraphs we see some of the main problems of theory for the social sciences, for in the fascinating tour on which Hall and Lindzey take us we go on a conceptual hop-scotch. Two ideas are presented: first, that theory can be heuristic, that is merely to say productive or useful, rather like a tool, in generating ideas for testing; second, that theory is a kind of Heath Robinson contraption – a cross between vacuum cleaner and card-index file, sucking up ideas and then sorting them and accounting for them.

Although it is untidy as a way of understanding theory, it's worth running with the exegesis of Hall and Lindzey for a while, for in it we see some of the problems of allowing theory to mean so many things. In the heuristic notion of theory they put forward is the idea that theory is valuable in its capacity 'to generate research by suggesting ideas or even by arousing disbelief and resistance'. They conflate Darwin's and Freud's theories in making this point. They are saying, as many say, that theory – folk theory, myth or accurate model – generates ideas and is thus to be welcomed. Well, we can all generate ideas that may arouse disbelief, but the difference between a theory in the sciences (e.g. Darwin's) and one in what Popper (1977: 264) calls the pseudo-sciences (e.g. Freud's) is in the nature of the evidence adduced in support or refutation of the theory. Popper suggests that so called theorists in a pseudo-science can interpret 'any conceivable event as a verification of their theories' (p. 264). His claim is that a theory is scientific if and only if it is *falsifiable* by empirical evidence:

the acceptance by science of a law or of a theory is tentative only; which is to say that all laws and theories are conjectures, or tentative hypotheses (a position which I have sometimes called 'hypotheticism'); and that we may reject a law or theory on the basis of new evidence.

(Popper, 1953/1974)

But if the evidence constitutes 'any conceivable event' as Popper suggests, there is no way of falsifying the theory. The need for falsification is entertainingly described in the physicist Wolfgang Pauli's quip about scientific work that he took to be unworthy of consideration. Pauli had three levels of insult for what he saw as bad science: 'Wrong!', 'Completely wrong!' and 'Not even wrong!' – the last meaning that the work couldn't even be shown to be wrong.[5] In psychoanalysis, and much the same could be said of much supposedly theoretical endeavour in education, there is no way of falsifying the putative theory. It is *not even wrong*. Even if natural scientists cannot lay claim to some particular and discrete methods of discovery (something I discuss as the book progresses), they work within certain parameters of expectation about the generalizability of their theories. Whether, as Fuller (2003) suggests, those parameters are set individually as in the Popperian model, or by the broader community, as in the Kuhnian model, is less important than the fact that they exist.

Let me return to the idea of theory as a generalization with predictive power. It is one raised by MacIntyre, who suggested in his seminal work *After Virtue* (1985), that this conception of social science has dominated the philosophy of social science for two hundred years. According to the standard account, suggests MacIntyre, the aim of the social sciences is to explain social phenomena by supplying generalizations that do not differ in their form from those applicable to natural phenomena in general. MacIntyre's assessment of the achievement of the social sciences here, though, is damning, as I have already noted. Pring (2000: 125) makes much the same point, specifically about education, when he says that 'Claims to "theory", especially in education, are often rather spurious because they are expressed so vaguely or blandly that it is not at all clear what would count as evidence against them'.

Why should social scientists, and in particular educators, want to generalize in this way? This is a question that I examine in more depth in Chapter 3, but suffice it to say for now that it is a subject about which Donald Schön has made interesting contributions. In the following quotation from one of his lectures, he draws a valuable distinction between knowledge as it is used in everyday life and knowledge as it is seen in schools. Knowledge in school, he notes, is formalized in the way that it is not in everyday life, and this formalization, he seems to feel, has not a little to do with the way that theory is elevated in the academic community of education:

> The categorization of knowledge in terms of a category like 'tool,' as distinct from the ordinary, familiar coherences of objects as they go together in our everyday life, is what I mean by the formal categorical character of knowledge. And it *is* one of the key features that separates schools from life. The ways in which things are grouped together, the way in which things are treated as similar and different, are not the way

in which they are grouped and treated as similar and different in our ordinary life experiences. There is also, in this view of school knowledge, the notion that the more general and the more theoretical the knowledge, the higher it is. I remember once being quite recently at a school of education, and a graduate student was in a seminar that I was doing, and she was working with nurses, and she said something I thought was interesting. And I asked her if she would give me an example. And she then gave me a proposition which was just as general as the first proposition. So I asked again for an example, and she gave me a proposition which was just slightly less general. And I asked again, and I finally got an example. And I asked her afterwards if she thought it was strange that it took three or four tries to get an example, and she said she did think it was strange, and she didn't understand why she'd done that. And I think it is because she had been socialized to an institution where, tacitly and automatically, we believe that the only thing that really counts and the only thing that's really of value is *theory*, and the higher and the more abstract and the more general the theory, the higher the status it is. Under such conditions it's very difficult to give more or less concrete examples.

(1987)

Schön's observation is by no means new. In Chapter 2 I comment on how Dewey (1920) expressed his concern about theory in education, saying that what was needed instead of general theory was more specific inquiries into a multitude of specific structures and interactions in education. It seems to me that Schön and Dewey are saying much the same here, namely that we should inhibit a first impulse to attempt to make abstract, to generalize, to find principles, to synthesize and predict on the basis of the synthesis. All of these restrain our capacity to examine the individual, the idiographic. The impulse to make abstract curtails any immediate desire to look more deeply at the individual situation (in Schön's example of the teacher in the classroom) and to reflect on that situation in order to improve practice. They are both saying much the same as the French revolutionary, Louis Saint-Just (1976): 'Too many laws, too few examples'.

Crosby (1993: 5–6), in a classic work on European expansion across the world, says much the same about his own work in the humanities:

Let us begin by applying to the problem what I call the Dupin technique, after Edgar Allan Poe's detective, C. Auguste Dupin, who found the invaluable 'Purloined Letter' not hidden in a bookbinding or a gimlet hole in a chair leg but out where everyone could see it in a letter rack. A description of the technique, a sort of corollary to Ockham's razor, goes like this: Ask simple questions, because the answers to complicated questions probably will be too complicated to test and, even worse, too fascinating to give up.

Much the same applies in education. Many of the questions we would like to ask are too complex for satisfactory answer, and it is here that theory is so tempting. We are tempted to oversimplify, generalize and theorize; tempted as Barrett (1978: 149) suggested to 'twist' experience so that it fits our framework. So, to go back to the Dupin technique, let us ask simple questions and use simple methods – let us realize that most of the evidence is in front of us, not concealed; let us *read* the letter (by all means reading between the lines), but go no further than this (and certainly not attempt graphology).

* * *

This book, then, represents a taking forward of the journeys in understanding that I have just touched on. I begin by looking at what theory is, and what use it is in education and by examining some theoretically significant influences on educational thought and practice in the twentieth century. In doing this, I shall explore the nature of the theories in question and examine their status and legitimacy as theories. To do this, I shall compare theory and theoretical analysis in education with that in the humanities and the natural sciences. I look at the arguments of those who have claimed that theory in fields like education is in fact a misnomer: that theory, whether 'personal theory' or 'grand theory' is not really theory at all. I shall argue that the elevation and privileging of theory has as its most serious effect the downplaying and relegation of practice, for its potential for distortion of educational practice is manifold. My contention is that such distortion has indeed occurred over the twentieth century and that it is time for a discussion and appraisal of theory's origins in education and its consequences – time for discussion about how values, evidence and ideas can more straightforwardly guide educational practice.

All of this, I believe, has significance for researchers, tutors, teachers and students of education, all of them inducted in the belief that theory is a *sine qua non* of scholarship and personal development. Whether one uses theory as a platform for further research (in testing or developing it), or as a validation for doing qualitative research (in 'discovering' it), or whether one sees it as the core of personal development (in formulating 'personal' or 'practical' theory), it is taken to be essential. I believe that these different formulations about the meaning of theory, juxtaposed with the high status given to theory in most methodological deliberation confuses students and researchers, much in the way that I described my own confusions at the beginning of this chapter.

Throughout my discussion I draw upon ideas about the nature of tacit knowledge, 'know-how', everyday knowledge in practice, and I conclude on the benefits of more 'bricolage' in enquiry: the need as I see it to trust in the reflective lessons which emerge from one's practice. In the penultimate chapter I make a case study of 'grounded theory' to bring together points of discussion from earlier in the book and in particular here, I look at the methodological accompaniments of what goes under the name of theory. I exemplify some of this discussion in the final chapter with some self-critical discussion of my own research, focusing on the benefits that may come from having confidence in one's own straightforward understandings.

Notes

1 Interestingly, Einstein, having flirted with logical positivism, rejected the significance of observability – even in physics (as distinct from psychology or education). In a letter to Karl Popper (Popper, 1968: 458) he says, 'I really do not like at all the now fashionable "positivistic" tendency of clinging to what is observable'. He goes on to say that in physics 'theory cannot be fabricated out of the results of observation ... it can only be invented' (p.458).
2 One of the messages of this book is that these analyses have been mistakenly referred to as 'theory'.
3 It is interesting to note that psychoanalysis and Rorschach tests were taken by Deutsch et al. at the time to be 'substantial contributions' (1971: 457). See Wood et al. (2003) for contemporary assessment and comprehensive critique of Rorschach.
4 Hammersley (2005b) questions the primacy of doubt. Noting that a willingness to be sceptical is important, he goes on to say that the academic's function should not be to doubt everything or to attack cherished beliefs for the sake of it. (Interestingly, Marx's favourite maxim is reputed to have been *De omnibus dubitandum*: One ought to question everything).
5 See Peierls (1960: 186) for reminiscence on Pauli: 'a friend showed him the paper of a young physicist which he suspected was not of great value but on which he wanted Pauli's views. Pauli remarked sadly "It is not even wrong" '.

2

What's the use of theory in education?

Researchers in the social sciences have, within arms' reach, just at their fingertips, preconstructed facts which are wholly fabricated: so many terms, so many subjects. At conferences, you can listen to these preconstructed concepts being exchanged, dressed up in theoretical tinsel, and having the air of scientific facts.

(Bourdieu, 1992: 42)

I should start this chapter by saying that its title isn't one of those questions that pretends naïvety, only to present you ultimately with the right answer, namely, that there really are *lots* of uses to theory in education. That's not the purpose at all. The question is genuinely put. I really am seriously wanting to question the purpose of theory in education.

The question needs asking because theory holds a central place in educational inquiry. Tutors exhort students to embed their work in it; grant-giving bodies demand that research proposals be contextualized in it; at conferences on educational research its importance is asserted and reasserted; complete journals are devoted to its discussion. Some commentators have even claimed that what they call 'atheoretical research' in education is impossible. Non-theoretical research seems taboo for the research community in education.

The allure of theory is puzzling given that a developing theme of contemporary commentary on methods of inquiry has concerned theory's fragility – not its utility. Despite the emergence of strong anti-theoretical strands in contemporary thought in the humanities and social sciences (and to an extent in the natural sciences), the reputation of theory in education persists with its lustre untarnished. My aim in this chapter is therefore to examine the tenacity with which education adheres to theory.

I seek reasons for this tenacity partly in the absence of a community language system by which educational researchers and academics understand theory; the word has a multiplicity of meanings popularly constructed for it. The thesis I shall put is that theory has come loosely to denote intellectual endeavour, and in such benign garb it has been awarded unwarranted acclaim. Many kinds of thinking and heuristics have come to be called theory. But why should they be entitled to this guise? It is rather like wanting to call a pig a cat. A cat is certainly a more elegant animal than a pig, but this is no reason to call one's pig a cat. The point I shall try to make in this chapter is that theory, if it is to be used and defended seriously, cannot describe *any kind* of intellectual endeavour.

I contend that the allure of theory – and the desire of educators to call their ideas 'theory' – rests historically on its success in other fields, most notably natural science. It was from this success that theory drew its epistemological legitimacy. Many educators appeared to have at the back of their minds the idea that theory represented the clearest distillation of intellectual endeavour; the conceptual and epistemological cream of the various disciplines from which it had been borrowed. But my argument is that these successes provide no good reason for contemporary education's romance with theory. The domains in which theory has been useful find no congruence in education. Indeed those domains where theory is valuable are more limited than one might imagine, and I plead for more of the methodological anarchy which Feyerabend (1993), the iconoclastic philosopher of science, pleaded for scientific research.

Theory's acquired potency for bestowing academic legitimacy is troublesome, for it means that particular kinds of endeavour in educational inquiry are reinforced and promulgated, while the legitimacy of other atheoretical kinds is questioned or belittled.[1] Educational inquiry is thus distorted; within educational inquiry strange interstices are created by the hegemony of theory.[2] I argue that theory – of any kind – is thus a force for conservatism, for stabilizing the status quo through the circumscription of thought within hermetic sets of rules, literatures, procedures and methods; seen in this way, theory – far from being emancipatory as some have claimed (e.g. Carr, 1995), or a vehicle for 'thinking otherwise' (Ball, 1995) – is in fact an instrument for reinforcing an existing set of practices and methods in education.

In the sub-sections of this chapter I look first at the problem of the meaning of theory in education by outlining a number of ways in which the word is used, and ideas about theory thereby confused, in particular a distinction between grand theory and personal theory is drawn.[3] I go on to suggest that theory circumscribes methods of thinking about educational problems and that it inhibits creativity among researchers, policy makers and teachers. This case is made both for personal theory and for grand theory and I give case studies of theory construction and theory use which I consider to have influenced practice in education for the worse. I finally make a case for *ad hocery* rather than theory, arguing that creativity and progress are rarely the fruit of theory and more often the product of anarchy in thought.

What is theory in education?

Some words become so flexible that they cease to be useful ... Like an amoeba they fit into almost any interstice of the language.

(Illich, 1979: 32)

As I noted in Chapter 1, any superficial examination (or, indeed, detailed examination) of educational literature discloses little consensus about the meaning of theory. There is no bond between 'theory' and the constellation of meanings it has acquired. The reader or listener, when encountering the word, is forced to guess what is signified by the word through the context in which it is applied.

But the problem for the reader or listener is different from that facing the reader who has to interpret the meaning of 'red' in reading about a red rose or a red herring. There, context tells the reader or listener something unequivocal. Yet the meaning of 'theoretical' is given scant distinction by the contexts in which it may be found in educational discourse: a theoretical article has no *a priori* distinction from a theoretical view, a theoretical background or a theoretical position. I have no way of knowing what the speaker intends to convey when the signifier 'theoretical' is used in any of these contexts. Given the importance attached to theory in education, the relation of signifier to signified is worryingly unstable, and it is this relation I shall attempt to begin to disentangle in the first part of this chapter.

Defining theory is a problem, and given the significance attached to theory, this is serious, since the message from commentators such as Ball (1995) is that while theory is essential, we must be discriminating in our selection of theory. 'Will any theory do?' Ball asks, and answers himself emphatically 'I think not!', warning against 'theory by numbers' (p. 268). Others have made similar warnings: the historian Namier (1955) has dismissed general social theories as 'flapdoodle'.

This seeming ambivalence about what counts as Good Theory, and what should be discounted as Bad Theory is confusing for students of education, for education abuts a range of different kinds of theory: learning theory, attribution theory, Freudian theory, Rawls's theory of justice, critical theory, activity theory, personal theory, practical theory or Marxist theory, to name just a few. Even chaos theory is taken by LeCompte (1994) to be a valid source from which to draw. Education may attempt a theory of instruction. Sociologists such as Glaser and Strauss (1967) who have questioned traditional development of theory and its uses have nevertheless shown a loyalty to the notion of theory and have attempted to develop grounded theory (of which more in Chapter 6). More recently, students of education have been encouraged to develop their own personal or practical theories.

Pring gives a lucid account of this variety and its frailties. He first notes,

> 'Theory' would seem to have the following features. It refers to a set of propositions which are stated with sufficient generality yet precision that they explain the 'behaviour' of a range of phenomena and predict what would happen in future. An understanding of those propositions includes an understanding of what would refute them – or at least what would count as evidence against their being true. The range of propositions would, in that way, be the result of a lot of argument, experiment and criticism. They would be what have survived the constant attempt to refute them. But they would always be provisional.
>
> (2000: 124–5)

He notes that with this sort of quasi-scientific notion (my characterization, not his), the more wide-ranging the theory the better. It is difficult, though, to assess the validity of a 'theory' such as this, since, he says, it is difficult to know in education what may count as evidence against it. It is also difficult because exceptions cause problems (as MacIntyre noted in all of social science, a problem I examine further in Chapter 3). Pring proceeds to discuss theory in relation to practice:

> First, theory supposes that one can express propositionally one's understanding of that which is to be researched into. Second, those propositions are expressed in such a way that they can be hypothesized and put to the test against experience. Third, the interpretation of those tests and that experience can be examined critically by others in the light of the data. Fourth, although it is desirable to make one's theories as all embracing as possible, it is often necessary to be satisfied with small-scale and rather tentative and provisional theoretical positions. Fifth, therefore, the growth of knowledge lies in the constant formulation of the assumptions and beliefs and in the criticism of these in the light of evidence or their implications.
>
> (2000: 125)

But, he goes on, there is something 'wrong about theory being formulated prior to practice and as a well formulated guide to practice ... Theory and practice are not necessarily related in this way' (2000: 126). Because practice is infinitely complex it must always be bound up with the teacher's beliefs, values, experience and context, and this 'might or might not be called theory, depending on the level of reflection or articulation' (2000: 126). So 'No practice stands outside a theoretical framework – that is, a framework of interconnected beliefs about the world, human beings and the values worth pursuing, which could be expressed propositionally and subjected to critical analysis' (2000: 127). Certain kinds of 'theory', Pring appears to be saying, are untenable. What remains are sets of beliefs and values – or 'personal theory', which I shall discuss in more detail later.

To begin to understand how students of education might divine the meaning of theory (and whether the meaning they come up with gets the seal of approval from academics), given these many and varied uses, one can do no better than to go to a popular textbook on educational research to see how academic discussion has been synthesized. Cohen and Manion (2000: 12) provide one such. They say that while theories in the natural sciences 'are characterized by a high degree of elegance and sophistication', educational theory is 'only at the early stages of for-mulation and ... thus characterized by great unevenness'.

These comments, if unpacked, exaggerate rather than attenuate the definitional burden which I set out to lighten. The opposition of 'elegance and sophistication' to 'unevenness' betrays the expectations of the wri-ters about the nature of theory. Indeed, the positing of this opposition falls into the trap of what Medawar (1974) has called 'poetism', namely the adoption of a theory because of its elegance, attractiveness or romantic appeal.[4] Theory in its purest form, they seem to be saying, should be precise and succinct, like scientific theory. The 'thus char-acterized' between 'only at the early stages of development' and 'unevenness' reveals the authors' judgement that unevenness is unde-sirable. Unevenness will with time, they appear to say, be ironed out. The conclusion to be drawn by the reader is that evenness in theory – and by extension smoothness, elegance – is desirable.

'Unevenness' perhaps is serving as a euphemism for confusion, which makes itself manifest in two definitions of theory Cohen and Manion (2000: 15) offer. The first, from Kerlinger (1970), says that theory is 'a set of interrelated constructs, definitions, and propositions that presents a systematic view of phenomena by specifying relations among variables, with the purpose of explaining and predicting the phenomena'. The other (from Mouly, 1978) says that 'theory is a convenience – a neces-sity, really – organizing a whole slough of facts, laws, concepts, constructs, principles into a meaningful and manageable form'. This latter is similar to O'Connor's, 'a set or system of rules or a collection of precepts which guide or control actions of various kinds', quoted by Hirst (1993: 149).

Now, the definitions of Kerlinger on the one side and Mouly and O'Connor on the other do not simply lack congruence. Rather, they describe intellectual processes as different as chalk and cheese. The first acknowledges theory's traditionally held purposes of explanation and prediction in science, while the latter could be said to take a tool-shed view: theory is a repository – a way of tidying the various bodies of knowledge and analytical instruments which might be used in education. The first is active, while the latter is passive.

However, it is true to say that each definition does provide a satisfactory descriptive account of a way in which theory is sometimes used (as a word) in education. If this is the case, there is a serious problem. 'Theory' as a word must be one thing or another. It cannot – if it is to be used seriously to describe a particular kind of intellectual construction in education – have two or more meanings, unless the context in which it is used can universally and unequivocally distinguish those meanings. If we are to understand what 'pipe' means, the word must refer only to that class of objects normally thought of as pipes; it must not also refer to dogs, vacuum cleaners and trees. And if 'pipe' does happen to be inconvenient enough to refer, as my dictionary tells me it does, to a musical wind instrument, to a tube or to the note of a bird, I can be confident that the context – sentence, paragraph or longer passage – will disambiguate and furnish the right meaning. I cannot be so sure with 'theory'. For it is my contention that the context cannot distinguish the strong colours of meaning that alter with use of 'theory', since the users themselves are rarely aware of the meaning they intend.[5]

For the situation is indeed far more complex than Cohen and Manion describe. The broad-ranging definitions they offer are insufficient to explain what is popularly meant by theory in education and a further disentangling of meanings is necessary.

Let us take another text-book definition. Bryman and Cramer (1994: 2), for instance, say that, 'Theories in the social sciences can vary between abstract general approaches (such as functionalism) and fairly low-level theories to explain specific phenomena (such as voting behaviour, delinquency, aggressiveness)'. Note, again, the opposition of adjectives such as 'abstract' and 'low-level'. There seems to be the feeling that theories which are to be awarded high marks are those which are refined, parsimonious, elegant and capable of wide application. On the other hand, theories which still need a bit of work done on them are those that are capable of applicability only in a narrow range of cases.

However, an examination of text-book definitions does not complete a deconstruction of popular meaning. There is a widely held view, for instance, that theory is anything that isn't practice: a simple theory–practice continuum is implied. Theory is at one end of the continuum; practice is at the other. When theory is used in this way – as the opposite of practice – it seems to be used to convey not merely child development theory or Marxist theory (for example) but, more generally, book learning and speculation. This undifferentiated nexus of mental activities appears to be put forward as the opposite of doing and learning-on-the-job. The notion is a powerful one, shared even by academics. Skinner (1990), for example, even suggests that those whom he calls the 'anti-theorists' of post-modernism[6] are in fact 'the grandest theorists of current practice'. This perplexing assertion is supported by no more than the fact that these individuals (Wittgenstein, Feyerabend, Foucault, Derrida) have done a lot of critical thinking – and thinking has apparently come to be congruent with theorizing. If 'theory' really can mean any kind of intellectual endeavour (and 'theorizing' any kind of thinking) then one would be forced to accept that any conjoining of words is a theoretical enterprise, and even that this book is a theoretical one – I discuss this further in Chapter 3.

Defenders of theory in education also take this expansive view that theory means any kind of structured reflection. Carr, for example, prior to the revisions to his thinking articulated more recently (Carr, 1995, 2006) suggested that the ambit of theory encompassed a wide range of critical activity concerned with 'intellectual resources'. He worried about a concern over the relation of theory to practice and the discontinuity between the two in education. The problem, he felt, was attributable to the fact that educational theory has in the past been seen as an attempt to derive practical principles from general philosophical beliefs, and more recently to a Hirstian belief that educational theory should draw on various forms of knowledge, particularly history, philosophy and the social sciences. Carr said that this was mistaken; that educational theory does not have to conform to conventional criteria of academic legitimacy, but should rather demonstrate 'a capacity to explore a particular range of problems in a systematic and rigorous manner' (Carr, 1995: 32). In dismissing the relevance and utility of traditional notions of theory, there seemed to be the attempt here to rescue the word 'theory' from its past and apply it to simple, critical reflection and thinking. But why the temptation to call this 'theory'? Why not use simpler terms? More recently, Carr has revised his views on theory. He now states that those who discuss and promote theory 'no longer appear as contributors to some timeless philosophical argument about how educational theory is to be conducted and understood but as the unconscious inheritors of a flawed intellectual project whose faulty presuppositions were to ensure its eventual and inevitable demise' (2006: 137). More of the revisions in Carr's thinking later.

The foregoing only begins to unravel the multiple meanings of theory in educational discourse. A useful overview is provided by Chambers (1992), who asserts that he can distinguish no fewer than nine meanings. First, he says, there is theory contrasted with fact; here theory is used simply to mean a hunch, a loose explanatory idea. Second, there is theory as the opposite of practice, as I have already described. Third, theory may be used to mean evolving explanation; he gives Bruner's

Theory of Instruction as an example. What is meant here is an accumulating body of knowledge which, in contrast to scientific theory, has become more diffuse (not more precise and succinct, note) as it has tried to accommodate more facts. Bannister and Fransella (1971) liken such theories to stalactitic growths, which have accumulated over the years. This kind of theory is closest to the grand theory about which Wright Mills (1959) objected.

Fourth, he identifies practical theory, by which he (or at least those who use it this way) means reflective practice; this is what Carr (1995) was referring to, and what Hirst (1993: 152) refers to when he says, 'Any adequate account of educational theory must, I now consider, reject more firmly than I once saw certain central tenets of rationalism in favour of a more complex theory of rational action'.

Fifth, theory is taken to have a cluster of meanings surrounding the idea of hypothesis, model or heuristic. Sixth, theory may mean presupposition: a set of orienting principles or epistemological presuppositions. Seventh, he suggests that people may be talking about what he calls normative theory – a clearly developed argument that has evolved under the pressure of rigorous criticism; Rousseau's individualism is given as an example. Eighth, there is empiricist theory, which seems to be the equivalent of craft knowledge, or the accumulation of technical knowledge through doing (see Naughton, 1981, for a discussion of craft knowledge). Last, there is scientific theory, the most complex of all, comprising interrelated sets of propositions, and rational and empirical connections between concepts.

Chambers's codification is interesting as an unusually detailed acknowledgement of the diversity of uses of the word 'theory' in education, and it is valuable as such. However, before proceeding with it some refinement is necessary. For my purposes here, I shall query several of his categories, conflate others, and add one. The first and fifth uses he identifies – theory as hunch, and theory as hypothesis – may be conflated as looser and tighter versions of the same notion. The third and seventh uses – theory as evolving explanation, and normative theory – may also be conjoined.

There is one meaning to be added, which exists in weaker and stronger forms. This is of theory as some kind of sieve, manufactured from intelligently reflected-on experience, filtering information to allow through only that which has passed muster according to the filtration proffered by the theory. Here, theory is acting as a template, a way of viewing and understanding the world. In its most simple form this takes its form in grounded theory (Glaser and Strauss, 1967). The central difference that is supposed to exist between grounded theory and other kinds of intellectual endeavour labelled theory is the temporal placing of the intellectual organization – in most theorizing one might say that presupposition exists, while what is supposed to occur in grounded theory might be called post-supposition, with an iterative visiting of the data to refine the theory. (Whether the post-supposition occurs in the way that grounded theorists claim is a major issue, and one that is examined in detail in Chapter 6.) In its stronger, more sophisticated forms, this sieve-like theory takes the form of a complex set of hypothetical formulations built out of a practitioner's experience – and these may exist in the form of beliefs or as presuppositions shaped by more formalized models such as those found in Freudian theory. Crews speaks disparagingly of such constructions as being 'epistemic sieve[s]' saying that they provide 'algorithms for making something happen with maximum complication … [the] theory is a display of ingenuity unencumbered by recalcitrant data' (1997: 12). He proceeds to note that the constructions set up in this kind of theory are 'merely a lavish set of options for creating, not detecting, thematic links [and] …the application of these tools by different interpreters yields a cacophony of incompatible explanations' (1997: 297).

I'm getting ahead of myself, though, with my disquisition on the diverse ways in which the word is used. Let me return to Chambers's typology. If one boils down my comments on it, four broad uses of 'theory' in education can be distilled out. Those four uses are:

1. *Theory as the obverse of practice*: Theory is thinking and reflecting (as opposed to doing). This encompasses personal theory, Carr's notion of structured reflection, Hirst's rational action (both referred to earlier) and McIntyre's (1995) practical theorizing.
2. *Theory as generalizing/explanatory model*: Theory is an idea that may be followed up, embracing looser or tighter hypothesizing, modelling, heuristics and thought experiments. The temporal placing of the theoretical element – the bringing together – is a moot one. Whence does it emerge? It will certainly emerge from experience and intuition, but does this come before or after the events that go under the research title of 'data gathering'? Grounded theory puts itself in a peculiar position, claiming that researchers clear their minds in order for theory to emerge not out of previously constructed ideas but just out of the research experiences to hand (and more on this in Chapter 6).
3. *Theory as developing bodies of explanation*: this category embraces the broadening bodies of knowledge developing in particular fields, which may or may not have come to be associated with labels such as 'learning theory', 'management theory' or 'Piagetian theory'.
4. *Scientific theory*: theory here may ultimately exist in the form of ideas formally expressed in a series of statements. It is part of the process of normal science critically described by Kuhn (1970), and involved in it is Popper's (1968) notion of theory developed in such a way that it is falsifiable.[7] What constitutes scientific thinking and scientific theory is discussed further in Chapters 3 and 4.

A simple description of common usage comes if these four categories are further conflated to form two separate continua. One of these continua represents theory versus practice (see Figure 2.1), where theory in its purest form exists as elegant description of knowledge; incorporated along its length is the notion of the hunch or hypothesis which has crystallized out of practical experience; at the other end of the continuum is practice and doing.

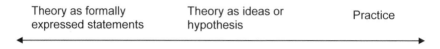

Figure 2.1. Theory versus practice

Thus, at the far left of the continuum, theory exists in the form of ideas formally expressed in a series of statements, (as, for instance, in Kelly's Construct Theory[8]). Toward the centre-left, and less formal, there may be theories such as attribution theory which seek to account for behaviour under an overarching idea (that idea in attribution theory being the dispositional-situational divide). Towards the centre, theory may be used to mean an idea – based on observation, and open to being tested – about some aspect of the way the world works. Here the word is used in the loosest sense (as it might be used in action research or in practical theory) almost as an alternative to 'hypothesis'. To the right of the line would be practical and craft knowledge in its various forms.

The other continuum may be described as theory as plural *versus* theory as singular. Certain theories are in fact single formally stated ideas or loosely stated hypotheses. Or they may have the precise, succinct character of scientific theory. The common element in these diverse notions is that of singularity. At the other end of the extreme, theory in education may comprise broadening bodies of knowledge or collations of cognate knowledge.

If these continua are now presented orthogonally, the position of various theories (and other epistemological tools with more or less right to call themselves theory) may be situated within the resulting frame (see Figure 2.2).

Thus, for instance, Kelly's Construct Theory might be placed in the top left corner – unitary and formal – while half-way down and nearer the centre one might place attribution theory, a reasonably tight collection of ideas with a single explanatory theme. Along the bottom left we might draw sausage shapes representing the more amorphous and ill-defined learning theory or child development theory.

This looseness – this straying along and between the continua I have described – is a cause for serious concern. If theory's use and inter-

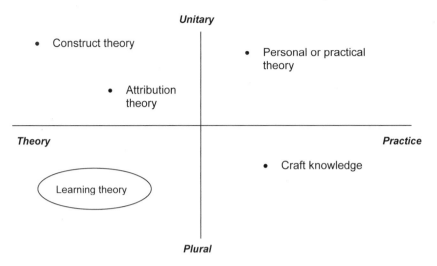

Figure 2.2. Theory or practice? Unitary or plural?

pretation slips arbitrarily this way and then that, its potential utility (assuming for a moment that it might have any utility) is compromised: its possible usefulness as a construct may be diluted. Conversely, and worse, its possible lack of utility may be camouflaged. It is one of the shibboleths of educational research that theory, its construction, development and testing, are valuable – if not essential. But if the morphology of theory is inconstant – if it takes on a number of shapes and hues in people's understanding – its chameleon-like nature will allow it to escape serious scrutiny.

However, perhaps the most serious problem concerning theory is its encouragement to particular kinds of thinking and to the discouragement of diversity in thought. To argue the point I shall take very different kinds of theory from my earlier taxonomy – personal on one side and grand on the other, both central to contemporary theorizing in education – and argue that they suffer the same problems arising from a discouragement to diversity in thought. I shall do this in a moment. Before doing it, I wish to examine why education has come to be in such thrall to theory, and why its confidence in theoretical endeavour may be misplaced.

The problem with theory

I noted in Chapter 1 the various rebirths of theory in education. One could place the original provenance of the supposed need for theory down to nineteenth-century reformers' conjoining of rationalism to theory. Theory was what was needed to make educational practice rational. Since that time, as that view in its original form became less tenable, theory's nature has undergone a number of metamorphoses. But its putative place at the summit of epistemological activity probably rests historically on its supposed success in one particular form: that manifested in science. It is as though the new disciplines – education, psychology, sociology – in their adolescent years suffered from a collective inferiority complex about their epistemological pedigrees, and to inoculate themselves against potential criticism sought to assume the epistemological clothes (with theory as the essential garment) of the disciplinary giants. The non-contiguity of scientific theory and educational theory (and the impossibility of emulating scientific theory in education) is discussed interestingly by MacIntyre (1985), Hirst (1993), Chambers (1992) and others, and I shall return to it briefly later in this chapter, and more fully in Chapter 3. To spend too long now discussing the non-contiguity itself would be to distract from my main point here, which is simply to establish the genealogy of the allure of theory. My point is that education has come to be in thrall to theory.

Being in thrall to theory means that education is preoccupied with the paraphernalia of theory and its development and that it eschews alternative currents of thought which offer it much. While educators have occasionally bounced up against these currents of thought and considered them cursorily, they appear to have dismissed their potential. Dismissed is perhaps too positive a word. They have sniffed at them, as a dog sniffs at a tree in the street, and have passed on uninterested.

One of those currents of thought is articulated in the work of those who suggest that thought usually progresses unpredictably and in a less orderly way than methodological discourse suggests. Feyerabend is one such. Feyerabend's position is not simply that theory is no use, or that its users should be more fastidious in their verbal hygiene. It is that the trappings of theory are harmful, actively destructive of thought and progress. Theory is harmful because it structures and thus constrains thought. Thought actually moves forward, Feyerabend (1993: 14) says, by 'a maze of interactions ... by accidents and conjunctures and curious juxtapositions of events'. The naïve and simple-minded rules that methodologists use cannot hope to provide the progress which we wish for. He quotes Einstein as saying that the creative scientist must seem to the systematic epistemologist to be an 'unscrupulous opportunist'. Holton also draws on Einstein as saying that the essence of scientific method is in the seeking 'in whatever manner is suitable, a simplified and lucid image of the world ... There is no logical path, but only intuition' (1995: 168).[9] In other words, Feyerabend concludes, 'the only principle that does not inhibit progress is *anything goes*' (1993: 4).

Alongside Feyerabend, it is worth touching on Foucault's views here. Looking at an entirely different set of issues and problems, Foucault emerges with an analysis that is directly comparable. Foucault concentrates on areas more directly akin to education – psychiatry, sociology, economics. His conclusions, though, are remarkably similar. As Philp (1990: 69) puts it, 'He [Foucault] rejects the traditional units of analysis and interpretation ... as well as the postulated unities in science – theories, paradigms and research programmes'. Theory and theorizing, in almost any of the forms which I identified in the earlier typology, are about the construction of ideas into a framework. The problem with such frameworks, in looser or tighter forms – in either the mental model notion of theory or in grand theory – is that once they exist they constrain thought within their boundaries. The refreshing and enlightening aspect of Foucault's work is its homelessness; its theoretical and methodological anarchy. In, for instance, *Discipline and Punish* (1985) he cuts a swathe through the theoretical understandings which have guided psychological and sociological understanding of deviance.

But the point I am making is not about the veracity or interest of Foucault's substantive position here. It is rather about his techniques for approaching and thinking about the problem. It is not by coincidence or by serendipity that he comes to such insights. It is by deliberately walking theoretically unarmed into the territory which he explores. It is, he says, the rules and constraints – the archive – of particular discourses which force thought into stereotypical channels. Assumptions and certainties should be questioned as we try to 'breach self-evidence ... [to] construct around the singular event a "polyhedron" of intelligibility' (Foucault, 1981: 4).

Douglas (1975) contrasts Foucault and Durkheim. She makes the point that for both Foucault and Durkheim 'controls, boundaries, prohibitions and privileges' were crucial. The difference between them, she says, was that whereas Durkheim venerated the system of controls, Foucault savagely denounces it. Her conclusion appears to be similar to that of Foucault: that this system of controls – in which I would place theory at the apex – is a means of controlling what is permitted to count as knowledge.

Against personal or practical theory

There are two grounds for mistrust in the line of reasoning that leads to notions of personal theory. The first lies in what are taken to be its unwarrantedly foundational roots. By 'foundational' is meant the assumption that beliefs, claims or behaviour *x* are justified by lodging them some way in belief, claim or 'theory' *y*, which is more reliable or better than *x* (see Van Goor et al., 2004). Thus one's practice in the classroom is justified by one's personal theory (refined after searching reflection, self-criticism, etc.), which is taken to be more secure or reliable than the practice and context from which it was generated. But, as Carr (2006: 150) now puts it, 'our assumptions and beliefs cannot be made the object of our "practical theorizing" because they provide the indispensable precondition to our "practical theorizing" '. It is impossible to separate the one from the other, a case Ryle (1949: 26) makes when he says that 'intelligent practice is not a step-child of theory'. Stanley Fish is probably the most articulate critic of the foundationalist approach to personal theorizing. In his essay *Dennis Martinez and the Uses of Theory* (1989) he takes as his opening vignette a TV interview with the famous baseball pitcher, Dennis Martinez. The baseball star is being asked by a reporter about the supposedly inspirational and facilitative dialogue between him and his coach. The reporter receives in response a two-stage narrative:

> In the first stage he [Martinez, the baseball player] reports the event. 'He [the coach] said, "Throw strikes and keep 'em off the bases," ... and I said, "O.K." ' This is already brilliant enough, both as an account of what transpires between fully situated members of a community and as a wonderfully deadpan rebuke to the outsider who assumes the posture of an analyst. But Martinez is not content to leave the rebuke implicit, and in the second stage he drives the lesson home with a precision Wittgenstein might envy: 'What else could I say? What else could he say?' Or, in other words, 'What did you expect?' Clearly, what Berkow [the reporter] expected was some set of directions or an articulated method or formula or rule or piece of instruction ...
>
> (1989: 372)

The reporter had expected the personal theory articulated by the coach, assimilated in some way by Martinez and reflected on by him. But as Ryle, Polanyi and others would have predicted, the personal theory, if it were possible to articulate it, could never be of any use.

> What they [Martinez and his coach] know is either inside of them or (at least on this day) beyond them; and if they know it, they did not come to know it by submitting to a formalization; neither can any formalization capture what they know in such a way as to make it available to those who haven't come to know it in the same way.
>
> (1989: 373)

As Fish goes on to make clear, there are two activities: playing baseball, and explaining (either to oneself or to others) playing baseball, and there is no relationship at all between these two activities. There are some baseball players who are better at discoursing on their play than other baseball players, but this doesn't make them better baseball players. Similarly, there are some teachers who are better at discoursing on their teaching than other teachers, but this doesn't make them better teachers – something I realized from being a parent governor in my daughters' secondary school: could the reflective, sensitive, articulate, confident, thoughtful super-teacher I had witnessed talking to the governing body really be the same persistently late, disorganized, rude, unhelpful teacher that they described? (It was.) Fish explains, 'the practice of discoursing on practice does not stand in a relationship of superiority or governance to the practice that is its object' (1989: 377). No one consults the formal model of the skill one is exercising in order to exercise it, or exercise it better. As Ryle (1949: 296) puts it, that model is merely a 'muttered rehearsal'. The conclusion that one is driven to about personal or practical theory is well outlined by Carr in his recent thinking on the subject:

> What practitioners are committed to is not a theory but a set of beliefs and, in reflecting upon these beliefs, what they are making explicit is not their theoretical assumptions but that cluster of related beliefs which provide them with their interpretive understanding of their practice and the context within which their practice takes place. In 'articulating' their beliefs in this way, practitioners are neither engaging in 'theoretical activity' nor articulating their 'theoretical position'.
>
> (2006: 149)

The second reason for mistrusting personal theory lies in the procedures that are made to accompany it. We should be concerned, Oakeshott says, to consider the role of 'procedures, methods and devices' and we should notice how in recent times these procedures and devices have broken loose from their subordination as a means of 'finding out' and have 'imposed themselves on our understanding of the transaction itself, with unfortunate consequences' (1989: 63). The problem with theory here – particularly theory as the word is used in education – is that it accretes these procedures and 'correct' methods. It pays too much heed to that which is established. This is a theme that has exercised literary scholars as well as those in the social sciences. Knapp and Michaels (1985a: 25) go so far as to suggest that the goal of theory in literary studies *is* the goal of method, 'the governance of interpretive practice by some larger and more principled account'.

These procedures accompany not only the certainties of 'grand theory' (which I shall examine in the next section) but also the system of rational ideas and accepted methods which lie at the root of our latter-day 'theorizing'. If one is wanting to reflect on one's personal experience, then 'theory' and 'theorizing' are the wrong words for the process. As Eagleton puts it,

> Entomologists study insect life, but they would not study a single spider and nothing more. Theory is general, culture is specific. Even if we take culture in a wider sense, to mean the ways in which a group of people make symbolic sense of their situation, we are still talking about their lived experience. And it is hard to see how there can be a theory of this.
>
> (2004: 74)

And it is hard, as a corollary, to see how there can be any procedures associated with such putative theory. In such circumstances Foucault's (1981) 'eventalization' would be more appropriate.

Looking both at student essays and academic articles in education, one of the dangers of structured reflection (as represented by personal theory in education) is in its conformity to the archive, its desire not to be original or radical but rather to cleave to the structure of established and respectable methods, literatures, rules and procedures. Once the formulae are followed, the structured reflection becomes as tedious as a model railway journey, forever chugging along the same route, forever passing the same dusty scenery. One can understand this conservatism on the part of students, since one of the commonest criticisms of the student dissertation is that the work is inadequately located in theory. Students, if they are wise, do as they are told by their supervisors. Even in their reflection, they understandably seek the right way.

Foucault shares with Feyerabend a predilection for anarchy in this kind of personal thought, for a distaste for theory. Unusual and different opinion, local and specific knowledge should be given free play. 'Rupture, contingency and discontinuity' (Philp, 1990) should be afforded more status than the structure of theory. We should rediscover fragmented, local and specific knowledge. Progress comes through 'critique', through those who 'fight, those who refuse and resist what is.' It comes through 'conflict and confrontation' (Foucault, 1981: 13). This is in contrast to the often anodyne reflections that pass as theorizing in education.

It is the placement of personal educational theory within the archive which surely makes it so often anodyne. It is thus also at the political level that personal theory or practical theory should be seen as suspect. Carr (1995: 127) at one time suggested that it was in 'confronting the postmodernist challenge' that educational theory could 'best defend Enlightenment ideals by seeking to multiply and extend emancipatory educational practices'. Although he has revised his views on the place and possibilities of theory (Carr, 2006), it is difficult, for me at least, to see how theory could be could have ever been enlisted to this aim.

Foucault is just one proponent of anarchy and discontinuity, yet the intellectual current that has delivered discourse on the benefits of disorder comprises thinkers from far and wide. From the philosophical contributions of Nietzsche, Heidegger, Wittgenstein, Gadamer, Husserl, Ryle and Oakeshott, to the offerings of Feyerabend, Kuhn, Popper and Polanyi in science, to the less classifiable contributions of figures such as Derrida, Foucault and Fish, the broad theme is one which emphasizes the situatedness of thought, the intersubjectivity of understanding and the fragmentary, contextual nature of knowledge. The common theme is the ephemeral, and the construction of meaning by the individual. It is about subjective understandings and the building from bottom up of collective understandings: the ways in which Berger and Luckmann, describe the 'intersubjective commonsense world' being constructed [(1979: 20)]. I shall return to the importance of this personal construction in Chapter 7.

Some commentators find the general mood created by this collection of ideas too anarchic. Brooker (1991), for instance, suggests that this mood is one of 'radical indeterminacy, [with] a tone of self-conscious parodic scepticism towards previous certainties in personal, intellectual and political life' (cited in Selden and Widdowson, 1993: 175). This may have given rise in education to an impression of the 'easy oppositionalism' of a post-foundational position (Green, 1994) – an undisciplined contrariness. It has led to a fear of nihilism, a fear that systematic inquiry will be rejected (see also Hill et al., 1999). There may indeed have been some nihilism associated with the flotsam and jetsam of such criticism, but this should not detract from the wholly legitimate critiques of theory that it implies. In his defence of such critique, Smith (1995) argues for a new vision of practice liberated from theory – a view owing its provenance to Polanyi's (1969) 'tacit knowing' and Oakeshott's (1962, 1972, 1989) views on the development of practice distinct from theory.

Against grand theory in education: some case studies

The anti-theoretical thrust of late twentieth-century thought has osten-sibly been invisible – or at least it has appeared only wraith-like – to educators. Wright Mills (1959) warned how inimical such a search was to the development of imagination. His warning specifically concerned the enervating effects of the search for grand theory and I offer here some support for this thesis in education by looking at some grand theory which has influenced education significantly.

I start with Piagetian Theory because it provides good examples of many of the problems to which I have referred. In the formidable and powerful figure of Jean Piaget one also sees a forceful construction – reinforced by the solid status of theory – of the power/knowledge nexus to which Foucault alludes and the dangerous fixity of theoretical knowledge within an institution committed to certain ideas. One can see the process clearly in an account from Gruber and Vonèche (1977) in which the accretion of funds and power to the *International Centre for the Study of Genetic Epistemology* is described. Between the lines, one can almost hear the hushed tones in which discussion about Le Patron is conducted.

We in education should be concerned about the methods and the consequences of theory, since those consequences are in the real world of classrooms and the real lives of teachers and children. Theories are not simply the playthings of bored academics. Piaget's thinking has been responsible for many of the ideas in discovery learning and some of those ideas have been remarkably helpful, such as the idea that children are the constructors of their own mental worlds, though this idea – the rawest, most basic of Piagetian tenets – emerged, one imagines, from the fertility of the man's creativity, almost as an 'Ah Ha!'. It is difficult to see how it could be called a theory.

But the power of the theory in its more detailed expositions has meant that other Piagetian notions – which would not without the legitimization and lustre of theory have made it to the light of day – have been wholly destructive. One can think, for example, of the stage-based notion of development and the notion of 'readiness' for reading, which his interpreters have drawn from his ideas. It is surely not too soon to say that certain elements of the theory proffer a serious misrepresentation of the way children think. This has happened for two main reasons: from unrealistic expectations about the place and limits of theory in education, and from the understandable fascination of professional and academic communities by a particularly powerful nexus of theoretical knowledge. I shall examine these briefly.

In the accumulating body of knowledge surrounding Piagetian theory is the realization that there are not simply odd observations for which Piaget has not been able to account. Rather, it now appears that many of his ideas were wholly mistaken. Donaldson (1978) summarizes well the arguments against Piaget's conclusions, for instance those of McGarrigle and Donaldson (1974), and others. And Nisbett (1993: 7), in relation to Piagetian theory, states that 'Psychological and educational positions, as well as philosophical positions, that assume a universal adult competence with respect to reasoning must give way to the recognition that adult inferential competence is highly variable and highly dependent on educational history'.

Indeed, a significant amount of evidence continues steadily to accumulate against the conclusions and explanations Piaget draws from his theory. Yet the resilience and putative solidity of the theory as a basis for further study continues – because of the status of theory as received knowledge. I have referred to some of the evidence against Piaget. One can, of course, continue, and in that continuation one is struck by the simplicity of the ideas and experiments which have challenged Piagetian theory. It is almost as though educators in continuing defence of Piaget were hypnotized by the theoretical power nexus which surrounded the man, finding it difficult to accept a challenge to what became almost canonical. The significant worry in all of this is that what invariably characterized those challenges was a more positive and optimistic view of children's capabilities than that which inhered in Piagetian theory. Bower's (1982) most important experiment, for instance, conjoined commonsense logic with measures of infants' heart-rate to demonstrate that infants' supposed egocentricity is in fact an artefact of their undeveloped motor system, not their knowledge of the world. Wason and Johnson-Laird (1972) and others subsequently have shown that logic – even in college students – is more elusive than Piaget imagined, while paradoxically logic can be shown to exist in young children (Hughes, 1975) if the circumstances are propitious. The paradoxical (and wholly age-inappropriate) appearance and disappearance of logical thought appears to depend more on social and other circumstances than on the passing of developmental marker-posts. Indeed, the success of very young children in the use of deictic shifters[10] (words like 'I' and 'you' that change their meaning depending on who is uttering and who is listening) is elegant enough proof of the young child's ability to decentre, without recourse to any experiments.

Convinced by the elegance of his theory, Piaget (and others subsequently) found it legitimate to ask 8-year-old children (as a demonstration that formal operations do not occur until the conditions are correct) questions such as 'Are there more primroses on this table or more flowers?' (Piaget, 1973: 23.) Not surprisingly, the ingenuous youngsters – eager to please – would give a helpful response such as, 'It's the same thing because there are six on one side and six on the other'. This seems to me to be a perfectly reasonable response, and a far more polite one than would be obtained from a confident adult confronted with a similar question. If someone came into my garden and asked me 'Do you have more lupins in your garden or more plants?' I should think that they were suffering from some fairly serious thought disorder, probably schizoid in origin. However, the baffled response from the youngsters is taken as support for the theory. Adherents of the theory – contrary to all expectations about falsifiability – seem to find it legitimate to give in support of the theory the fact that children cannot answer silly questions.

The elegance and significance of the theory meant that the absurdity of such question wording was not challenged until relatively recently. Indeed, questions of this kind even made their way into serious tests such as the British Ability Scales.[11] It seems that the power of a good theory is enough to subvert the reason of hardened psychological scientists.

Many of Piaget's conclusions arise from a theory-first view of the world. The theory is foremost and the experiment is ostensibly designed to support (rather than refute) the theory. In Kuhn's terms, the data are products of the activity and artefacts of the scientific culture in which the experiment is set. As Bryant (1984), whose work more than 20 years ago was among the first seriously to challenge Piagetian orthodoxy, has pointed out, the failure of young children to perform adequately in Piagetian experiments is more likely due to their being flabbergasted by the task they are being asked to complete. Or there are more straight-forward and more parsimonious explanations for children's behaviour which are simply unconsidered since the children's behaviour is taken as confirmation of a powerful theoretical explanation. The work of Bryant and Kopytynska (1976), for instance, shows that Piaget's supposition that young children would not 'logically' reproduce a tower with bricks by not taking the logical path of using available measuring equipment is the case because they reasonably consider that the evidence of their eyes is satis-factory evidence. If the top of the tower is not actually visible, however, children will use available measuring tools. The original experiments were self-validating; they produced a world in which they were true.

Others of course have shown Piagetian conclusions to be mistaken. Elkind (1967) and Gelman (1982) in well-known work have shown that children are quite able to conserve (that is, to hold on to the idea of constant amount, in spite of presentation) if given the right circum-stances. Work continues to show the same thing: that children's thinking is characterized by adaptability and plasticity rather than fixity. Glenn (1993) and Lawson (1992) are just two of the many who have done more recent work to show that children's learning is dependent on context and use of language. Bryant sums up the situation:

> In fact every one of the many claims that Piaget made for some glaring
> logical gap in young children is now hotly disputed, and in every case
> some evidence has been produced which appears to show that young
> children can manage the logical move in question.
>
> (1984: 225)

The purpose of presenting this discussion is not to harangue Piagetians. It is rather to demonstrate the power and resilience of theory – of a tota-lizing discourse in Foucault's terms. Despite being shown to be mistaken in some very important respects Piagetian theory has influenced (and is still influencing) two generations of early childhood educators. Haack (2005) summarizes an element of Popper's position on falsifiability as 'in deciding how to act we can do no better than go with theories we don't so far know to be false'. The trouble is that we do know Piaget's theory to be false in important ways, but the defences continue. According to Feyerabend, a certain form of oppositional discourse may even perpe-tuate the theory, leading to it becoming an 'obstacle to thought':

> [a] quite uninformed desire to be on the right side is taken as a further
> sign of the importance of the theory ... [But] Problematic aspects which
> were originally introduced with the help of carefully constructed argu-
> ments now become basic principles; doubtful points into slogans;
> debates with opponents become standardized [and] only serve as a
> background for the splendour of the new theory.
>
> (1993: 30)

Feyerabend here describes an academic socialization of knowledge, and strong connections can be drawn between the 'archive' and 'totalizing discourse' of Foucault, and the paradigm of Kuhn (1970). Kuhn describes the way that the paradigm is used consensually. It is what is agreed to be correct rather than the product of compelling justifications. If experiments are done which confirm the paradigm, all is well and good and knowledge is added to. However, if experiments fail to confirm existing theory in the paradigm it is taken to be because of the incompetence or stupidity of the scientist or some problem in the design or interpretation of the experiment. Thus Finn (1992) accuses those who interpret and criticize Piaget of 'clichéd description' and 'malign misinterpretation'. Even those who have followed Piaget (but emerged with mistaken and attack-prone conclusions) are accused by Finn of a process akin to raiding a goodie-bag for support for their ideals (such as discovery learning). But it should surely come as no surprise, given the creed-like status which is ascribed to knowledge when it achieves such theoretical heights, that supporters may wilfully misinterpret it.

Indeed, those who have found the theory wanting are taken to be guilty of a process which is familiar to Kuhn: Finn (1992) says that 'precociously successful conservation' may be noted (as it has often been in the critique of Piaget) but he puts this down to the 'specifically advantageous situations' in which children have been placed. The problem here, as Kuhn predicts, is taken to be in the design of the challenging experiment or in its interpretation. Although Kuhn's target is the influence of 'existing custom, convention, inherited knowledge, current procedures and current interpretations' (Barnes, 1990: 89) in science, the defences of Piaget give ample evidence for the same process in education.

Not only has Piaget's theory influenced education; it has also influenced other theories – themselves with their own influences on the world. Webs of theories arise, with each strand of the web depending on other strands, which in turn depend on others. Never mind that the original strand may be wildly off the mark or even hopelessly wrong. For instance, Habermas relies extensively on Piaget as showing that the child gradually decentres, and the notion of decentring has been one of the most conclusively attacked aspects of Piaget's work. Habermas (1991) maps Piaget's three main developmental stages to three main stages of social evolution: the 'mythical', 'religious-metaphysical' and 'modern'. Decentering, and the movement of the child from stage to stage, is seen to be also at the root of the move of small, traditional cultures dominated by myths (which represent concrete thought), eventually to societies which develop forums in which debate and argument are possible, and ultimately to society in which the development of religion signifies a move to rationality. The linkage of societal development to individual development and its dependence on Piagetian Theory is tortuous and is evidence of the 'profoundly appealing' yet 'profoundly unsound' process of theoretical development about which Medawar (1974) warned. Even if taken metaphorically, Habermas's ideas in this respect already appear at best mistaken and at worst insulting.

Habermas relies heavily on Freud's psychoanalysis (itself surely mortally wounded[12]) as a vehicle for demonstrating the reconcilability of the positivist and hermeneutic traditions. Habermas sought to show that the interpretative elements of psychoanalysis (e.g. via the analysis of dreams) and its simultaneous assumption of impersonal, anonymous forces (e.g. in the unconscious forces of the id) were signal evidence of the assumptions of two supposedly irreconcilable traditions (positivist and hermeneutic) in fact complementing one another.

Looking at Habermas's position and his reliance on both Piaget and Freud, it is possible to see that a vast intellectual superstructure is constructed on what is now recognized to be, at best, shaky foundations. If the theories on which the arguments are based can be shown to be so fundamentally mistaken then we must surely look with a more sceptical eye at the arguments based on those extended theories. In both of them the fault lies with theory being taken to be the substantial representation of our best knowledge.

Let us move on to Chomsky and his 'theory of mind' (1980: 50). Chomsky argues in his theory for physiological correlates to thought. He tries to make the point through drawing on a passage from Wittgenstein, who takes the opposite view: that mental capacities lack locally structured vehicles. Wittgenstein illustrates his point by drawing an analogy with the contents of a plant's seed, arguing for the anarchy in the germ:

> I mean this: if I talk or write there is, I assume, a system of impulses going out from my brain and correlated with my spoken or written thoughts. But why should the *system* continue further in the direction of the centre? Why should this order not proceed, so to speak, out of chaos? The case would be like the following – certain kind of plants multiply by seed, so that a seed always produces a plant of the same kind as that from which it was produced – but *nothing* in the seed corresponds to the plant which comes from it; so that it is impossible to infer the properties or structure of the plant from those of the seed that comes out of it – this can only be done from the *history* of the seed. So an organism might come into being even out of something quite amorphous, as it were causelessly; and there is no reason why this should not really hold for our thoughts, and hence for our talking and writing.
>
> (cited in Chomsky, 1980: 49)

Clearly Wittgenstein is not arguing for the complete absence of physiological correlates for thought. He is arguing from analogy that there is no necessary central or localized form of organization which corresponds to the thought. It is this which jars with Chomsky – because it contradicts his theory.

Genetic science shows Wittgenstein to be right about forms of organization (or the lack of them) and one wonders why Chomsky chose the quotation; there are no obvious (or indeed covert) connections between the coded message in the seed and its phenotypic effects. Indeed pleiotropy is a key feature of geneticists' current understanding of the way that the coded message has its effects; Dawkins defines pleiotropy thus:

> The phenomenon whereby a change at one genetic locus can bring about a variety of apparently unconnected phenotypic changes. For instance, a particular mutation might at one and the same time affect eye color, toe length, and milk yield. Pleiotropy is probably the rule rather than the exception, and is entirely to be expected from all that we understand about the complex way in which development happens.
>
> (1982: 292)

Further evidence against Chomsky's simple LAD – against the notion of simple mapping of language to neurological hard-wiring – comes from the application of insights from quantum physics to the workings of the brain (see Penrose, 1994). Penrose points to the strong likelihood that the cyto-skeleton – that is, the level of interconnections of microtubules below that of neurons (which are explicable in terms of classical-level physics) – operates at a level where quantum laws rather than classical-level laws apply. With quantum laws applying, with multiple possibilities and ultimately with what Penrose calls 'non-computability', the likelihood of Chomsky's 'device' – localized in some discrete organizational centre – seems even more remote.

Back in the world of classical physics, Chomsky's theory has recently been questioned following the research of those who are conducting work into the learning of language in non-human primates. It now seems likely that other primates have the mental apparatus to learn vocabulary and syntax, albeit at a far more primitive level than in humankind (see, for example, Fouts and Fouts, 1993; White-Miles, 1993). The notion of a brain centre exclusive to *homo sapiens* for the learning of language has had to give way to the notion of plasticity in thinking and learning – to a generalized ability to learn something even as complex as language in the higher primates, albeit at not such a sophisticated level as that developed in humans.

The point of using Chomsky's ideas to exemplify this debate is, as with Piaget and Habermas, to signify the nature of the wrongness of the theory The 'structural theory of mind', if it is wrong, is not simply slightly off the mark; it is seriously mistaken and it will not lead to explanations or predictions that are any more helpful than, for example, Leonard Schatzman's (1991: 304) 'common interpretive acts'. And yet, partly because of the allure of theory and theory's accompaniments, it has, like Piaget's theory, influenced a generation of educators. In parenthesis here one might mention that on the question of the 'wrongness' of theories the very cases of Piaget and Chomsky are taken by Smith (1992) to be examples of the incompatibility of two explanatory frameworks. In discussing a debate between Piaget and Chomsky, Smith says that their views were not even complementary: 'at least one of the major protagonists has to be wrong, and they both labored mightily to prove it was the other' (1992: 156). See also Piattelli-Palmarini (1980). Of course, the fact that one has to be wrong does not preclude the possibility that both may be wrong.

The committed theoriphile might defend the process rather than the actual theories in the examples I have used and point to the value of the cut-and-thrust of discourse in providing better ideas. But the problem with the legitimacy ascribed to theory is that for substantial periods, social, psychological and educational theory is taken to be the best representation of our knowledge. Even if assumptions are shown to be mistaken or conclusions flawed, if alternative explanations or everyday knowledge seem more robust, strange loyalty is shown to the ailing theory. It is treated not as tentative or once useful, but something to be supported, even when the contradictory evidence and challenging arguments assume substantial weight. The legacy in education is not simply the débris of academic debate, but practice in classrooms. Both Piaget and Chomsky can leave the educator with a less than optimistic view as to the potential of the teacher; a view that emphasizes the fixedness of development. As Bryant (1984) says in the specific case of Piaget, the message for the teacher is 'a pretty bleak one'. Although one side of Piaget's theory has been helpful (i.e. in the way in which children construct the world for themselves) Bryant avers that 'there can be no question that the implication of Piaget's theories about children's logical skills is, as far as teachers are concerned, restrictive and negative' (1984: 257).

I re-emphasize here that the point is not to attack these specific theories, but rather to challenge the process of theorizing in education. Theory may exist in various forms along the continua I have drawn, and its value, respectability and putative validity will be determined irrespective of its positioning here, since those who speak of theory and theorizing in education often use the word indiscriminately, with little attention to its use from one moment to the next. Perhaps most seriously though, theory in all forms has acquired a respectability and a glamour: theorizing, and thought which is located in theory, is taken to be legitimate and acceptable and we may ask questions about how limiting such a set of theories may be to fertility in thought about education. One might also ask who benefits by the reinforcement of that archive – that notion of correct ideas, correct ways of interpreting, correct procedures and processes to structure one's thought. Given the nature of theory in education, its veracity is difficult to gauge yet its influence may be significant. Whether that influence is benign or malign will be open to test; my point is that power has been located in theory and those who are associated with it. If theory is then seen as the engine of ideas and change, particular kinds of idea, particular ways of thinking and particular methods for structuring research have legitimacy bestowed upon them.

Grand theory – and its non-contiguity with scientific theory

> ... it is the vocabulary of practice rather than that of theory, of action rather than contemplation, in which one can say something useful ... we want to know in what sense Pasteur's views of disease picture the world accurately and Paraclesus' inaccurately ...
>
> (Rorty, 1982: 162–3)

> We shall not think there is or could be an epistemologically pregnant answer to the question 'What did Galileo do right that Aristotle did wrong?' ... We shall just say that Galileo had a good idea, and Aristotle a less good idea; Galileo was using some terminology which helped, and Aristotle wasn't.
>
> (Rorty, 1982: 193)

Rorty believes that there is no special way of doing things that characterizes science, and he has differences here with Popper on the status of theory and the ways in which it is used in the natural and the 'pseudo' sciences, as I discussed in Chapter 1. Rorty suggests that any notionally methodological differences may be down simply to vocabulary – that we are all doing essentially the same thing. But it's the 'essentially' that is the key word here – differences of degree. Bruner (1986: 13) points out that natural science is marked by what he calls the paradigmatic mode, concerned with formal systems of explanation employing categorization with a language regulated by the requirements of consistency and non-contradiction. Here, development of theory involves 'higher and higher reaching for abstraction', and this reaching may take different forms in different arenas.

One of the problems with grand theory is that it is in this theoretical form that there are the clearest pretensions to the kind of 'language requirements' or methodological requirements expected in the natural sciences. But the pretensions (the easy bits) are matched neither by the checks and controls (the hard bits) self-imposed by natural scientists nor by assumptions about falsifiability. On the contrary, the tendency can often be to treat theory as though it is a fixed framework faithfully to be followed in the planning of research, and the research in turn can be seen as an instrument for the verification and support of the theory. As Bruner (1986: 48) puts it, the aim seems to be to construct 'theory that can be ... carefully guarded against attack'. If this criticism is valid, it is of course one – as Kuhn (1970) has noted – which applies also to 'normal science' which proceeds by seeking confirmation of established theory rather than its refutation. The shortcomings of 'normal science', though, are at least acknowledged and acted upon in practical as well as in methodological discourse. Theory is treated differently in the methodological literature of education, where there is an expectation that it will be a reliable instrument for scaffolding thinking, for driving forward knowledge and ideas.

To contrast the progress of theory in science it is worth taking two well-known developments: those of the Einsteinian revolution and neo-Darwinian development. When a theory of relativity superseded a theory of mechanics, it did so because the latter was unable to account for various paradoxical observations and phenomena at the edges of the measured world. But until the new theory was proposed, Newton's theory had sufficed (and continues to suffice) quite satisfactorily for most scientific purposes. So Einstein's theory did not replace the theory of mechanics because the latter was hopelessly and spectacularly wrong. As Feyerabend puts it, 'The trouble is not ... the result of sloppy procedure. It is created by experiments and measurements of the highest precision' (1993: 39). Similarly, we are now seeing a replacement of traditional Darwinian theory. Although neo-Darwinian theory is a revolution in thinking, it retains and cleaves to the central tenet of molecular biology that nucleic acids act as templates for the synthesis of proteins, but never the reverse – in other words that acquired characteristics are not inherited. It is essentially and fundamentally Darwinian in character.

Each of these cases – of the replacement of Newtonian and Darwinian theory – is a well-known example of the progress of science. The point of giving them is to show the contrast between the progress of these theories in natural science, and the progress (if it can be called that) of theories in education. When theories in education are shown to be wrong, they are shown to be not simply unable to account for a minority of paradoxical observations but mistaken in their fundamentals, as for example elements of Piagetian theory have proved to be.

Theory versus *ad hocery*

None of this is new. Dewey railed against certain kinds of theory nearly a century ago, but such is the glamour and resilience of theory that few seem to have heard him. This is to such an extent that the journal that is the organ of the John Dewey Society actually calls itself *Educational Theory*. His own views on this matter seem a generation or two ahead of his time. Indeed, Rorty (1991: 193) suggests that 'Foucault can be read ... as an up-to-date version of John Dewey'. Take Meiklejohn's (1966) summary:

> It is unwise, Dewey tells us, to philosophize, to have and to use 'general theories' ... 'What is needed,' Dewey says, 'is specific inquiries into a multitude of specific structures and interactions. Not only does the solemn reiteration of categories of individual and organic or social whole not further these definite and detailed inquiries but it checks them. It detains thought within pompous and sonorous generalities wherein controversy is incapable of solution.' Such theorizing tends to substitute mere abstract ideas for concrete, specific investigations.
>
> (cited in Dewey, 1920: 189–99.)

Dewey is saying that investigations should be specific. They should not derive from theory, nor should they be aimed at establishing theory. In particular, he warns that education's predilection for theory may not merely lead to pompous banality, but that it is actually dangerous. It 'detains thought'. Elliott has recently said something similar:

> With respect to research methods I now see 'educational research' as an eclectic and heuristic form of inquiry. It is not necessary to justify such methods 'methodologically' ... Whatever helps practitioners to develop a reasoned capacity for action in the service of their educational values will do.
>
> (2006: 178)

Garforth (cited in Dewey, 1966: 16) asserted that Dewey concluded that, 'Philosophy's primary purpose is that of rationalizing the *possibilities* of experience, especially collective human experience; it is practical, not theoretical, in intention'.[13] In this, Barrett (1978: 149) is at one with Dewey. Barrett warns specifically of the simplifying tendency of theory in the social and symbolic sciences: 'The greater and more spectacular the theory, the more likely it is to foster our indolent disposition to over-simplify: to twist all the ordinary matters of experience to fit them into the new framework, and if they do not, to lop them off'. The theme is that theoretical moulds, from wherever they derive, are the Procrustean bed of the educator; there is the danger that in compacting, trimming and generally forcing the worlds with which we work into theoretical moulds we distort and misperceive those worlds. Education is not alone in this respect: Wright Mills (1959/1970) described and attacked this theoretical tendency more broadly in socio-historical analysis, where he suggested that theory (in particular in the philosophies of Comte, Marx, Spencer and Weber) creates a 'trans-historical strait-jacket' into which the evidence of history is coerced.

Naughton (1981) suggests that our aim should not be to establish all-encompassing theories, with their strait-jacketing qualities. He quotes Checkland (1972, 1981) and Popper (1966) in saying that our orientation ought to be towards 'piecemeal social engineering'. Others have spoken similarly: Kuhn (1970) saw progress as a series of non-cumulative developments; Toffler (1985) talked of *ad hocery*, and Quinton (cited in Magee, 1982) suggested that Wittgenstein saw progress as the piecemeal dissipation of confusion.

These notions – of piecemeal dissipation of confusion, of *ad hocery*, of craft knowledge and of piecemeal social engineering – although from different stables (or from none), are congruent in one important respect. Central to these notions is the belief that Dewey expressed long ago that problem solving – particularly of the kind engaged in by educators – requires a different kind of understanding of the world from the one that educational research, and theory deriving from and driving educational research, has traditionally offered. It needs to be less structured, less constrained. In the next chapter I give some examples of less structured inquiry and of atheoretical progress outside and inside education.

Theory in education is antagonistic to pluralism in ideas. With commitment to it, fertility is sacrificed to orderliness. What is needed is more *ad hocery*, more thought experiments, more diversity. I return to Carr's original appeal for theory – where theory is reflection and thought. I agree on the merit of reflection and thought, but why call reflection and thought 'theory'? In his recent revision to his thinking, Carr (2006: 137) says that educational theory's claim to make a unique contribution to educational practice is mistaken, and rests on unrealistic and outmoded premises: 'what I am going to argue is that educational theory is simply an expression of a widely felt need to ground our beliefs and actions in knowledge that derives from some authoritative, external and independent source'. He argues that no such authoritative, external and independent source exists, and that 'educational theory is nothing other than the name we give to the various futile attempts that have been made over the last hundred years to stand outside our educational practices in order to explain and justify them'.

Carr's discussion focuses on contemporary understandings of theory in 'personal theory'. But 'theory' is understood as more than this: it denotes also an idea, a grand theory, a body of knowledge, or – even more widely – a safe conceptualization, a packaging of experience and ideas into circumscribed form and language. Teachers and researchers are supposed to have theories, but if academics cannot agree on what a theory is, then it is reasonable to assume that 'theory' will come to assume the status of received, acceptable schemata. In the next chapter I seek to expand on some of the issues that emerge from this.

Notes

1 For example Suppes (1974) and Garrison (1988). Ball (1995) characterizes atheoretical research as 'technical rationalist' and contrasts this with theoretically grounded research which concerns 'intellectual intelligence'. He associates atheoretical technical rationalism with isolation and the neglect of significant ideas and concepts.

2 For 30 years or more Piagetian theory, for example, has dominated child psychology courses in teacher education. Its status has meant that other kinds of explanation about children's cognitive development have found difficulty emerging, and small-scale enquiry by student teachers is often conducted in Piagetian terms. Its status has meant that new or different ideas may be ignored or rejected because they fail to conform to received wisdom.

3 'Grand theory' is a term coined by Wright Mills (1959/1970: 23) to describe the expectation among social scientists that their disciplines should attempt to build systematic theory of 'the nature of man and society'; he saw this effort as an obstacle to progress in the human sciences. By contrast, personal theory and 'practical theorizing', discussed by Carr (1995) and McIntyre (1995), concerns using 'intellectual resources that will enable them [educational practitioners] to take their activities more seriously' (Carr, 1995: 36). At its core is the notion of emancipation from habit and tradition via critical examination of existing belief.

4 Medawar and Medawar (1977: 10) give examples of elegant theory being 'profoundly appealing' yet 'profoundly unsound'. They record that the once attractive but now discredited notion of protoplasm led Victorian biologist Thomas Henry Huxley in a paper for the *Quarterly Journal of Microscopical Science* to give a detailed account of an organism dredged from deep in the Atlantic and consisting of naked protoplasm. The new organism was given a Latin name (*Bathybius haeckeli*) after the eminent zoologist Ernst Haeckel who first proposed the existence of a group of organisms, the Monera, consisting entirely of Urschleim, or primitive slime. The whole episode is an example of the consensual construction of supposedly scientific knowledge based on simple, romantic theory.

5 Illich and Sanders (1988: 106) discuss the misuse of words such as 'theory', which they say are used without thinking in academic, professional and lay circles, almost as a 'sublinguistic grunt'. They give the word 'energy' as a detailed example, recording how its early sixteenth-century English use as 'vigor of expression' altered in the nineteenth century as it acquired a technical meaning culled from physics. Later, concurrent with Marx's ascription of 'labour force' to the proletariat, German physicists described a general potential to perform work and called it 'energy', and this transferred itself to English. The continual accretion of technical and non-technical nuance and meaning, and the inaccurate vernacular use of the word in pretending technical expertise or scientific knowledge is troublesome. These 'sublinguistic grunts' (and I would put theory at the head of the list) are used, they say, 'neither with common sense, nor with the senseless precision of science' (1988: 106).

6   Skinner (1990: 12) aligns anti-theory with 'conceptual relativism'. He says that it is the project of these thinkers (Foucault, Feyerabend, Wittgenstein) to demolish the claims of theory and method to organize the materials of experience.

7   ' "Normal science" means research firmly based upon one or more past scientific achievements, achievements that some particular scientific community acknowledges for a time as supplying the foundation for its further practice' (Kuhn, 1970: 10). It is the conservatism of this process of which Kuhn was critical, as was Popper. Hence the latter's emphasis on developing theory in such as way that it can be falsified. The aim is to avoid ossification; nothing should be allowed to become sacred, so we must develop a theory in such a way that it can be knocked down and replaced. Wittgenstein also was concerned about not only the practice of science, but also its influence on philosophy. Ayer (1985: 143) puts it thus: 'he [Wittgenstein] thought that the prestige of science misled philosophers into fabricating explanations [theorizing?], whereas what was needed was an assortment of careful descriptions'.

8   Kelly's Construct Theory sees people as self-inventing explorers and interpreters of their worlds. It has a formal structure with a fundamental postulate and eleven elaborative corollaries. Bannister and Fransella (1971: 15) emphasize this formality and contrast Construct Theory with other putative theories, which they claim do not deserve the name 'theory'. They say, for instance, that a 'theory of memory can be no better than the concept of memory itself'.

9   This is somewhat different from Popper's (1968: 32) translation of this quotation, namely: 'Einstein speaks of the "search for those highly universal laws ... from which a picture of the world can be obtained by pure deduction. There is no logical path", he says, "leading to these ... laws". They can only be reached by intuition, based upon something like an intellectual love ("Einfuhlung") of the objects of experience'.

10   Deixis is the use of words relating to the time and place of utterance, for example, personal pronouns, demonstrative adverbs, adjectives and pronouns. The use and understanding of personal pronouns requires that users put themselves 'in another's shoes' (and is notably lacking in autistic children, though present in normal development from the very early years).

11   The British Ability Scales were devised during the late 1970s to assess ability without necessary recourse to the production of an IQ score. One element, devised on Piagetian principles, involved children answering questions of the kind described earlier.

12   Interestingly, Wittgenstein seems to have found Freud entertaining but fundamentally wrong. He says, 'Freud's fanciful pseudo-explanations (precisely because they are brilliant) perform a disservice' (quoted in Bouveresse, 1995: 3).

13   Bouveresse interprets Wittgenstein as thinking something similar. Bouveresse suggests that Wittgenstein's view was that 'the difficult thing in philosophy is not to produce theories – we do that quite naturally – but to resist the temptation to do so' (Bouveresse, 1995: 5).

3

Where's the theory? Behind you! (Oh No It Isn't!)

'When I use a word,' Humpty Dumpty said in rather a scornful tone, 'it means just what I choose it to mean – neither more nor less'.
Lewis Carroll: *Alice Through the Looking Glass*

As I mentioned in Chapter 1, my interest in theory arose principally from confusion about what educators were talking about when they included this ubiquitous phenomenon in their discussion. The interest has developed over a couple of decades into an academic pursuit in itself, turning from interest into obsession. While many have listened to my expositions on theory with seemingly genuine interest, I have to note that there are others who have responded to my questions about meaning and my injunctions to be less theoretical with less equanimity. Some of that defence comes from colleagues who see theorizing as synonymous with 'thinking'. So when I've given talks or written about this theme, people say, 'But this is all contradictory, hypocritical even: there you are saying we shouldn't theorize, and you're theorizing yourself!' So let me start by saying that I don't see theorizing as equivalent to thinking or arguing.

Clearly it would be preposterous to complain about or deprecate thinking. I can make it clear at this point that I am not averse to thinking, nor cogitating, pondering, guessing, hypothesizing, reflecting, considering, having a good idea, contemplating, musing, or having inspiration; all these are wonderful things. But to my mind it helps not a jot to call them 'theorizing,' however much more impressive the latter sounds. To call all geese, ducks and other waterfowl 'swans' not only fails to transform the geese and ducks into swans, it also points unerringly to the possibility that one thinks that the geese and ducks are in need of some transformation. To want to call all thinking 'theorizing' not only destroys the useful distinctions that different words make between different kinds of thinking, but by implication it also relegates those other kinds of thinking to thinking's second division. Frank Smith in his excellent book, *To Think* (1992), identifies no fewer than 77 thinking words, all with different nuance – some about 'forward' thinking (e.g. *expect, imagine, foresee*), some about 'current' thinking (e.g. *analyse, argue, examine*), some concerning 'past' thinking (e.g. *deduce, review, reflect*). It doesn't help to call them all 'theorizing'. Indeed, it is confusing to call them 'theorizing', yet this is what much of contemporary discourse in education does: it labels all thinking, pondering, considering, reflecting, synthesizing as 'theorizing'.

We can't mean just 'thinking' – and, indeed, when you examine the question closely, when you examine what 'theory' means, we *don't* mean just *thinking*. We mean even more. So here, in looking at usage and definition, problems become compounded rather than resolved. This chapter aims to consider this and some other criticisms that have emerged about the kinds of arguments posed so far in this book. There have been two main criticisms of the kinds of arguments I have made:

1. The fact that my difficulty with an eclectic understanding of 'theory' is unnecessarily limiting and betrays my supposed allegiance to particular folk understandings about a scientific model of theory; theory and theorizing should relate to all kinds of structured thinking, the criticism goes;
2. 'Theory' generates thought and is productive of ideas – this in itself is enough to validate theory. Theory is the inevitable product of thinking. In fact, theory is ubiquitous in thinking, reflective professionals.

My response has centred around four themes:

1. If theory applies to all structured thought, it confuses us. We may be distracted or diverted from straightforward practice by its allure and by its promises for suggestions, plans and action;
2. Theory may be talked about because it sounds impressive. Used thus, the word is hollow. As with the first theme, what is presumed to be 'theory' can divert from more straightforward – possibly less appropriate – practice;
3. Recognition that there is no special scientific method is not to reject all of the claims of natural science to certain kinds of precision. It is not, in other words, to accept all of the arguments of those whom Haack (2003) calls the 'Old Cynics'. There *are* differences between the use of theory in education and in the natural sciences.
4. Ubiquitous theory relegates the position of practice.

So, on to those themes.

1. If theory applies to all structured thought, it confuses us

The concern I have expressed is that 'theory' in educational discourse has come to denote just about any kind of intellectual endeavour. In this happy guise it has acquired a falsely deserved reputation and has led us into dead-ends in our thought about matters educational. Against my argument, some people have gone on to argue that theory should indeed be seen loosely, broadly to mean any intellectual construction. Rajagopalan (1998: 337) refers to this as the 'generic sense' of theory and avers that it is absolutely defensible to talk about theory in this sense. Rajagopalan's is a commonly held position and this section therefore addresses his assertions.

It is first necessary to reiterate a point made in the last chapter: if people argue for a loose, eclectic, generic usage of 'theory', then it has to be recognized just how many meanings are being elided with such eclecticism. When I've tried to get closer to an understanding of this eclecticism, I've tended to rely on the list of uses of theory drawn up by American educator John Chambers, whose analysis I discussed in some detail in Chapter 2. To save the reader the trouble of going back to find them, I'll rattle through them as quickly as possible here:

- theory contrasted with fact;
- theory as the opposite of practice;
- practical theory or personal theory;
- theory as presupposition from a set of orienting principles;
- normative theory – a clearly developed argument;
- empiricist theory (or craft knowledge);
- scientific theory.

The point of giving these is to indicate just how many distinctions we gloss over when we talk about theory in education. It seems to me that useful distinctions between different kinds of enquiry, different kinds of thinking, are often slurred by the catch-all use of *theory*. Too often these very different kinds of thinking and enquiry are bracketed together.

Little thought is given to the consequences of using theory in a generic way. I'd like to give some attention to this bracketing of meanings – or rather the failure to disaggregate them. Illich and Sanders (1988: 106) have said something interesting here. They suggest that there comes to be employed a hybrid use of words like 'theory' in pretending technical expertise or scientific knowledge. And they come up with a very nice phrase to describe words that are used to convey that kind of pretended knowledge. They say that these words, such as 'theory', become merely 'sub-linguistic grunts'.

The use of a word like 'theory' in a field like education – which has at its centre a study of thinking – has surely to be something more than a sub-linguistic grunt. To make this suggestion is not, incidentally, to buy in to some attempt to legislate for correct language. I'm not setting myself up as a one-person *Académie française* for educators. Rather, it is to say that in our scholarly discourse and with an idea as important as 'theory' seems to be for education we'd better be sure what we're talking about. Thus, for the educator and the social scientist, a loose, vernacular use of 'theory' is more important than it is for Popper (1968) in his discussion of the word. For the educator it refers to a population of meanings relating to thinking itself – meanings that are relatively unimportant for Popper, in his discussion of theory in the natural sciences. He can therefore say, as he does, that the logic of scientific knowledge is a 'theory of theories'. Referring to his differences with Mach, Wittgenstein and Schlick on this issue of what 'theory' can be permitted to mean he says,

> My point of view is, briefly, that our ordinary language is full of theories; that observation is always *observation in the light of theories;* that it is only the inductivist prejudice which leads people to think that there could be a phenomenal language, free of theories, and distinguishable from a 'theoretical' language.
>
> (1968: 59nn, emphasis in original)

This position is explicable if Popper is talking about 'our ordinary language' in natural scientific discourse. If, however, he is talking about theory in everyday language outside this discourse – the language of going to the shops, watering the pot plants, taking the register and thinking about one's thinking – it leads him into trouble. For if he also says, as he does, that certain elements of psychiatry constitute only pseudo-science (Popper, 1977) because their 'theories' are verifiable by any conceivable event, (Popper, 1953/1974) he is drawing a *de facto* distinction between the theories in those pseudo sciences and those in the natural sciences. They are different beasts. One is the pointless theory of the pseudo-sciences; the other is the falsifiable theory of the natural sciences. The conclusion one comes to is that the 'instrumentalism' of Wittgenstein, Mach and Schlick is indeed significant.

The general issue is about the significance (or insignificance) of eliding meaning. As educators – thinking about thinking, about learning, about performing – we must surely be confident of our ground when we use a word which comes in as many varieties as 'theory'. Otherwise, our analysis and discussion of thinking and learning may go down some unfruitful avenues. When I say to my daughter, 'I've got a theory why the dog has been sick' no one is going to worry about my epistemological premises. But the language in which we choose to discuss teaching and learning must surely be more precise. The words we employ are the *tools* we use for our thinking about thinking. If a surgeon, on a whim (perhaps after having read a paperback on the later Wittgenstein), were to decide habitually to call all surgical instruments 'scalpels', or a greengrocer to label all vegetables 'asparagus' (or, as a more exact analogy with the case of talk about theory, to label potatoes, asparagus, tomatoes and everything else 'vegetables'), they would surely soon be out of business. And it's the same with educators and theory. Apart from any other considerations, I don't think we can afford to call all words to do with thinking and enquiry 'theory'.

And I repeat that the point is not to legislate for what is correct, but rather the obverse: the point is to counter an academic tendency to want to scoop up all thinking words and paint 'theory' over them in metre-high red letters.

Terry Eagleton, made an identical point about the grossly overworked word 'ideology':

> Any word which covers everything loses its cutting edge and dwindles to an empty sound. For a term to have meaning, it must be possible to specify what, in particular circumstances, would count as the other of it ... if any piece of human behavior whatsoever, including torture, could count as an instance of compassion, the word compassion shrinks to an empty signifier.
>
> (1991: 7–8)

Sadly, 'theory' seems already to have achieved the status of 'empty signifier'. Stanley Fish (1994: 378) has had a lot to say about the over-use of 'theory' and its use in fields like the law and literary studies. He highlights the highly varied activities shoved under the billowing cloak of 'theory', concluding that 'to include such activities under the rubric of theory is finally to make everything theory, and if one does that there is nothing of a *general* kind to be said about theory'. As he notes,

> Am I following or enacting a theory when I stop for a red light, or use my American Express card, or rise to speak at a conference? Are you now furiously theorizing as you sit reading what I have to say? And if you are persuaded by me to alter your understanding of what is and is not a theory, is your new definition of theory a new theory of theory? Clearly it is possible to answer yes to all these questions, but just as clearly that answer will render the notion 'theory' *and* the issue of its consequences trivial by making 'theory' the name for ordinary, contingent, unpredictable, everyday behavior.
>
> (1989: 327)

He distinguishes between theory and what he calls *theory-talk*; the latter being 'any form of talk that has acquired cachet and prestige' (1989: 14–15).

And this brings me on to my second point ...

2. Prestigious theory: its pompous use and its camouflaging effects

> Theoria *is the highest form of activity*
> *Aristotle*

Aristotle is a pretty big cheese to gainsay, epistemologically speaking, and sadly his pronouncements often reverberate as The Truth through the history of thought. If he says that *theoria* is the highest form of activity, it's a strong endorsement. If one is unsure of the status of one's thought there is some epistemic ground to be claimed by calling it 'a theory'. By calling constructs, reflections and ideas – indeed any kind of structured thinking – 'theory' or 'theorizing', we can claim some powerful legitimacy and explanatory currency for them. Use of the word 'theory' is often about the need to associate oneself with something heavy sounding and explanatory. 'Theorizing', after all, sounds a lot better than 'pondering'. If theory is the clearest distillation of intellectual endeavour, then theorizing of course is an appropriate activity for serious scholars. Rather in the way that English ballerinas early in the twentieth century took on Russian names to make themselves sound more impressive, it seems to me that thinking, when given the title theorizing, is similar: while the roots of *think* are traceable only to the dull Old Saxon *thenkian* and Old Norse *thekkia*, meaning 'to know' – theory has a far more impressive pedigree out of *theoria*. Ancient Greece and Rome glitter with the names of philosophers, but how many Old Saxons can you name – other than Hengist and Horsa, who are well known for their insights in the thinking department.

I'd put the pompous use of theory into the category of theory despised by Richard Rorty (1998), who recently let loose a fierce onslaught on academic theorizing. He said that academics since the mid-1960s became so preoccupied with the weighty matters of theory and theorizing that they now no longer bothered to concern themselves with the mundane matters of reform and social justice. Reform has become submerged under theorizing. He says that academics nowadays, being so fascinated with what passes for theory, have turned away from secularism and pragmatism. Academics seem to want always to see things 'within a fixed frame of reference, a frame supplied by theory' (Rorty, 1998: 36).

Michael Ignatieff (1997) has said much the same about the academic fascination with theory and the theoretical:

> We know too much, understand too little, and when we turn to the humanities and social sciences for help, what do we get? The tenured radicals who went into academe after 1968 were supposed to free the university from the conformist functionalism of American social science. Instead, they set to work erecting new stockades of conformism: neo-Marxist scholasticism; deconstruction; critical theory – the games people play when they have given up on public debate.

These critiques are made in the context of what are seen to be an abdication by the academy from reform. Rorty contrasts the contemporary academy with pre-1960s reformers whose agenda was simply to protect the weak from the strong. His message, if it is right, surely has particular resonance for educators. The message is that for those in fields like education, the priority should be change, not theory. Change is effected only through an unremitting focus on the particular – by concentrating energy on a detailed, difficult agenda of practical matters. But a focus on these mundane but necessary matters is subverted by the contemporary intellectual's obsession with theory. The product of the theorizing academy has been '... many thousands of books which represent scholastic philosophizing at its worst' (1998: 93).

3. a) Theory in education doesn't get treated or tested like theory in natural science; b) in any case, scientists don't use theory in the ways that we presume, and theory discourages innovation

This section is about the similarities and differences between theory in education and theory in natural science, for a criticism of my take on theory is that it is underwritten by an unnecessary and unwarranted separation of the *Geisteswissenschaften* and the *Naturwissenschaften*, or the 'soft' and the 'hard' sciences. Rajagopalan (1998: 345) suggests that this putative separation reveals my view to be underwritten by a 'Cartesian dualism between mind and matter' and he proceeds to talk of my 'strong' and 'weak' views about theory. His criticism gives me a chance to expand on these issues.

a) Theory in education doesn't get treated or tested like theory in natural science

First, there is the issue of dualism, whether it be 'Cartesian' or otherwise. I see no problem in distinguishing between different forms of activity in the management of inquiry, and I fail to understand how the drawing of such distinctions invokes any disaggregation of mind and matter. The problem here is partly, I think, with the century-old invocation of the distinction between *Geisteswissenschaften* and *Naturwissenschaften*, or rather the words used to describe the putative distinction.[1] *'Wissenschaft/en'* comes from the German *'Wissen'* meaning 'knowledge' and *'schaften'* meaning 'to produce', and thus the 'production of knowledge'. From here, while *'Naturwissenschaften'* relates reasonably unproblematically to the natural sciences, *'Geisteswissenschaften'* translates literally to 'sciences of the spirit'.[2] It is in the contradistinction of these terms, particularly with the literal translation of the latter, that the potential for mind–body dualism is invoked – at least in those wishing to find it. But one does not need to translate one's vocabulary into another language in discussing these matters – and if one avoids the complication of so doing one can discuss different kinds of practice in inquiry without being haunted by fears of dualism.[3]

Second, there is the issue of the strong and weak views of theory. Rajagopalan (1998) suggests that I have two incompatible views, which I straddle uncomfortably: a weak view and a strong view. The weak view of theory is that it is useful in natural science, but not in education or the social sciences; the strong view is that theory is no use anywhere. Since this caricature exists, it will perhaps be helpful to expand a little on the issues. Taking the caricature at face value, it is correct – on the 'weak' issue – to say that I understand theory to be working in the natural sciences in ways that it cannot work in the social sciences, for the reasons I give later in discussing the role of generalization. On the 'strong' issue, it is not the case that I see it not working anywhere. Rather, I take its role to be overplayed everywhere, even in the natural sciences.

This is all within the context of a scepticism about claims to special method in science, a point that I make throughout this book. I cannot, however, help but note differences between natural scientists' working practices and those of social scientists. The similarities and differences are well summed up by Turney in his discussion of Susan Haack's (2003) work.

> Many who think about science for long probably settle somewhere near the view that it is closely akin to other forms of inquiry, albeit with a much more powerful toolkit ... there is nothing special about science, no distinctive scientific method. All empirical inquiry, whether under-taken by a detective, an investigative journalist, an anthropologist in the field or a physicist in the lab, demands the same epistemic virtues. Look for evidence as hard as you can, judge carefully what it is worth, and pay scrupulous attention to what it tells you. Then add this evidence to existing experience and use it to reason out your best-informed con-jectures ... What makes science and scientists stand out from this more general set of more or less disciplined investigations of the world, she [Haack] argues, is the large set of 'helps to inquiry' that the various sciences have developed – ever-more powerful instrumental aids to observation, experimental routines, models and metaphors.
>
> (Turney, 2004)

There are, in other words, both overlaps and distinctions between what happens in natural scientific inquiry and other inquiry. To assume otherwise – either to take an unyieldingly monistic view about the enterprise of inquiry on the one hand, or to draw sharp divisions on the other – is untenable.

On the issue of similarities, the celebrated biologist Sir Peter Medawar noted – in discussing what scientists say they do – that the special methods and procedures that are supposed to be associated with scientists' work represent merely 'the postures we choose to be seen in when the curtain goes up and the public sees us' (1982: 88). The theme is common in the sociology of science, as Becker notes, citing the work of those such as Latour and Woolgar (1979) and Lynch (1985), who have shown how natural scientists work 'in ways never mentioned in their formal statements of method, hiding "shop floor practice" – what scientists really do – in the formal way they talk about what they do' (Becker, 1998: 5). (I examine the nature of scientists' notional use of particular methods further in Chapter 6.)

One accepts that this is the case, especially in respect of the intuitive and discovery stages of natural scientific endeavour, a point that is important for my argument about the value, or non-value, of theory in these processes. To accept that it is the case, though, is not to deny that real differences exist between the 'materials' and the findings of natural scientific and social scientific endeavour and the ways that these can be handled and reported. As I mentioned in Chapter 1, Alasdair MacIntyre (1985) provided an important exegesis on the differences between what goes on in the natural sciences and the social sciences, and I think it is useful now to look at this more closely. Much of MacIntyre's thesis rests on the nature of generalization in the different fields, and since generalization – the drawing of an essence – is what theory is about in one of its most important meanings, from the natural sciences to the social sciences to the arts, it is crucial to understand this capacity in these different fields. In seeking theory, scholars of one kind or another are often (but not always) seeking something that brings information together, organizes it, seeks generalization on the basis of that organization, then explains and/or predicts on the basis of that generalization. One could even provide a tentative working definition of the most important way in which theory is thought about as: *a generalization abstracted from empirical study or personal experience that enables one to explain or predict.*

With this in mind, what are MacIntyre's reasons for suggesting that there are differences between the legitimacy of generalization – and thus theorization – in the natural sciences and in other areas of inquiry? He argues that conventional social science seeks generalizations, or at the least 'probabilistic generalizations' and in this, he says, it has failed: it has provided nothing in the way of generalizable knowledge in two hundred years. He proceeds to compare generalizations in the social sciences with those in the natural sciences, noting the role that *counter-examples* play in each. In the natural sciences counter-examples are treated entirely differently from those in the social sciences. The attitude in the social sciences, MacIntyre says, is 'tolerant' to counter-examples – very different from the attitude in the natural sciences. He suggests that social science's generalizations lack not only universal quantifiers, but also scope modifiers, that is to say 'they are not only not genuinely of the form "For all x and some y if x has property φ, then y has property φ," but we cannot say of them in any precise way under what conditions they hold' (1985: 91).

This is in contrast to generalizations in the natural sciences, where the characteristics of the counter-examples are well known and understood, and where a law is modified in the light of the new knowledge. The example he gives is of gas law equations relating pressure, temperature and volume where it is known that they apply for all gases under all conditions, *except* those of very high and very low temperature. This is not possible with social science generalizations. MacIntyre follows with an important point about social science generalizations, noting that an attenuated proposition about social sciences is that they provide *probabilistic generalizations*. These, he says are no better. Asking what the status of social science generalizations can be, he says,

> To respond to this question is not going to be easy, because we do not possess any philosophical account of them which respects them for what they are ... Some social scientists, it is true, have seen no problem here. Confronted with the kind of consideration which I have adduced they have thought it appropriate to reply: 'What the social sciences discover are probabilistic generalizations; and where a generalization is only probabilistic of course there can be cases which would be counter-examples if the generalization was non-probabilistic and universal.' But this reply misses the point completely. For if the type of generalization which I have cited is to be a generalization at all, it must be something more than a mere list of instances.
>
> (1985: 91)

He proceeds to note that the probabilistic generalizations of natural science – for example, of statistical mechanics – are more than this:

> They possess universal quantifiers – quantification is over sets, not over individuals – they entail well-defined sets of counter-factual conditionals and they are refuted by counter-examples in precisely the same way and to the same degree that other law-like generalizations are. Hence we throw no light on the status of the characteristic generalizations of the social sciences by calling them probabilistic; for they are as different from the generalizations of statistical mechanics as they are from the generalizations of Newtonian mechanics or of the gas law equations.
>
> (1985: 9)

He suggests that the standard Enlightenment reasoning behind the relationship between explanation and prediction is that *explanation* involves the invocation of a law-like generalization retrospectively, while *prediction* involves the invocation of a similar generalization prospectively – and the diminution of predictive failure is the mark of progress in science. But there has been no diminution of predictive failure in the social 'sciences': there has been no progress.

Why have the social sciences been so unsuccessful in their mission to provide not only generalizations, but also probabilistic generalizations? He gives four reasons, all resting in 'systematic unpredictability' in the social world.

1. The nature of radical conceptual innovation. It is impossible to predict (except in very mundane ways, for example to predict that the suicide rate rises at Christmas time), because a necessary part of any kind of noteworthy prediction must involve the incorporation of the prediction itself;
2. Individual agents are unable to predict their own behaviour (let alone that of others). This introduces radical contingency into any event.
3. The illusoriness of the game-theoretic character of social life. This illusoriness is in three parts:
   a) there is an indefinite reflexivity in game-theoretic situations, wherein each party is trying to predict what the other is about to do; thus, the rules of the 'game' are always changing;
   b) game-theoretic situations are characteristically situations of imperfect knowledge, and further, these imperfections will often be deliberately magnified by each party;
   c) a universe of unknowns exists in any social situation (an example he gives is of the impending retirement of a party in an industrial negotiation).
   In short, MacIntyre says, 'Not one game is being played, but several, and, if the game metaphor may be stretched further, the problem about real life is that moving one's knight to QB3 may always be replied to with a lob across the net' (1985: 98). In any social situation, he is asserting, not only are participants not playing by the same rules; they are not playing the same game. He proceeds: 'There is at the outset no determinate, enumerable set of factors, the totality of which comprise the situation. To suppose otherwise is to confuse a retrospective standpoint with a prospective one' (1985: 99);
4. Pure contingency. These are the galaxy of minor and major things of everyday life that cannot be factored into any social situation: power failures, the colour of the paint on the walls, the morning's argument with the spouse, or – a specific example that MacIntyre gives – the length of someone's nose: 'J.B. Bury once followed Pascal in suggesting that the cause of the foundation of the Roman Empire was the length of Cleopatra's nose: had her features not been perfectly

proportioned, Mark Antony would not have been entranced; had he not been entranced he would not have allied himself with Egypt against Octavian; had he not made that alliance, the battle of Actium would not have been fought – and so on' (1985: 99)

He then goes on to note that there are predictable elements in social life:

1. That which arises from the scheduling and coordinating of our social actions: the daily things of life, structured by timetables and so on;
2. That which arises from statistical regularity (e.g. that your spouse is more likely to murder you than a stranger);
3. That which arises from the regularities of nature, (e.g. the coming of winter);
4. Those which arise from people's knowledge of the first three.

Examining both the unpredictable and predictable elements, he goes on to say that in the relationship between the two, unpredictability will always win over predictability as far as the matters of social science are concerned. It is only the trivial things that are predictable, and we don't need any kind of sophisticated social 'science' to tell us about these. What characterizes the subjects of social science is 'pervasive unpredictability'. This renders all projection in social life 'permanently vulnerable and fragile' (MacIntyre, 1985: 103). Though he does not draw on it, MacIntyre's analysis is similar to that of Gilbert Ryle in the latter's discussion of the ability of the natural scientist to employ induction and issue 'inference tickets' (discussed further in Chapter 6 in relation to the claims of 'grounded theorists'). Social scientists don't have the wherewithal to issue inference tickets on the basis of their work.

It had been assumed by social scientists that with progress in the 'science' – as its achievements were systematically built upon, bit by bit, and as techniques developed – unpredictability would diminish. But it hasn't, and this, says MacIntyre, is why the 'scientific' project of social science needs to be abandoned. Such is the character of the counterfactuals in social science generalizations, that these generalizations are in fact no better than their predecessors: the proverbs of folk society, the generalizations of jurists, the maxims of Machiavelli.

MacIntyre's criticism of generalization in social science is compelling and its implications for any process of theorizing that rests in generalization are far-ranging. Bassey provides a useful overview of the ways in which generalization has been thought about specifically in education, and the fragmentary nature of discussion on this important issue:

> Perhaps Yin's concept of an 'analytic generalization' is very similar to Stenhouse's 'retrospective generalization', Erickson's 'assertion' and Stake's 'propositional generalization'. ... Perhaps Tripp's 'qualitative generalization' is akin to Stake's 'naturalistic generalization'. But to

draw such comparisons is a dangerous game for I cannot be sure that I have correctly elicited what these writers have meant by the terms they have used and, dare I say it, neither can we be sure that these writers themselves had clear, unambiguous concepts in their minds and managed to express them coherently.

(2001: 7)

In reviewing the idiosyncratic and disconnected vocabulary of generalization, Bassey shows how each contributor to the debate offers a new spin and some new vocabulary. His general point, though, is that generalization in education and the social sciences is of a different character from that in the natural sciences: it is 'fuzzy' rather than precise, and as such should be accompanied by a 'best estimate of trustworthiness' (2001: 19). This best estimate of trustworthiness (BET) would be based on researchers' insights, so that they might be able to say that an outcome is likely to happen about 19 times in every 20, which they might express as a BET of 90–9 per cent. The problem surely to be faced here is that if the calculation of such an important qualifier is to be based on the insight of the researcher, one wonders why the conduct of empirical research should be necessary at all. If the researchers' insights are to be afforded such significance in the reporting of findings, why should one not proceed in formulating policy and advice about classroom practice solely on the basis of those insights and researchers' accumulated knowledge and experience?

In any case, assuming for a moment that such estimates were necessary, they would be properly conducted, as Hammersley points out, by the academic community, rather than the interested researcher. Hammersley's wider critique of Bassey's fuzzy generalization concerns the status of social scientific generalization vis-à-vis generalization in the natural sciences. All such generalizations should be seen, says Hammersley (2001: 220), as 'cautious formulations' about what might happen based upon *any* kind of generalization in any kind of inquiry. There are no clear distinctions to be made between natural scientific and other endeavour in this respect. While this is certainly the case up to a point, one has to return to the critique that MacIntyre makes of the social sciences, a critique that rests principally on the quality of generalization in different fields of inquiry and the confidence that can be placed in each. On the basis of this, one needs to ask whether the *degree* of caution needed about one's formulation in each is not in fact very different. If MacIntyre's analysis is correct, there are systems and conventions for accepting or rejecting generalizations in the natural sciences that simply have no parallel in the social sciences, and nor could they have, given the circumstances he outlines. I examine Hammersley's thesis in more detail in Chapter 5.

Many would no doubt go along with the short-story writer Damon

Runyan and his comment in *A Very Honourable Guy*: 'The race is not always to the swift, nor the battle to the strong. But that's the way to bet'. In other words, one's generalizations may be far from perfect as ways of judging the future, but one can, to varying extents, rely on them as heuristics or rules of thumb in ordering one's life or the findings from one's research. This is the essence of ideas such as the practical syllogism (Russell, 1992), the heuristic, the rule of thumb, bounded rationality (Simon, 1983) – all of which describe much the same kind of rough and ready process but which do not pretend to be theory, with all that this implies. The appropriateness or otherwise of gathering this extended family of thinking tools and harbouring them under the capacious frocks of 'theory' is a theme to which I shall return throughout this book.

b) In any case, scientists don't use theory in the ways that we presume, and theory discourages innovation in ideas

A key feature of the work of those upon whom I have drawn so far is that the theoretical components of natural scientists' research do not conform to the folk models of that research, its processes and methods. Natural science works around, not within, theories – through processes of imagination, expectation, trial and error. The notions of 'theory' and 'theorization' can act, in our thinking about thinking, as a proxy for any of these processes, or indeed the generalization that follows from them, or, for that matter, for the explanatory system that follows the generalization, but if this happens it makes for a premature closure on our understanding of what is happening when thought moves forward.

As an illustration of the process of new thought and discovery, one can take the story of the discovery of the shape of the benzene molecule. We now know, thanks to the work of the German chemist Friedrich August Kekulé, that its shape is like that in Figure 3.1. Kekulé, in 1865, made several discoveries which Paul Hoffman (1989: 112) in his book *Archimedes Revenge* calls 'the basis of organic chemistry'. How did he do it? How did he realize that it was this shape – a realization, a conclusion that eluded his contemporaries and predecessors?

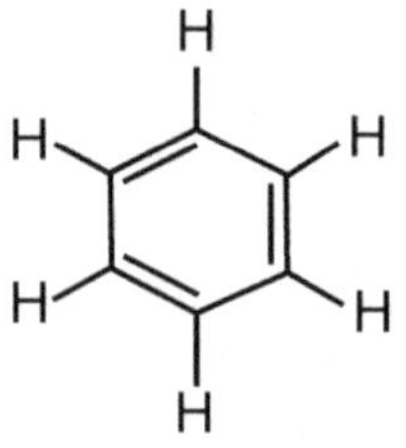

Figure 3.1 The shape of benzene, as discovered by Kekulé

He seems to have done it not after painstaking theoretical endeavour (though he was of course a highly skilled chemist, and he stood, in Newton's words, on the shoulders of giants – on the work of those who preceded him, and was steeped in the tacit knowledge that he had acquired by, as Kuhn put it, 'doing science')[4] but he made his original insights after dreaming. Kekulé described how he first contemplated carbon chains after having a daydream on a London bus. To quote from his journal:

> One fine summer evening I was returning by the last omnibus ... through the deserted streets of the metropolis, which are at other times so full of life. I fell into a reverie and lo! the atoms were gambolling before my eyes ... I saw how, frequently two smaller atoms united to form a pair, how a larger one embraced two smaller ones; how still larger ones kept hold of three or even four of the smaller; whilst the whole kept whirling in a giddy dance. I saw how the larger ones formed a chain ... I spent part of the night putting on paper at least sketches of these dream forms.
>
> (in Hoffman, 1989: 113)

Eleven years later, a dream again provided the inspiration for the possibility that the carbon chains could curl around to form rings. To quote again from his journal:

> I was sitting at my textbook, but the work did not progress; my thoughts were elsewhere. I turned my chair to the fire and dozed ... [and he describes how he began again to dream] ... the atoms were gambolling before my eyes ... long rows sometimes fitted more closely together; all twisting and turning in a snakelike motion. But look! What was that? One of the snakes had seized hold of its own tail ... As if by a flash of lightning I woke'
>
> (in Hoffman, 1989: 113)

The dream had enabled Kekulé to solve the puzzle: benzene, which it was known comprised six carbon atoms and six hydrogen atoms, was shaped in a hexagon – the molecule 'had hold of its tail' – a simple pictorial metaphor had enabled his breakthrough.

It seems to me that when breakthroughs in thinking occur – when we are talking about inspiration and creativity – they almost always occur despite theory rather than because of theory. Progress in thinking seems to occur (to borrow a phrase from evolutionary biology) via 'punctuated equilibrium', punching through the existing lineaments of explanation following individuals' energy, curiosity, ingenuity and creativity. There are steps in knowledge, leaps forward. In almost any leap forward – the invention of the microscope, the discovery of penicillin, the development of nylon, the recent isolation of *helicobacter pylori* (of which more in a moment), the discovery of superconductivity (see De Bruyn Ouboter,

1997), the story is one of chance (one might say amethodological as well as atheoretical), discovery, pursued with creativity and intelligence, despite the rearguard action of theoreticians. There are thousands of examples of this creativity aside from the examples I've already given: the invention of the aeroplane by the Wright brothers was atheoretical and done, to quote Freeman Dyson, 'as a relief from the monotony of their normal business of selling and repairing bicycles' (1997: 17). What one might call 'intelligent noticing' was more important than theory and this seems to be common to all discovery.

More successes arise from accident – from the happy process of noticing (look for example at the way Kohler's apes 'noticed' that they could move a box to stand on, to reach the bananas – which Kohler called the 'Ah Ha!' moment – see Kohler (1925) – and it seems to me it's very little different in our own minor or major insights and discoveries). More successes arise from the unusual joining of ideas (sometimes outlandish ideas) than from the employment of theory. Looking at advances in knowledge from Archimedes's 'Eureka!' to Einstein's thought experiments, it is probable that the vast majority of successes arise from the Ah Ha! rather than from theory. Einstein (see Hoffmann, 1973), for example, describes how he performed what he called 'thought experiments' in developing the theory of relativity. He would imagine himself sitting on the end of a beam of light to make guesses about how the world around him would change visually as he surfed along near the speed of light. Neither theory nor the set of respectable methods associated with it were as valuable as these exercises in imagination. It is imagination that is the driver. Why is there this impulse to call this theory? Theory, (using a broad-based definition as the systematization of existing knowledge), can provide only a kind of platform for certain kinds of incremental accretion – and *that* only in particular kinds of knowledge and practice, as MacIntyre indicates.

In the development of *new* ideas – and I think this is as true in education as anywhere else (indeed perhaps more so) – theory rarely plays a part, and I think in education it often leads us on interminable wild goose chases. Theory can't act as a *vehicle* for creativity. When inventors and creative thinkers give us an insight into the ways that they think, it is clear that the role of theory is predicated to that of metaphor, inspiration, imagination and even dream. From the earlier examples to Watts's invention of lead shot and the pure mathematics involved in Andrew Wiles's solution of Fermat's Last Theorem, theory had zero significance. Watts describes the idea for making lead shot coming to him in a drunken dream – he dreamed that he was lying at the foot of his village's church tower and that his wife was pouring molten lead onto his head. Wiles describes his solution to Fermat's Last Theorem (see Millson and Singh, 1996), which had baffled mathematicians for 300 years, coming to him 'almost from nowhere' and against the grain of the most of the work he had been conducting in the seven years he had worked on the problem. The psychiatrist Anthony Storr in his book, *Feet of Clay* (1997), provides many examples of this kind of intuition in which a solution suddenly appears. He quotes from the mathematician Gauss: 'Like a sudden flash of lightning, the riddle happened to be solved. I myself cannot say what was the conducting thread which connected what I previously knew with what made my success possible' (1997: 176).

I have just noted some advances in understanding, and I'd like to look more closely at one of these: the discovery of the bacterium *helicobacter pylori* (Figure 3.2). It is worth going into this *cause célèbre* of atheoretical advance in a little more detail in the context of the development of new ideas and what that development owes, or doesn't owe, to theory. As I mentioned earlier, it's now known that this germ is the cause of the great majority of stomach ulcers, whose aetiology had mystified the medical profession until the 1980s. One possible cause – the presence of bacteria in the stomach – was discounted because it violated the established theory that no bacterium could tolerate the acidic environment of the stomach. 'Discounted' is probably too weak a word. When the Australian medics, Robin Warren and Barry Marshall, came up with the idea that bacteria might cause ulcers, they were a laughing stock. The idea was dismissed, sometimes with vitriol. Martin Blaser of Vanderbilt University School of Medicine (and a subsequent convert) thought a 1983 talk by Marshall was 'the most preposterous thing I'd ever heard. I thought: "This guy is a madman"' (Monmaney, 1993: 65). Subsequently, Blaser (1989; see also Cover and Blaser, 1992) has become one of the world's leading researchers on *helicobacter pylori*. David Forman of the Imperial Cancer Research Fund originally thought Marshall's claim that bacteria were responsible for ulcers was a 'totally crazy hypothesis' (Suzuki, 1995: 9).

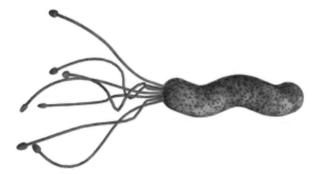

Figure 3.2. *Helicobacter pylori*, a *cause célèbre* in atheoretical advance
H. pylori image courtesy of Luke Marshall & Justin Kitson-Coombs

It is worth here taking a moment to look at some of the consequences of the crystallization of the existing knowledge into the well-established theory (Chambers's type 3 theory) that preceded Warren and Marshall's discovery. The following is a quotation from a paper in a highly respected journal, before the discovery was made of the role of *helicobacter pylori*:

> ... the mothers of ulcer patients tend to be striving, obsessional, and dominant in the home; fathers tend to be unassertive and passive ... ulcer patients tend to have a powerful mother and demanding adult roles. The variations in peptic ulcer in different geographical, historical, and social contexts are *unequivocal evidence* of the influence of ways of life in this disease. The specific elements that contribute to the variations probably include diet, alcohol, smoking, emotional strain, personality, and genotype.
>
> (Susser, 1967: emphasis added)

Now the interesting thing about this quotation is that a theory as to the psychogenic origin of stomach ulcers had taken on a life of its own. What little evidence existed from epidemiology was spun and twisted into what became the established position: that position being that stress (and its origins in family background) were the source of stomach ulcers. The meagre evidence – or perhaps it is truer to say non-existent evidence – was transmuted by the power of theory into what Susser in this paper called *unequivocal evidence*.

Not only was this theoretical position allowed to thrive apparently uninhibited by any self-conscious concern for the need for falsifiability, it was allowed also to influence a generation of up-and-coming medics in such a way that when the likely real cause of stomach ulcers was about to be discovered, those who were about to make that discovery about the real cause were met not only with disbelief but with hostility. Thus it was that the psychogenic theory as to the cause of stomach ulcers survived resiliently until Robert Warren decided to look at the bacteria that had occasionally been noticed in various medical examinations and post-mortems, but whose significance had been discounted (again because of the power of the theory) as an artefact of experimental procedures.

I can already imagine people saying, 'Well, this doctor was theorizing, surely'. I don't think he was. He was, by contrast, in Stanley Fish's terms 'not following a theory, but extending a practice, employing a set of heuristic questions' or as E.D. Hirsch (1976) puts it, 'making calculations of probability based on an insider's knowledge'. We can, says Fish, always call such kinds of practice 'theory' but nothing whatsoever will have been gained and we will have lost any sense that theory is special. I would add here that we'll also have lost any sense that practice is special – and I'll come on to this later.

In order to get further with their ideas Robert Warren and Barry

Marshall had first to obtain the grudging permission of hospital authorities to undertake a small piece of research in which they would try to culture a bacterium from an ulcer patient's stomach (grudging, of course, because it was too preposterous for words to assume that bacteria would set up home and live in the hostile, fiercely acidic environment of the stomach – on this the theory was absolutely secure. And, what's more, other rebel doctors had tried to be iconoclastic before and had looked for bacterial causes, but without success in culturing anything from ulcer patients' stomachs).

At first, unsurprisingly, no bacterium could be cultured, until by happy accident (the intervention of the Easter holidays) incubation was – completely accidentally – allowed for three days longer than normal. With the extra days, cultures did begin to develop. (*H pylori* is now known to be a uniquely slow-growing bacterium, which is why no one had managed to culture it before.) By happy accident, and by *intelligent noticing* (not theorizing), *H. pylori* – a now-notoriously acid-loving and slow-growing bacterium – was identified. An interesting offshoot of the story is that the maintenance of the pre-existing theory had not a little to do with drug companies' interests in maintaining it. When the theory was toppled, their profits from the sales of the drug *Ranitidine* slumped – the drug had made Glaxo handsome income; the slumps occurred because use of much cheaper antibiotics took over as the obvious, and one-off, permanent, treatment for ulcers.

Of course, the finding-out that occurred in the case of Warren and Marshall was not the only way of finding out, and the important point to make is that the labelling of this process as 'theorization' disguises for us in education rich and interactive varieties of thinking and reflecting. Thagard (1998) proposes the schema shown in Figure 3.3 to illustrate different processes of discovery and the interrelationships between and among them. The processes he describes are broadly of three kinds: search, questioning, and serendipity.[5]

- *Discovery from search*: Thagard uses the schema of Schunn and Klahr (1995) to describe search involving what he calls a moving from space to space – those spaces being a *data representation space*, a *hypothesis space*, an *experimental paradigm space* and an *experiment space*. Heuristics are important in this process – they are rules of thumb that make the search intelligently selective rather than random;
- *Discovery from questioning*: If there are not well-defined problems, search may not be the best way to come at discovery. Thagard suggests that in this case, deliberate questioning is necessary. Original questions arise from surprise, practical need, and curiosity. Surprise occurs when something is found that is not consistent with previous expectations and beliefs, for example when Darwin found an unusual distribution

of species in the Galapagos, and asked himself questions about why this should be. Practical need generates scientific questions when the accomplishment of some technological task is seen to require additional knowledge about how the world works, as when the Manhattan project gave rise to questions in atomic physics crucial to building an atomic bomb. Curiosity generates questions when there is something that a scientist wants to know out of general interest;

- *Discovery as serendipity:* Many discoveries in science are accidental. Roberts (1989) distinguishes between *serendipity,* where accidental discoveries are made of things not sought for, and *pseudo-serendipity,* where accidental discoveries are made within the more defined frame of a specific enquiry. Thus, Goodyear's discovery of vulcanization of rubber, involving the accidental dropping of a piece of rubber mixed with sulphur onto a hot stove, constituted pseudo-serendipity since it occurred within the specific frame of his enquiries: he had been searching for a way to make rubber useful for years. By contrast, George deMestral's noticing of how burrs stick to dog hair and subsequent invention of Velcro constituted serendipity, since he was not looking for a new fastener. Röntgen's discovery of X-rays and Fleming's discovery of penicillin were similar.

Thagard attempts to integrate these four models of discovery, which he says provide complementary aspects of the process of reflection in scientific discovery, as shown in Figure 3.3.

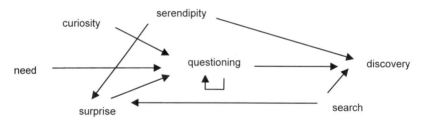

Figure 3.3. Thagard's interrelations of models of discovery

My point in having looked at the first and interrelating stages of scientific discovery is to indicate how thought stemming from established technology for finding out may be less productive than less orderly ways of thinking. It's important to remember that folk models about the development of theory have in their wake an entourage of methodological processes, supposedly 'right' ways of doing things – right ways of finding out. Most advance in thought and practice, though, comes *not* from paying due regard to what is established, *not* from conforming to correct procedure. It comes, rather, from the almost deliberate dismissal of that existing thought – from rupture rather than conformity. It is almost as if the deliberate casting-off of existing knowledge – and, by contrast, of the *acceptance* of ideas which arise from serendipity, chance, dream, metaphor and the process of sudden insight whereby ideas appear from nowhere – is helpful.

I contend that the creative events I have noted have not only been made in an atheoretical context, but in some cases are anti-theoretical, inverting received theoretical understanding. They were made by the chance confluence of noticing something unusual and a human quality that one might call creative intuition. The critic of social science Stanislav Andreski (1972: 108) says that how we achieve creativity 'is just as much a mystery [today] as it was in the days of Socrates: all that is known is that, in order to conceive fruitful original ideas, one must have talent, must immerse oneself in the available knowledge, and think very hard'.

I've been talking about creativity and inspiration mainly in the sciences, and there are those like Paul Feyerabend and Thomas Kuhn who have described the slow progress of innovation in science, resistance to new ideas, and the painful process of what's come, after Kuhn, to be called 'paradigm shift' there in the sciences. But it is important to note that theory in properly conducted science is open to attack via a reflexive and vigorous peer-review community. By contrast, in education, there is rarely any engagement in dialogue or dispute about findings that have emerged from theoretical endeavour and when there is it does little apparently to make people change their views or revise their theoretical positions. There is the tendency not only *not* to treat theory as something to be refuted – or even as tenuous, as a loose statement of where we are now – but to treat it as a sacred text: something to be cherished and protected. As I noted in the previous chapter, one can look, for example, at the discussion about the correctness or otherwise of elements of Piagetian theory (e.g. Bryant, 1984; Finn, 1992) (particularly notions of conservation and egocentricity) as the theory is 'defended' (and redefended) against perceived 'attack'.

Can the inspirational advance I've described ever happen *at all* in education? Not, I fear, if we rely on theory, because of the resilient, plastic, ill-defined nature of theory in education. There is no means in educational research of enabling the establishment of reliable information in MacIntyre's terms, or what Canguilhem (1994: 41) calls the 'elimination of the false by the true', and therein the verification or falsification of the theory. It's salutary to think back to the Wright brothers' plane: when it rose into the air and flew there wasn't much use anyone gainsaying the fact. It was no use someone saying, 'But this contravenes the theory! It can't be so!' The machine was in the air and flying – albeit not very far, but demonstrably flying. But if a new idea in education is good – or indeed bad – who is to validate it, or invalidate it? The stuff of education is so plastic that every finding, every conjecture can be interpreted and reinterpreted, constructed, deconstructed and reconstructed almost to infinity, with no resolution.

The aim in education often seems to be to construct theory that is unimpregnable, and if this criticism is valid, it is of course one that does in practice apply also to what Kuhn (1970) calls 'normal science' which proceeds by seeking confirmation of established theory rather than its refutation. But the fault of 'normal science' is at least acknowledged in its methodological discourse – it seems to me that there is no such acknowledgement in education. Indeed, not to put too fine a point on it, barmy ideas can be perpetuated for decades without effective suffocation. There are interpretative games which a non-science can forever play. As Popper (1977: 264) suggests, so called theorists in what he calls a pseudo-science can interpret 'any conceivable event as a verification of their theories'. So the false may never be eliminated by the true.

Educational theory is (and I'm thinking here of its 'grand theory'), unlike natural science's theory, non-progressive – in natural science there *is* an eventual elimination of false by true or at least (for those who balk at the starkness of false versus true) an elimination of less reliable knowledge by more reliable knowledge. But in education that process of elimination of less reliable by more reliable is far more problematic. And I think this says something about the knowledge we trade in, as educators. While today's school student knows more about electricity than Faraday, knows more about chemistry than Mendeleyev and more about genetics than Mendel, it's unlikely that today's student of education knows more about education than great educators such as Froebel, Pestalozzi or Rousseau. But today's experienced teacher in any and every school in the land may well 'know' more than these luminaries. The reasons for the contrast between the education student and the practising teacher lie in the difference between what Gilbert Ryle called know-*how* knowledge and know-*that* knowledge. The know-how knowledge is the practical knowledge behind which lurks the problematic notion of 'personal theory' – and the practising teacher's know-how knowledge may (or may not) be more sophisticated than that of Froebel. The 'know that' knowledge is the accreted knowledge of facts, collectable and progressive and clearly demonstrable in the sciences, but this latter has offered little progress that I, for one, can discern in education. There has been little conspicuous elimination of the false by the true – and nor should we expect there to be.

4. Ubiquitous theory relegates poor old practice

This is about the implications for *practice* if we put too much faith in theory. Schön (1991: 42) has contrasted the 'high ground of theory' to 'the swampy lowland of practice', and one needs to be aware of the consequences of the contradistinctions deliberately drawn between theory and practice. I return here to Terry Eagleton's point of identifying what the Other of something is if we want to know what it is about. The Other of theory is surely practice. Note that we don't talk about musing and practice, guessing and practice, hypothesizing and practice, saying 'Ah Ha!' and practice, or even thinking and practice – we talk about theory and practice. The simple existence of theory as a construct (irrespective of its validity) separates it from practice. And despite much talk about the integration of theory and practice, the *highlighting* of theory necessarily emphasizes their disaggregation. The theory that is hankered after by many educators, I think, sets a fault line between theory and practice.

And once theory has been separated it is set on a pedestal. The distinction created between it and practice manufactures a relationship between the one and the other, and that relationship is one of priority and subservience. Theory is first; practice follows. This fracture is important for education, for theories of whatever kind – grand theory or personal theory – are taken to inform practice, and in this informing process some explanatory value is made to reside in 'theory'.

Rajagopalan (1998) has asserted that almost anything we do involves theorizing. Even in the simple processes of selection and structuring, something above practice is occurring: theorizing is occurring. In looking in one's rear-view mirror on the motorway, for example, there is some mental transmutation taking place, Rajagopalan says, which involves both seeing and the assimilation into this process of already acquired knowledge of the world – 'theorizing' is the name given to what follows. We all do it, he asserts, and it is the defining characteristic of human beings. (I have to ask, as an aside, why just humans are theorizing when we do this kind of thing. Since dogs, chickens, frogs and sticklebacks all see, why aren't they and, for that matter, the entire animal kingdom with any visual apparatus, inside or outside a brain, also theorizing when they make judgments about how to move from here to there? But I'll leave that for a moment.) Whatever its problems, this invoking of theorizing seems benign enough. But incorporated into it is the unavoidable separation of theory from practice. Once invoked, theorizing sits stubbornly there like an incubus, pushing practice away and demoting it. Once theory is summoned, theory and practice forever remain separate, in a relation of priority and subservience.

For a profession like teaching this raises some profound questions concerning not only the contribution of theory to practice in education but also concerning the way we as teachers think about our own thinking and that of our pupils and students. The issue at stake is thus not simply the relatively trivial one of what we *call* this or that process, but what we conjure up when we rub the theory lamp.

When we conjure up the 'thinking theory' or 'personal theory' on which contemporary educators have been so keen, a key question has to be posed: do people deliberately theorize in such a way that their practice is affected, and hopefully bettered (if 'personal theory' is to live up to the hopes educators have for it) – are there, in other words, two distinguishable and separable processes? Or, or is *'tacit knowing'*, a phrase coined by Michael Polanyi (1958), a kind of knowing out of which theory cannot be drawn? Gilbert Ryle, in his masterpiece *The Concept of Mind*, made a crucial distinction here between different kinds of knowing – separating 'knowing how and knowing that' (1949: 27). Knowing how to do something is not dependent on knowing principles for doing it nor on the possession of articulated knowledge. As Ryle put it, 'Intelligent practice is not a step-child of theory' (1949: 26). Stanley Fish says much the same thing in talking about his book's title, *Doing What Comes Naturally*. He intends it 'to refer to the unreflective actions that follow from being embedded in a context of practice . . . what you think to do will not be calculated in relation to a higher law or an overarching theory but will issue from you as naturally as breathing' (1989: ix).

In fact, if all our practical movements and thoughts depended on theorizing and planning we should never move or think at all, for the planning would have to be planned. You'd thus have to have a theory about your theory, and so on . . . and on and on and on. Ryle proceeds thus, 'if, for any operation to be intelligently executed, a prior theoretical operation had first to be performed and performed intelligently, it would be a logical impossibility for anyone ever to break into the circle' (1949: 30). Practical knowledge and practical competence and proficiency cannot, in other words, be governed by a theory – by, in Ryle's own metaphor, a ghost in the machine. As Quine (1963: 48) puts it of the similar word 'idea': 'The evil of the idea idea is that its use . . . engenders an illusion of having explained something'. 'Idea', like 'theory' is some imagined (but assumed to be existing) positioned object – some engram – used to explain some action, but in reality it is nothing more than an explanatory fiction.

The problem with personal theory is precisely this: that it seems to want to evoke some arcane explanatory process lying behind the action itself. Behind the driving mirror manoeuvre is . . . what? A theory! Behind the teacher's skill lies what? A personal theory! The American philosopher Daniel Dennett (1993) uses the metaphor of the homunculus to describe the fallacy in this kind of analysis. A homunculus (from the Latin meaning 'little man') is postulated in some models of mind to explain the process of thinking by putting a little person in our heads who 'sees' inputs, and arranges for outputs (movements, speech, skilled action or whatever) to happen. No one, of course, has ever actually believed that little people live in our heads: the homunculus is shorthand for any postulated *agent* which performs these functions. It's an appealing notion and psychologists and educators have a predilection for inventing ever-newer and ever-better forms of homuncular metaphor. Dennett notes that the ghostly notions of mind once held are updated in the paraphernalia of Artificial Intelligence (clever-sounding things like micronemes, censor agents and suppressor agents). He notes that what has happened is merely a change in the 'grain size' (1993: 262) of homunculi, so that these new forms now replace the ghosts of yesteryear. Now it seems to me that *theory* (having a good long epistemological pedigree and an etymology stretching back to ancient Greece) is an entirely appropriate homunculus for serious academics.

All this is important for education, since teaching and learning are about intelligent performances and there is a common misconception that, as Ryle puts it, 'the execution of intelligent performances entails the additional execution of intellectual operations' (1949: 49). This is the case whether or not one wants to bother about calling those intellectual operations 'theory'. When someone does or thinks something in the practical world, asking them to reflect or theorize on it produces merely Ryle's ghostly double, the 'soliloquized or muttered rehearsal' (1949: 296). He asks, 'Why are people so strongly drawn to believe, in the face of their own daily experience, that the intelligent execution of an operation must embody two processes, one of doing and another of theorizing?' (1949: 32).

So the problem as I see it is not simply with grand theories inhibiting our creativity as educators. The problem with personal theory is the invocation of theory as the other of practice: theory as the point around which explanatory ideas crystallize – personal 'theories' which suppo-sedly help us to develop our practice. The problem, in the context of teacher development, is the belief that one's own observations and reflections can be rounded up, cleansed and transformed to provide an improved explanatory structure and practical guide for one's professional life. It is the idea that following the injection of suitable kinds of knowledge and training in reflective methods and theorizing, *experience* is elevated by some alchemy to 'personal theory' and that this furnishes us with some glittering epistemological sword.

Is the teacher who is encouraged to engage in this 'personal theorizing' really a better teacher? As Isaiah Berlin (1979: 86) says, 'What do the greatest classical scholars of our time know about ancient Rome that was not known to Cicero's servant girl? What have they added to her store?

What, then, is the use of all these learned labours?'. The student of education, armed with the theoretical and methodological tools of the trade, is in danger of becoming a latter-day Midas, unable to touch anything without turning it into a theory.

To call all structured thinking 'theory' is unnecessary. More than this, it is misleading, for it leads us into assuming that the hollow theorizing of the kind Rorty despises is in some way the proper activity of scholars and professionals. Rorty (1998: 93–5) says that theory often offers 'the most abstract and barren explanations imaginable', that 'Disengagement from practice produces theoretical hallucinations', and that 'in committing itself to what it calls "theory", this [cultural] Left has gotten something which is entirely too much like religion'. But, more importantly for the educator, it also leads us into well-worn ruts about the assumption that an ability to engage in advanced personal theorizing should in some way be the hallmark of the successfully developing teacher. Practice is therein demoted to its opposite and other, as though practice were forever dependent on superior theoretical processes.

This, of course, is only to be thinking about 'theory' as it is employed as a construct – as it is sought by social scientists. But this theory, whatever its form, even if it is only Fish's 'theory-talk', becomes separated out from practice and rises above it. The separation can only do harm since:

> The distinction between theory and theory-talk is a distinction between a discourse that stands apart from all practices (and no such discourse exists) and a discourse that is itself a practice and is therefore con-sequential to the extent that it is influential or respected or widespread. It is a distinction between the claims often made for theory – that it stands in a relationship of governance or independence to practice – and the force that making those claims (which are uncashable) may have acquired as the result of conditions existing in an institution.
>
> (Fish, 1989: 14)

In a particular discipline, he says, theory-talk may well have con-sequences but these will be no different from, nor any more predictable than, the consequences of any form of talk that has acquired cachet and prestige.

A crucial issue for education, which stands in importance well above the relatively trivial one of what we call this or that, is the lowly place made for practice if we spend too much time genuflecting before theory. Talking about theory is not, in other words, just talking about what we name thinking. In summoning theory lies the potential for artificially separating and ranking the intelligent performances demanded of all of us in education – children, students, teachers and researchers – and subjugating those performances to some elusive, illusory explanatory phenomenon to which we give the name 'theory'.

Notes

1. See Dilthey (1883/1989).
2. I am indebted to Birgit Pepin (2006) for her help in the translation, use and understanding of *Wissenschaft* and its variants.
3. Popper (1968: 251-2nn) raises the dangers in translation when he outlines what he describes as his own mistake in his acceptance of Carnap's translation of 'my term "degree of corroboration"*("Grad der Bewahrung")* as ... "degree of confirmation"'. He says, 'I did not like this term, because of some of its associations ("make firm"; "establish firmly"', etc) the latter having better equivalents in German (*'erhiirten'* or *'bestatigen'*). He suggested a change to Carnap, but implies that he was almost bullied into acceptance of the misleading translation.
4. As Kuhn (1970: 191) puts it, Polanyi's '"tacit knowledge" ... is learned by doing science rather than by acquiring rules for doing it'.
5. He actually describes four processes, but the fourth, 'blind variation', arising from genetic mutation and used by computer programmers in the creation of genetic algorithms is unlikely to be of interest; indeed, as Thagard (1998) himself says, there is no psychological or neurological evidence that such algorithms are part of human cognition. (One wonders therefore why he includes it in his model.)

4

Theory and the rational mind

If he had been asked whether he liked the peasants, Levin would certainly not have known what to answer. He both liked and did not like the peasants, just as he liked and did not like men in general ... With Koznyshev it was the reverse ... he liked the peasantry as opposed to the class of men he did not like ... His methodical mind had formulated definite ideas about peasant life ... He never altered his opinions about the peasantry or his sympathetic attitude towards them.

In the discussions which took place between the brothers on their views of the peasantry, Koznyshev was always victorious, precisely because he had definite ideas about the peasant ... while Levin had no definite and fixed views on the subject, and so in their arguments Levin was readily convicted of contradicting himself.

(Tolstoy, *Anna Karenin*)

Rationalism, consistency and educational theory

The kinds of enquiry and theorization so beloved of contemporary educators involve the formalization of ideas and knowledge. They involve categorization, crystallization, codification, making things clear, taking a line, developing constructs through which the world can be viewed. They are logical, clear, tidy, parsimonious, rational, consistent. The disordered or undisciplined is frowned upon and rejected. The result of such a process is the making consistent of knowledge which resists consistency. It is no coincidence in the contrast Tolstoy draws between brothers Levin and Koznyshev that the latter is an academic. And of course the academic always wins the arguments because his opponent displays the worst of intellectual sins: inconsistency.

In short, Koznyshev is a rationalist, and he shares this faith (I use the word advisedly) with modern educational researchers of whatever hue.

A faith in rationalism is no strange thing. Indeed, Berlin (1979: 80-1) asserts that the assumption that 'the method which leads to correct solutions is rational in character' is part of a central tradition in western thought which extends back as far as Plato.

The question, however, is not whether what is taken to be rational enquiry is valuable in answering some questions (for its success with certain kinds of question is palpable), but whether it is valuable for all questions – and in our case, most educational questions. I share Berlin's confidence in rationalism's manifest value in the natural sciences and his view that the sciences' espousal of and successful use of rationalism probably mark the major achievement of the human mind. But the problem arises, as he asserts, from the assumption that 'the world is a single system which can be described and explained by the use of rational methods' (Berlin, 1979: 81). It comes from the Enlightenment assumption that rationalism, 'while it may not lead to absolute certainty, attains to a degree of verisimilitude or probability quite sufficient for human affairs' (1979: 88).

My thesis is that if educators take this world-view they are wrong. The insight may not seem too iconoclastic, for it has been at the core of much criticism about empirical/analytic educational research in the positivist tradition. My argument, however, is that it is not only educational inquiry and its 'theory' in the positivist tradition that suffers from rationalist delusions of utility. It is that both positivist research and the proffered alternatives to positivist research in education tacitly share the same faith in rationalism: a faith that good, logical reflection and thinking can result in theories – of whatever kind – that will explain and predict aspects of the educational world. As part of the debate about appropriate methods for educational research a false opposition has been set up wherein one cluster of ideas – positivist, normative, experimental, objective – has been set against another: interpretative, subjective, intuitive. It is almost as though positivism with its transparent weaknesses as a paradigm within which to study education has become the whipping boy behind which the assumptions and shortcomings of alternative paradigms may pass unexamined. My argument is that a belief in a certain kind of objective rationality unhelpfully persists after the critiques of positivism are complete. This belief tacitly but firmly inheres in many forms of educational research and enquiry which avowedly eschew the simplicities of positivism.

The belief in objective rationality is accompanied by sequelae, most notably in the need for theorizing. And by theorizing here I mean tidying, generalizing, making sense, being systematic and being logical. A confidence in rationality therefore has two important products, at least as far as this chapter is concerned. First, there is an injunction upon researchers to adopt conventional, theorizing, tidying methods in their own thinking, their own analysis and synopsis. And second, these methods construct assumptions about mind in general and about the accessibility and the rationality of others' minds. I am thinking here not just of the methods, assumptions and findings of interpretivist research, but also of psychological research such as that which purported to discover sub-skills in children's learning of reading. Every assumption was of compartments, definition and logic (see Newcomer and Hammill, 1975; Brown and Campione, 1986; Anderson and Pellicer, 1990, for reviews and discussion). The assumption is also at the root of Piagetian theory, which sees logical thought at the zenith of development – the butterfly at the end of some ugly but necessary pre-logical stages. As many have now shown, the ability to unpick and respond 'logically' to syllogisms and other thinking puzzles may simply be one characteristic of developed thinking (see, for example, Wason and Johnson Laird, 1972; Nisbett, 1993) and assumptions about logicality may merely be by-products of the assumptions and methodology of the researcher (e.g. Elkind, 1967; Gelman, 1982; Bryant, 1984).

Academic education's persisting faith in a certain kind of rationality has important and, to my mind, unwelcome consequences. It legitimates certain kinds of knowledge and certain kinds of idea while restricting the opportunity for other less conventional kinds of knowledge and ideas to develop and come to fruit. Associated with the faith there has developed a technology of rationality and theory associated with educational research, as it is practised both by students and educational researchers, which is destructive of imagination, curiosity and innovation. I suggest that the structured reflections – the 'personal theory' – into which students of education are encouraged are less fruitful than more unstructured alternatives. In short, my thesis is that with our lingering attachment to the paraphernalia of rational thinking and theorizing, fertility gives way to tidiness in contemporary educational inquiry.

The problem with an elevation of the benefits of theorizing in seeking to answer educational questions is that inconsistency is the hallmark of the human worlds in which educators are interested. The reason that our theories about people and their social milieux so persistently bear mediocre fruit (see MacIntyre's, 1985 analysis in Chapter 3) is because we have the incorrigible expectation that rules, essences and explanatory themes – what have come to be called 'theories' – will be discovered in domains that are anarchic, or at least ineffably complex. In the passage from *Anna Karenin* (at the beginning of this chapter) Koznyshev's confidence that he has won arguments with Levin rests entirely in his confidence in consistency and other canons of correct thinking. The tacitly held archive of correct ways of thinking boosts Koznyshev's confidence at the same time as it saps Levin's.

But a faith in rational analysis has long had its antagonists – before the now-fashionable critiques of Foucault, Derrida and Deleuze – even though these antagonists were often seen as 'queer visionaries' (Berlin, 1969: 14). In one of the more recent assaults by these queer visionaries on the self-confidence of rationalists, Oakeshott (1967) makes a number of points. He claims that rationalism is merely a post-Renaissance intellectual fashion and that people who call themselves Rationalists have unjustly claimed to have cornered the market on all kinds of positive attributes. They are *for* independence of mind, but *against* authority, prejudice, the traditional, customary or habitual. The rationalist is sceptical and optimistic, and never doubts the power of 'reason'. But the big problem, says Oakeshott, is that the rationalist has

> none of that *negative capability* ... the power of accepting the mysteries and uncertainties of experience without any irritable search for order and distinctness, only the capability of subjugating experience ... [The rationalist has] no aptitude for that close and detailed appreciation of what actually presents itself ... but only the power of recognising the large outline.
>
> (1967: 2, emphasis in original)

My plea in the rest of this chapter is for enquiry that lessens the fervour for that 'irritable search'.

Rational research, theory and models of mind

Much of the debate in educational research over the past few decades has centred on the value of what usually goes under the name of 'positivist' research. (In fact, the agglomeration of all systematic, normative and experimental research and its imputation to positivism represents a frequently made over-simplification.) The 'given' has been the artificial simplicity of the positivist world-view. It has been the inappropriateness of assuming that the social world is reducible to the kind of laws that explain the physical world and the inappropriateness of assuming that the set of methods for finding out about those laws is good for education. But a belief in theory – and the order and rationality that accompanies it – persists in the critics' minds. Underneath all of their criticism of positivism there appears to linger a belief in an order (or at least a set of orders) underpinning the social world, and in the power of our rational thought in explicating this world. There appears to linger what Derrida (1978: 280) calls 'a desire for centre in the constitution of structure'. It is the fruitlessness of hankering after and perpetually seeking that kind of centre – that kind of order – that I now wish to examine by making specific reference to the assumptions about mind that appear to me to inhere in interpretative enquiry and personal theorizing. As part of this discussion I shall examine the methodological and technological accompaniments of those assumptions.

Interpretative enquiry and its rational technology

After all the interpretivist criticism of positivist research is complete there loiters Derrida's desire for 'centre' in much of the discussion about how to do interpretivist research. There lingers an assumption of order and structure that can be accessed via methods and techniques. Behind an interview (to take an often-used example of the genre) we can somehow 'get at' what a person really means; we can contextualize what they are saying and interpret it to emerge with categories, themes and 'grounded theory'. Indeed, there are now even computer programmes which can assist in the establishment of these themes by systematically searching, sorting and counting strings of text. All the paraphernalia of positivist research has resurfaced; all that has been lost, apparently, are its tenets.

But much of the bedrock upon which hermeneutics rests is that meaning is personal to the speaker. A corollary of this position is surely that there is nothing in a set of thoughts or articulated ideas – which might be obtained from research using interviews or participant obser-vation – that necessarily can be captured by themes; no categories which will express better what has already been expressed. What is said is in an interview is coded in intonation, in personal history. It is coded in what Oakeshott (1989: 65) called 'historic languages of feelings, sentiments, imaginings, fancies, desires, recognitions, moral and religious beliefs, intellectual and practical enterprises, customs, conventions, procedures and practices, canons, maxims and principles of conduct'. Its expression through language is infinitely complex. Literally infinitely: there will be an infinite set of meanings built into a complex utterance, resting in the 'language games' that a speaker is using – meaning hidden in what Giroux (1988: 20) calls the 'shifting, changing relations of difference that characterize the referential play of language'. Deleuze (1993: 30) puts it thus: 'A semiotic chain is like a tuber agglomerating very diverse acts, not only linguistic, but also perceptive, mimetic, gestural and cognitive: there is no language in itself, nor are there any linguistic universals, only a throng ...'. Listeners interpret more or less well on the basis of the quality of their shared knowledge, shared history and shared under-standings. The listener is therefore, in Wittgenstein's words, 'haunted by explanations' (Kenny, 1994: 221). If listeners are so haunted, their angst is at least demonstrative of a healthy self-doubt. By contrast, the con-fidence of the interpretative researcher in an ability to process interviews and discover themes and theory – especially via a computer programme – might be thought presumptuous.

But this is not to say that the understanding of others is, as Berlin

(1996: 24) puts it, a 'special act of magical divination not describable in the language of ordinary experience'. Rather, it is that our everyday understanding is 'a kind *of automatic integration of a very large number of data too fugitive and various* ... Our language is not meant to catch them' (1996: 24, emphasis added). The understanding of others takes place as part of what Claxton (1997) calls the 'undermind'. Capturing others' meaning will depend on all kinds of unarticulated and half-articulated signs – the gaze that is a second too long, the gesture, the tone, the intonation, the word used in a special way, the 'Yes' said to mean 'No'. These 'fugitive data', the evidence of cognitive science seems increasingly to agree, are processed without conscious deliberation and they are inaccessible via the weapons of our rational armoury. Giddens makes the point well:

> Oakeshott's critique of rationalism, which has affinities with the later Wittgenstein and with Hans-Georg Gadamer, is not directed against 'reason' as such, but against the identifying of reason with technique. All forms of knowledge ... are saturated by practice, by what cannot be put into words because it is the condition of linguistic communication.
>
> (1994: 29)

Elsewhere, Giddens (1996: 69) calls this 'practical consciousness ... The idea refers to all the things that we know as social actors ... but to which we cannot necessarily give discursive form'.

There may be more prosaic reasons for mistrusting our interpretations of what people say, for our respondents are themselves victims of their own educational histories about the legitimacy of rational explanation. So, when asked why they feel the way they do about something, people will focus on the rational and plausible – they will *rationalize* – even though these rational, plausible explanations can be shown to have had no effect on their actual behaviour and attitude (e.g. Nisbett and Wilson, 1977).

Complexity and plausibility apart, there is moreover no reason to assume that some shadowy organization, some Rylean ghost, underpins people's thought or behaviour in any of the social phenomena in which educational researchers are interested. What respondents say and do in interviews, and what teachers say and do in their work are what they say and do. We have no right to impute more; no right to impose 'theory'. We can certainly listen, empathize and try to understand. But to superimpose a theory – to lay some rational framework over the 'raw data' of their words – is going too far. We cannot get at some underlying truth which will be more or less well discovered via a research method, irrespective of how well we acknowledge our own pre-judgements and prejudices and irrespective of the satisfactoriness of our genuflection to Habermasian reflexivity or to Gadamerian *Sprachlichkeit*.[1]

The rules of the rational-theoretical game are given away in the title of Glaser and Strauss's *The Discovery of Grounded Theory* (1967). The assumption behind the title is that there must be a *theory* there somewhere, if only we look hard enough, and it's waiting to be *discovered*. Note that the word 'discovery' is used in preference to 'invention'. That choice to describe the putative process is revealing. For 'discovery' is the uncovering of already existing phenomena, as opposed to the creation of new, previously unimagined phenomena. *Discovery* is of things which exist; *invention* is of things that exist only in an infinite universe of possibly existing things. I explore these issues in more detail in relation to the specific case of grounded theory in Chapter 6.

And the term 'theory' – whether it's a set of orienting principles or epistemological presuppositions (see Chapters 1 and 2), or something even looser – implies that something has crystallized out of the inchoate data. The researcher 'discovers' it. But what if there is nothing to be discovered? What if that in which we are interested is shapeless? Does the educational researcher say, 'I haven't found anything: there is no pattern here – no "theory" '. It's unlikely. For *Homo Sapiens* is a pattern-finding animal whose facility to divine patterns where there aren't any is prolific. It requires only the mildest encouragement for a person to see a pattern.[2] We are predisposed to prefer to see form where there is none, rather than not to see form. Popper (1977: 270) suggests that this faculty may be inborn; it is due, he suggests, to 'mechanisms which make us search for regularities' and is responsible for 'the dogmatic way of thinking'. In the modern circumstances of the education academic this predisposition provides a predilection to make shape and theory out of that which is shapeless. And having once manufactured shape we of course have to start being analytic and rational about it. We have to have theory.

The ordered mind and personal theory: the rats become footmen and Cinders shall go to the ball

Why should a theory be behind the chaos, save to satisfy our lust for the rational and the ordered? It is worth taking a moment or two to look at the academic's devotion to theory and to wonder about its provenance. For instance, Carr (1987), in his earlier work, took issue with Ryle's subjugation of theory to practice on the grounds that if a teacher merely 'knows how' to practice in a Rylean sense one could assume that the teacher may be acting without reference to an ethical framework – and that this would not be practising educationally. This misses Ryle's point and distorts his argument. To quote from Ryle: 'Knowing how, then, is a disposition, but not a single-track disposition like a reflex or a habit. Its exercises are observances of rules or canons or the applications of criteria, but they are not tandem operations of theoretically avowing maxims and then putting them into practice' (1990: 46).

Another interesting example of theory worship comes in academics trying to prove that luminaries like Bourdieu are really theorists, even though they protest that they are not. Take what Bourdieu has to say about his own work:

> Let me say outright and very forcefully that I never 'theorize', if by that we mean engage in the kind of conceptual gobbledygook ... that is good for textbooks and which, through an extraordinary misconstrual of the logic of science, passes for Theory in much of Anglo-American social science ... There is no doubt a theory in my work, or, better, a set of *thinking tools* visible through the results they yield, but it is not built as such ... It is a temporary construct which takes shape for and by empirical work.
>
> (cited in Jenkins, 1992: 67)

Jenkins (1992) cannot believe that Bourdieu means what he says here, even though Bourdieu's disavowal of theory and theorizing is unequivocal and emphatic. For Bourdieu to *reject* theory presents cognitive dissonance on a grand scale for the commentating sociologist. Jenkins resolves the dissonance by saying that Bourdieu is being 'too modest' when he says that he is not a theorist. The 'too modest' discloses Jenkins's view that theorizing represents the pinnacle of intellectual achievement. Thus, for theory to remain with its epistemological lustre untarnished Bourdieu has to remain a theorist, but be too modest to admit it!

As Ryle (1949: 32) asks, 'Why are people so strongly drawn to believe, in the face of their own daily experience, that the intelligent execution of an operation must embody two processes, one of doing and another of theorizing?'.

Theory stands as the central problem in all of this. Theory forms the point around which explanatory ideas will crystallize. As I noted in Chapter 2, many have pointed to the problem of 'grand theory' in forming a kind of formal grammar within which the narrative of our thought is constrained. But the problem is not simply with grand theories. It is also with the belief that one's own observations and reflections can be corralled, cleansed and transformed to provide an improved explanatory structure and practical guide for one's future professional life. Following the injection of suitable kinds of knowledge and training in reflective methods, thoughts and experience are elevated to 'personal theory' or 'practical theory' (McIntyre, 1993; Carr, 1995). The essence of the process, LaBoskey asserts, is that 'The tacit assumptions, values and intuitions of teachers, particularly novice teachers, need to be *surfaced* and analyzed' (1993: 34, emphasis added). In this 'surfaced' one finds the heart of the problem. To posit a surface is to impose an almost tangible membrane between theory and practice in which the former informs the latter, and the latter informs the former in a consciously reflexive process.

The key question here is whether we can deliberately theorize in such a way that our practice is affected; whether there are two distinguishable and separable processes, or whether 'tacit knowing' (Polanyi, 1958) is a kind of knowing out of which theory cannot be drawn. In dealing with the world we do not consciously gather evidence and place it in a theoretical or heuristic framework for practical purposes. Polanyi notes:

> We cannot learn to keep our balance on a bicycle by taking to heart that in order to compensate for a given angle of imbalance α, we must take a curve on the side of the imbalance, of which the radius (r) should be proportionate to the square of 5th the velocity (v) over the imbalance: $r \sim v^2 / \alpha$. Such knowledge is ineffectual, unless known tacitly.
>
> (1969: 144)

The identical bike-riding point is made, more prosaically, in *Butch Cassidy and the Sundance Kid*. Sundance's girlfriend, Etta, is watching Butch ineffectually trying to ride a bike.

> *Etta*: Do you know what you're doing?
> *Butch*: Theoretically.

The same kind of thing could be said of much professional knowledge in teaching. That knowledge in the classroom – whether to make eye contact, how to respond to an interruption, what sort of question to ask, what kind of language to employ in developing a theme – is ineffectual unless known tacitly.

Oakeshott's views are relevant here and predate the discussion of Schön (1991) and other contemporary thinkers on this subject. His message is that the skills of the teacher or physician can be shared only by a process similar to apprenticeship – in the same way that knowledge about language use is shared with the developing infant. They are reducible neither to technique nor to theory. The analogous distinction made by Ryle (1949: 27) is between 'knowing how and knowing that'. Knowing how to do something, in other words, is not predicated on knowing principles for doing it or the possession of articulated knowledge. As Ryle put it, 'Intelligent practice is not a step-child of theory' (1949: 26).

This is not to deny the value of intellectual operations, but only, as Ryle puts it, 'to deny that the execution of intelligent performances entails the additional execution of intellectual operations' (1949: 49). When someone does or thinks something in the practical world, asking them to reflect or theorize on it merely produces what Ryle calls a ghostly double, 'a soliloquised or muttered rehearsal' (1949: 296). Ryle's position is now supported by a great deal of psychological research indicating that personal attempts to organize cognition are often counter-productive (see Claxton, 1997, for an overview; this will be discussed further in the final section of this chapter). The notion that some rational 'otherness' exists behind our practical competence is part of what Hoy (1990: 46) calls the 'grand tradition' of metaphysics – a tradition that Derrida attempts to deconstruct by examining the falsity of supposedly natural oppositions such as speech and writing, mind and body, literal and figurative. One might add theory and practice to the list.

Once theory of this kind has been created in the academic consciousness it takes on a life of its own. By calling the collection of vernacular constructs, reflections and ideas 'theory' we claim some epistemological legitimacy and explanatory currency for them. But personal views culled from everyday experience are not theory. To elevate ideas, impressions and transient hypotheses to 'theory' dilutes the word theory to such an extent that it ceases to be of any value. Merely to call these cognitive phenomena 'theory' blesses them with neither validity nor utility. Musings are not theory. Unless our personal musings are subjected to rigorous criticism – and survive – they may constitute no more than prejudice, dogma, or the weakest kind of generalization. As Russell (1956: 91) notes, the person who says that unsupported bodies in the air fall, 'has merely generalized, and is liable to be refuted by balloons, butterflies and aeroplanes'. The problem with personal theory is that legitimation may be conferred on what is no more than hunch, orienting beliefs, personal generalizations and prejudice.[3]

It is worth here pausing to examine Habermas's views on this, for he offers a way of smoothing out the imperfections of this kind of personal 'theory'. But he does this only to proceed with a notion of 'critical theory'. He offers a way of seeing our everyday thinking and theorizing as disordered and in some way flawed. Though flawed, it is, he says, transformable – and faith in rationality and order lie at the heart of the transformative process. Carr and Kemmis (1986) provided an excellent and sympathetic account of this process and its potential in education. Although superseded by Carr's (2006) recent comments it is worth examining this, since it still very much occupies the standard ground on personal theorizing. Rejecting bodies-of-knowledge theories and 'positivist theories' Carr and Kemmis offered a detailed exposition of the new understanding of theory in education. In a practical activity like teaching, they argued, theoretical formulations are the personal formulations of the do-er. The beliefs and personal histories of practising teachers are in fact the theory that informs their practice. But these 'theories', they went on to say, may not be true: they are the product of 'habit, precedent and tradition' (1986: 123). The value and purpose of research is to adopt a scientific approach which will provide the skills and resources for practitioners critically to examine practice. Thus, the irrational is transformed into the rational and bad theory is transmuted to good theory via the impedimenta of educational research.

So experience is sculpted into the more respectable 'theory' via the academic educator's favourite tools: location of the idea in established literature, procedure and analytical technique, and consistent, clear, rational argument. The rats have become footmen in shining livery. Teachers are thereby 'emancipated' from their dependence on habit and tradition. Cinders becomes a princess.

Carr and Kemmis developed an intricate argument for following this Habermasian notion of critical theory, that is, an approach which goes beyond the confines of the purely interpretative to one which is critical, enlightening and emancipatory. They put it thus: 'This requires an integration of theory and practice as reflective and practical moments in a dialectical process of reflection, enlightenment and political struggle carried out by groups for the purpose of their own emancipation' (1986: 144). Rationality is at the core of this, and in particular a Habermasian understanding of the means of getting at rationality via an idealized form of communication. The key to this position is that while there may not be any universals or absolutes in knowledge, 'the canons of rationality', as Giddens (1990: 132) puts it, *are* universal. If discourse could only take place in these terms, bad ideas could be separated out from good ideas. Or, as Carr and Kemmis put it, we would be able 'to distinguish ideas and interpretations which are ideological or systematically distorted from those which are not' (1986: 149). Thereby, 'rational change' (1986: 150) would be enabled.

Now an intellectual construction as voluminous as Habermas's is bound to be vulnerable to puncture at certain points and a point at which it is most frequently stabbed is in this claim to access to a special kind of rationality via an idealized discourse and the sequel assumption of emancipation following that access. Fish puts it thus:

> critical theory is faced with two unsatisfactory alternatives: either it admits an inability to distinguish between its own agenda and the agenda it repeatedly exposes, admits, in short, that it is, like everything else, merely 'interested' and not possessed of a special interest called the emancipatory or it preserves its specialness by leaving its agenda without content, operating forever at the level of millenarian prophecy ...
>
> (1989: 455)

And given that its essence rests in rationality's elevation it is worth asking some questions about the internal consistency and rationality of Habermas's own work. These questions are summarized by Giddens:

> Why are there only three aspects of social life which generate knowledge-constitutive interests? Is the idea of knowledge constitutive

interests in fact compatible with the orientation of Habermas's later work on validity-claims, which do not seem to be tied to such interests? Why does Habermas refer so little to ... [his own] psychoanalytic model of critical theory in his more recent writings? How can he depend so much upon Piaget's writings in developing a theory of social evolution, when the empirical basis of those writings is notoriously insecure?

(1990: 137)

The point here is not to make a serious critique of Habermas's epic work but rather to illuminate the frailty of supposedly rational analysis, even analysis from a high priest of rational analysis. It is evident even from Habermas that the 'canons of rationality' rest not merely in pure, uncoerced reasoning but in some supposedly concrete yet, dare one say it, fallible intellectual constructions. These constructions – the theories of Freud and Piaget – are taken to be not merely tentative hopping-off points but the solid rock out of which supposedly rational ideas emerge.

It is useful to contrast Habermas with Foucault here. For Habermas, rationality is at the apex of ways of finding out, and there is no reason to assume that the rationality that has served the natural sciences (but not, of course, in the tenets of positivism or 'instrumental rationality') should not also serve the human 'sciences'. The process of mind can be rational and it is this rationality to which we should aspire in studying the human project. Rationality should be pulled as the single golden thread worth preserving from positivism. Rationality thus emerges – apparently, if one uses Habermas's own reasoning as an exemplar – from sound, theoretically based formulations, which give rise to careful, unforced discussion. Theory is interwoven with theory, idea is built upon idea and sound conclusions are therein drawn.

Foucault inverts this logic. For Foucault, while Piagetian or psycho-analytic theory may form useful stepping-off points, they are useful only in the sense that they are caricatured or theatricalized. The conclusions that one draws thus emerge from a cavalier tossing around of the notions of the grand theory builders. They cannot emerge, according to Foucault, from the very architecture of the theorists' palaces. To use theorists' ideas in this way, as totalities that provide a useful explanatory framework, can lead us on interminable wild goose chases and down infinitely long *culs de sac*. Foucault (1980: 81) suggests that when social theories have been used as explanatory frameworks they have proved a 'hindrance to research'.

The linkage of development, research and 'theory' too closely with the kind of rationality that disciples of Habermas would promote has two major consequences as far as education is concerned. First, the privileging of certain kinds of inquiry implies relegating the unconventional: the intuitive, the playful, the polemic, the dialogic, the practical. It sets certain kinds of 'theoretical' thinking on a pedestal and it eschews other kinds of thinking. Second, it links the putative fusion of theory and practice to the teacher's concerns, the teacher's values, and the university lecturer's notions of rationality. It thereby relegates (by implication, if nothing else) the place of others in the supposed dialectic. Of course, their views may *be taken account of* in the personal theorizing of the teacher (indeed, this would nowadays be taken to be obligatory), but the implication that the elevation of rationality carries with it is that the knowledge of these people will be contextualized and sanitized and become transparent to rational-minded people only in the dialectic which the 'emancipated' teacher is able to articulate.

None of this criticism of the supposedly rational is about justifying nescience or vindicating 'a lyrical right to ignorance or non-knowledge', as Foucault (1980: 84) put it. Rather, it is about guarding against the institutionalization of discourse (the university being the institution in question) which the following of Habermasian logic would imply. To set terms for what is rational, and then to set the putatively rational on a pedestal legitimates certain kinds of understanding about the world and reifies certain kinds of thinking.

Carr and Kemmis say that educational science should not be positivist but rather should be ' "scientific" in that it regards the purpose of theory to be one of criticizing unsatisfactory elements in practical thinking' (1986: 127). The task of Habermas, they assert has been to find 'a meta-theory' (1986: 133) in which the social sciences are rescued from the possible arrogations of the natural sciences by 'preserving the concerns of "practical philosophy" with the qualities and values inherent in human life'. By contrast, Foucault (1980: 197) aligns the elevation of these Habermasian assays on rationalism with *scientificity* rather than science. The project of the new rationalist, he asserts, is to legislate what are acceptable kinds of thinking: 'I would define the *episteme* ... as the strategic apparatus which permits of separating out from among all the statements which are possible those that will be acceptable within, I won't say a scientific theory, but a field of scientificity, and which it is possible to say are true or false'.

The elevation of the academic *episteme* means that the value of teachers' direct practical experience is minimized. It has to be theorized in a special way in order for it to become rational, meaningful and useful. As Oakeshott (1967b: 11) asserts, the rationalist assumption is that practical knowledge is not knowledge at all: it is really 'only a sort of nescience'. It cannot be allowed to exist in its unadorned form – it has to be theorized. The error lies, as Oakeshott makes clear, from the belief that nothing but benefit can come from making conduct self-conscious. The assumption is that the personal knowledge of the teacher can be cleansed, burnished and theorized via the tools of the academy and emerge as a shining epistemological sword.

Some people may occasionally use conscious, reflected-upon reasoning to solve the problems they confront – they may use principles 'to discover the truth by transmitting evidential support or probability from some cases to others' (Nozick, 1993: 35) – but there is little evidence that such principles can be used as anything other than rules of thumb to be accepted or rejected almost at whim. Herbert Simon, winner of the 1978 Nobel Prize in economics for his work on decision making, makes some interesting comments on such heuristics, pointing out that people never deliberately employ what he calls the Olympian model of rationality, which 'postulates a heroic man making comprehensive choices in an integrated universe. The Olympian view serves, perhaps, as a model of the mind of God, but certainly not as a model of the mind of man' (Simon, 1983: 33). If the mind of God is an appropriate metaphor for our pretensions in the thinking department, it is worth remembering Terry Eagleton's (2004: 58) comment: 'As Nietzsche admonished us ... we have killed God but hidden the body'. We have, in other words, believed our own rhetoric – we want to think of ourselves as rational beings, but in so doing behave in our reflection on our own reflections as though they were possessed of superhuman, or at least extra-human, qualities.

Simon (1983) goes on to suggest that human rationality is in fact very limited 'very much bounded by the situation and by human computational powers' and that decisions that are ultimately made consist of a hybrid of heuristic and intuitive processes – the kind of processes I examined in Chapter 3. Popper (1968: 32) says something similar: 'there is no such thing as a logical method of having new ideas, or a logical reconstruction of this process. My view may be expressed by saying that every discovery contains "an irrational element", or "a creative intuition" '. He proceeds to liken this to Einstein's comment (in an address on Max Planck's 60th birthday) that scientific advance depends on 'intuition, based upon something like an intellectual love (*"Einfuhlung"*) of the objects of experience'.

Simon puts such intuition down to what he calls 'recognition processes'. In some way, we recognize situations in which experience is relevant and appropriate and use it. But there is no rational 'theorizing' involved: the fallible processes and corrigible heuristics involved are a million miles away from the Olympian view of human rationalizing and theorizing that Simon dismisses.

The assumption that conscious 'cognizing' takes place is a construction of our own methods for thinking about thinking. It is what Ryle (1949: 291) calls a 'para-mechanical dramatisation'. Indeed, as Storr (1997) suggests, those who are best at this kind of thought (notably philosophers) often themselves seem incapable of producing original thought or ideas; they are too clever by half.

The tyranny of method

There are certain sequelae to the rational-theoretical way of going about things in educational enquiry. A 'given' is that it is wise – even necessary – to build carefully on what has gone before, to use existing knowledge as a platform on which new ideas can be built. In discussing methodology, careful regard is paid to what went before. There is a canon of appropriate methods and right ways of using them. Books on methodology give detailed genealogies of the methods and procedures being described. The whole process conspires to create an impression of correct and incorrect method. Each name in the family tree of ideas stands for the solidity of the idea, for its status in the canon of ideas. Names given in research papers and essays alike are offered as badges of honour, sufficient almost in themselves to vouch for of the validity of the knowledge or viewpoint being imparted.

The process of building 'correct' method is akin to the process of the construction of paradigms in science described by Kuhn (1970) and it is worth examining this, for Kuhn's meaning of paradigm is different from that which has come to be understood by the word in the educational community. In the educational community, 'paradigm' is often used to describe a set of ontological and epistemological suppositions within which research is framed. For Kuhn, by contrast, a paradigm is 'an example of good practice, which must be used directly as a concrete model of competent work' (Barnes, 1990: 88). This notion of paradigm is a far subtler but much more insidious constraint on practice than the one with which we have become familiar in education. For it contributes as a set of social constraints to what Barnes says is Kuhn's 'myth of rationalism' (1990: 86). He calls it a myth 'not simply to imply that rationalism is false, but to imply that it is generally believed in the way that a myth is believed, because of its happy congruity with other patterns of thought and activity'. In other words, the myth of rational process is perpetuated by belief in what-has-been and in what-has-worked, and by association with other intellectual virtues. The key to Kuhn's exposure of the myth lies in his assertion that rationality does not reside in universal laws of reasoning, which exist like some unvarying liturgy. Rather, what is presumed to be rationality resides in the expectations of the academic community about what is right, good and appropriate – and it is this which wins the plaudit 'rational'.

Kuhn (1970) draws on a fascinating experimental vignette of expectation and tradition to offer some kind of psychological explanation of the effect of these phenomena on individuals working in a community of inquiry. The experiment is that of Bruner and Postman (1949) in which playing cards were shown to people tachistoscopically (i.e. at extremely short exposures) with the colours of the spades and hearts reversed.

People found it impossible to notice the anomaly at short exposures. Even at long exposures some people simply could not notice it. One said, 'I can't make the suit out, whatever it is. It didn't even look like a card that time. I don't know what color it is now or whether it's a spade or a heart. I'm not even sure now what a spade looks like. My God!' (cited in Kuhn, 1970: 63–4). Kuhn goes on to say, 'In science, as in the playing card experiment, novelty emerges only with difficulty, manifested by resistance, against a background provided by expectation'.

The myth of rationalism, in short, is perpetuated by the traditions, training and socialization of the academic community. Paradigms – right ways of doing things – are consensual, social. They are maintained intact by cultural pressure – pressure to conform. And a serious corollary, Kuhn says, is that 'Normal science does not aim at novelties of fact or theory and, when successful, finds none' (1970: 52).

That process of maintaining tradition – maintaining the paradigm of the rational – exists in the research training courses of undergraduate, graduate and research degrees in education, courses that stress theoretical embeddedness (whatever 'theoretical' may mean in a particular context) and its methodological accompaniments. But, as I tried to show in Chapter 3, thought stemming from established technology for finding out may be less productive than more anarchic and idiosyncratic ways of thinking. Most advance in thought and practice comes not from paying due regard to what is established, from conforming to correct procedure. It comes from the dismissal of that existing thought – from rupture rather than conformity. Any brief examination of the history of creativity shows that progress is made by the almost deliberate casting-off of existing knowledge and, by contrast, of the acceptance of ideas which arise from serendipity, chance, metaphor and the process of sudden insight whereby ideas appear from nowhere.

The creative events of the kind noted in Chapter 3 were not only atheoretical, but in some cases anti-theoretical, with what might be called 'serendipitous noticing' inverting received theoretical understanding. They were made by the chance confluence of noticing something unusual and a human quality that one might call creative intuition. They certainly did not rely on the academic technology of rationalism, with its heavy emphasis on what-went-before and using the 'right' methods.

Educational research as it is currently practised places great store on what-is, and on the correctness of methods. Students on masters degrees and taught doctorates typically undertake an introductory course on research methodology where they examine words – theory, ontology, epistemology, reliability, validity – rarely in a questioning way but more usually as ingredients for obligatory inclusion in their dissertations. While this kind of information is undoubtedly helpful to students as an instrument for meeting their immediate ambitions, it can introduce a kind of stereotypy to their research, and – more seriously – to their own thinking about their practice. I discuss some less theory-privileged approaches to inquiry in Chapter 7.

None of this, incidentally, is to say that people should not have the wherewithal to dissect arguments and analyse them clearly. This is surely part of the cognitive equipment of any educated person. There are simple books that teach people how to spot, for example, the illegitimate intimation of causation from correlation or silly arguments of the kind 'if p then q; q therefore p' (e.g. Thouless, 1968; Thomson, 1996; Warburton, 1996). However, to be sensitive to this kind of educated reasoning does not require the industrial-scale training in epistemology, ontology and research method currently provided by higher degree courses in education. To say that thinking, and especially creative thinking, is seldom marked by rational process is not to imply that rational process is not useful in analysing and constructing argument. My point is not to suggest the elimination of rational thought (for this would be silly) but rather to mark the parameters of rationality's utility when we are thinking about teaching and learning.[4]

Emphasis on the legitimacy-of-the-existing in method leads to a certain inhibition to creativity in thinking about inquiry in education. Oakeshott (1989) was concerned with this obsession with method. He says that we should notice how 'procedures, methods and devices' in recent times have broken loose from their subordination as a means of 'finding out' and have 'imposed themselves on our understanding of the transaction itself, with unfortunate consequences' (1989: 63). He is surely right. The shelves of my university library bulge with books on procedure in educational research – what to do, what not to do, why normative methods are right or (more likely) wrong. It sometimes seems that there are more books on procedure than books on the findings of research. A corollary to obeisance to what are assumed to be the canons of rationality is that assumptions are made about accompanying procedures and methods. Canons, procedures, methods and techniques all belong to the same family. They exist in a happy symbiosis, each feeding the others' needs and collectively excluding the raw light of new ideas.

A mini case study of method

There have surely been some unfortunate consequences of education's preoccupation with method. Take, as a mini case study, modern education's romance with anthropology and ethnography, for anthropology and its methods have had a profound impact on contemporary educational enquiry. My concern is not that ethnographic research is insufficiently productive of 'emancipation' as the scholarly critique of

Gitlin et al. (1989) asserts. It is more prosaic. Why should the methods of anthropology have been any more appropriate than any other method – or indeed than no method? Giddens suggests that ethnography (as anthropology's central method) is unnecessary for understanding groups with which we are *familiar*: 'The mystique of field-work in anthropology was closely bound up with the idea that anthropology investigates the exotic; for the more alien a group or community appears, the more an immersion in its practices and customs is necessary to understand them' (1996: 123). Surely a self-consciously ethnographic approach is therefore unnecessary for the teacher-researcher, who is already steeped in the life and processes of the school. What, in other words, is the point of reflecting on it and calling it 'ethnography'? Why not just do it? What are the particular advantages of this *method* in our situation and what use is *methodology* which encourages us to such methods?

And, (to continue the mini case study) anthropology and ethnography are not immune from the naïvety, over-commitedness and entangling of power and knowledge which Kuhn and Feyerabend have noted in practitioners in the natural sciences. I outline in Chapter 5 Freeman's (1996) refutation of Margaret Mead's work. The interesting point to note here is the reaction that Freeman's work occasioned. It appeared for the academic community to suggest the gravest heresy; his analysis was the subject of the most determined vilification. The resolute defence put up by the committed supporters of established positions and methods is unsettling. If findings can be as mistaken as Mead's appear to have been, what value can there be in method*ology* which leads us to methods such as those she adopted?

My point is not to attack this particular method, but rather method in general. We do no service to students' personal development if we encourage them to wrap their ideas in shrouds of methodological non-sense, to weigh down new ideas with all the impedimenta of theory, procedure and analytical 'rigour'. How often have we seen a student idea – bright and exciting when articulated at first – so strangled by the dissertation procedure that it ultimately bores student and supervisor alike?

The people who will have the best ideas about teaching will surely never have heard of symbolic interactionism, hermeneutics, participant observation or logical positivism, let alone Habermas, Hans-Georg Gadamer, the Vienna Circle or the Frankfurt School. The best ideas are flashes – intuitions and insights – evanescent and fragile, to be captured, held and acted upon. They are the 'sagacity' of Aristotle, the 'hitting by guess upon the essential connection in an inappreciable time' (Pólya, 1945/2004: 58). They reside in the kind of practice that is separate from the reason implied in 'personal theory' and indissoluble in the unspoken and unacknowledged impedimenta of Simon's 'Olympian rationality' (1983: 33).

Creativity through anarchy

> Knowledge ... is not a series of self-consistent theories that converges
> toward an ideal view ... It is rather an ever increasing *ocean of mutually
> incompatible alternatives*.
>
> (Feyerabend, 1993: 21)

There is a strand in the criticism of the recent critical thinking that has
come to be associated with what Giddens (1991: 10) has called 'high
modernity' that seems to suggest that such thought is merely a kind of
academic graffiti, just a sort of nihilistic fooling-about which is all right as
long as it stays in its place but shouldn't be allowed to disrupt the serious
deliberations of rational thinkers and theorists. But the contemporary
rebels are not as new as one might think. There is a long tradition of
resistance to rational orthodoxy from those who have suggested that
thinking – thought itself – is not amenable to the rational gaze. Berlin
(1969: 13) calls them 'isolated thinkers' – people such as Carlyle, Dos-
toevsky, Baudelaire, Schopenhauer, Nietzsche, Büchner, Kierkegaard
and Leontiev – who 'said or implied that rationalism in any form was a
fallacy derived from a false analysis of the character of human beings,
because the springs of human action lay in regions unthought of by the
sober thinkers whose views enjoyed prestige among the serious public'
(1969: 13-14). Unfortunately, such thinkers have always been caricatured as 'queer visionaries, a little unhinged' (1969: 14), yet now
cognitive science (see Claxton, 1997, for a comprehensive overview)
increasingly appears to show that in many ways they were right.

If this is the case, the practical knowledge of teachers can and should
remain untheorized. It can remain unschematized, uncodified (and I
discuss in Chapter 7 some examples where I consider that the use of
theory in my own work has been unhelpful). The contribution of imagination and intuition are greater than thought which is organized and
homogenized following the precepts of educational research and the
technology of reflection. It is dangerous, I realize, for the credibility of
someone putting forward alternatives to orthodox epistemology to talk of
intuition or imagination but it is clear I hope from the examples I gave in
Chapter 3 that new ideas spring as much from these sources as from
rationality ordered toward theory or theorization. Simon puts it thus:

> What is intuition all about? It is an observable fact that people some-
> times reach solutions to problems suddenly. They then have an 'aha!'
> experience of varying degrees of intensity. There is no doubt of the
> genuineness of the phenomenon [and] intuitive judgments frequently
> are correct.
>
> (1983: 25)

He proceeds to discuss the intuition of chess players, which takes place outside any explicit calculus:

> The explanation for the chess master's sound intuitions is well known to psychologists, and is not really surprising. It is no deeper than the explanation of your ability, in a matter of seconds, to recognize one of your friends whom you meet on the path tomorrow as you are going to class. Unless you are very deep in thought as you walk, the recognition will be immediate and reliable. Now in any field in which we have gained considerable experience, we have acquired a large number of 'friends' – a large number of stimuli that we can recognize immediately. ... Intuition is the ability to recognize a friend and to retrieve from memory all the things you've learned about the friend in the years that you've known him. And of course if you know a lot about the friend, you'll be able to make good judgments about him. Should you lend him money or not? Will you get it back if you do? If you know the friend well, you can say 'yes' or 'no' intuitively.
>
> (1983: 25)

Much new thought on human intelligence stresses the importance of the chance, the intuitive, the serendipitous and the irrational. This new thought derives insights from far and wide – from cognitive science as well as from research on animal and artificial intelligence (e.g. Fouts and Fouts, 1993; White-Miles, 1993; Penrose, 1994; Vauclair, 1996) – and it attests to the power of insight rather than the 'Olympian rationality' of which Simon was so dismissive. As Yeats, puts it, '[I am] now certain that the imagination has some way of lighting on the truth that the reason has not (1980: 53). Or as Blake asserted, 'The tigers of wrath are wiser than the horses of instruction ... improvement makes straight roads, but the crooked roads without improvement are roads of genius' (quoted by Yeats, 1970: 281).

The ability to think creatively, Popper (1977) suggests, depends upon the ability to break through pre-defined parameters to a problem. This ability he calls 'creative imagination'. He suggests that the essential qualities of this creative imagination are an intense interest in a problem combined with a readiness to attack presuppositions and an 'imaginative freedom' (1977: 269). In Chapter 3 I gave some examples of this kind of creative imagination and intuition. An acceptance of the chaotic advancement (or *disjointed incrementalism*, as Lindblom, 1979, calls it) that is inevitably associated with the sequelae of such thinking is not simply an escape to nihilism, as some commentators have implied. Rather, it is a rejection of the assumption that highly ordered methods and the development or establishment of theory get us somewhere in education and the social sciences. We should be less self-conscious about our methods and use what seems best for answering our research questions. There are no right or wrong methods. This theme is an insistent one in much recent thought and is captured well in Derrida's discussion of Lévi-Strauss's *bricolage*:

> The *bricoleur*, says Lévi-Strauss, is someone who uses the 'means at hand', that is, the instruments he finds at his disposition around him, those which are already there, which had not been especially conceived with an eye to the operation for which they are to be used and to which one tries by trial and error to adapt them, not hesitating to change them whenever it appears necessary, or to try several of them at once, even if their form and their origin are heterogeneous ...

> (1978: 285)

The idea that finding out is best done via a letting-go of the boundaries that surround inquiry chimes with the ideas discussed in Chapter 3, where I suggested that significant additions to knowledge are characterized – if one examines their provenance – by departure from, as distinct from adherence to, method. There is no reason why thought in and about education should be exempt from the removal of such constraint. As I have been at pains to point out throughout, this does not imply an abrogation of serious thought about educational problems; rather, it implies a plea for such thought not to be constrained within the ligatures of particular kinds of supposed theory and putatively rational enquiry. It implies a remorseless agitation, an unapologetic use of fragments and ideas from here and there. It implies an encouragement of the student's and the researcher's unrestrained intelligence so that they do whatever seems best – not what is implied by some theory, or what is consistent with some existing body of knowledge.

Kant noted,

> Dogmas and formulas, those mechanical instruments for rational use (or rather misuse) ... are the ball and chain of ... permanent immaturity. And if anyone did throw them off, he would still be uncertain about jumping over even the narrowest of trenches, for he would be unaccustomed to free movement of this kind.

> (1784: 1)

In contemporary educational inquiry, theory has assumed equivalent status to Kant's 'dogmas and formulas'. Licence to think creatively requires freedom to let go of what passes for theory.

My point in this chapter has been to point out how educational research is constrained by its carefully accumulated procedures and methods for finding out and theorizing. My fear is that an education academy preoccupied with theory becomes introverted and unadventurous – that it becomes a profession obsessed with what-is and what-has-been. My fear is that theory encourages research in education too often to be research created in its own image, forever iterating its own findings and reiterating its own beliefs, obsessed with its procedures and locked in its own involuted literatures.

Notes

1. Knapp and Michaels (1987) explore these issues in depth in relation to text.
2. Barrow (1997) points out that the human brain detects patterns infinitely better than any computer ever constructed. But there has been an evolutionary imperative to *over*see patterns: the occasional seeing of patterns where they didn't exist (as 'false positives' – for instance, 'seeing' regular slender shadows as tiger stripes) would have an evolutionary advantage over the non-recognition of patterns where they in fact did exist (the actual stripes of the tiger).
3. Of course, drawing on the discussion in Chapter 3 about generalization, one could say that the generalizations of social science constitute little more than this.
4. To argue that those who urge such circumscription of rationality's remit have as their goal some grand anti-rational project (which appears to be the position of the writers of the reviews quoted on the back cover of Siegel's *Rationality Redeemed* (1997)) is preposterous. Indeed, it is an example of the kind of argument (the setting-up of a 'straw man') which simple educated reasoning should protect one from using. In a similar vein Habermas (1992) sets rationality against relativism in order to defend the former. And elsewhere he even suggests that a critic of rationality – Foucault – is in a difficult position if writing a 'history of the constellations of reason and madness' because such a history involves the writer moving about 'within the horizon of reason' (Habermas, 1990: 247). To do such a thing, Habermas calls a 'methodological problem' (1990: 247).

5

Theory's spell: on qualitative inquiry and educational research

Life is the art of drawing sufficient conclusions from insufficient premises
(Samuel Butler, *Notebooks*)

As I noted right at the beginning of this book, I soon learned that to question academic educators' attachment to theory is to swim in dangerous water. On submitting an article on the problems associated with the idea of theory to a major British education journal, I received the unusual response – actually, unique in my experience – of a phone call from the Editor, suggesting that I withdraw the article because if it were published it would be bad for my reputation and my career. This was not, she noted, a comment on the quality of the article – merely a comment on how it would be received. She was right: when the article was eventually published (in a different journal) it met with a combination of bewilderment and hostility.

If the most common reaction to this article was polite amusement, it became clear to me from the reflex response from several colleagues that they considered my action in publishing the article to be irreverent and disrespectful. I am unclear, though, why this reaction – the mild or the angry – to any questioning of theory occurs. Certainly, it is an appropriate response to a particular brand of philistinism about educational inquiry. But if it becomes a reflexive defensiveness to (and disdain about) any questioning of *theory* – theory's meaning, its uses and the consequences of our seeking it and its development – it means that a central theme in ways of understanding education is curtailed off from debate.

I have so far addressed theory in its relation to all inquiry in education, but the purpose of this chapter is to ask specifically what value there is in the association of theory with qualitative inquiry in education. For clarity's sake, some central definitional issues have again to be refined before attempting to begin to answer this question. When thinking about these one needs to start off with some broad definitional points and to narrow down to one or two key ones.

On the broad definitional matters, one first has to recognize that there exist the coarser lineaments of 'theory' as-it-is-used: the casual and vernacular uses of the word 'theory' in educational discourse. As I noted in Chapter 2, these casual uses are often at the root of the 'contradiction' claims of those who assert that the theoretical cannot legitimately be criticized in a discursive critique, for that critique is itself 'theoretical' and thus necessarily contradicts itself. But any supposed contradiction exists, of course, only because definitional boundaries have been pushed outwards so far that 'theory' comes to encompass any kind of reasoned discussion. 'Theory' widened in this way is merely the 'epistemic sieve' spoken of by Crews (1997) or the 'protoscientific' theory spoken about by Russell (1992). These vernacular uses of theory are distracting when thrown into discussion about inquiry, but they far from complete the definitional picture, for there are many other ways in which the word 'theory' is used in educational inquiry. In Chapter 1 I examined the many and varied intellectual constructions and heuristics 'theory' has come to denote: systems of evolving explanation; personal reflections; orienting principles; epistemological presuppositions; developed arguments; craft knowledge; and more.

The word theory has come to denote all of these in educational discourse, and its promiscuous use – with a failure to distinguish between meanings – leads to problems in relation to various kinds of educational inquiry. It is not, to be fair to education, only in education that one finds this promiscuity or these problems. Stanley Fish (1989) suggests that much discourse about theory in the academy generally is not really about theory at all, but rather about 'theory-talk, that is, 'any form of talk that has acquired cachet and prestige' (1989: 14–15). The cavalier way in which 'theory' is employed results in the word becoming impotent. And this is often merely in the attempt to add epistemic weight and gloss to what is otherwise mundane. 'Theory' is used, says Fish

> to designate high-order generalizations, or strong declarations of basic beliefs, or programmatic statements of political or economic agendas, or descriptions of underlying assumptions. Here my argument is that to include such activities under the rubric of theory is finally to make everything theory, and if one does that there is nothing of a *general* kind to be said about theory. (1989: 378)

Fish is surely correct to note that the indiscriminate employment of the word results in its becoming meaningless. The aim at this juncture in the book, though, is not to go into this general tendency to want to develop and employ 'theory' in a range of inquiry contexts but to examine specifically what I take to be a misplaced devotion to theory in one particular arena – that of qualitative inquiry.

That devotion undeniably exists. In their classic *The Discovery of Grounded Theory*, Glaser and Strauss (1967: 1) state that 'We believe that the discovery of theory ... is a major task'. Lincoln and Guba (1985: 41) give 'grounded theory' as one of the characteristics of naturalistic inquiry. Even Eisner, after persuasively arguing for a loosening of grip on the erstwhile tools of the educational inquirer persists nevertheless in a determination to seek theory. He notes that 'The arts and the humanities have provided a long tradition of ways of describing, interpreting, and appraising the world' (1991: 2), observing that inquirers into education have largely rejected these forms of description and interpretation because of 'a limited and limiting conception of knowledge'.

But quarantined away from consideration in the contrast between educational inquiry and that of the humanities is the disputed place of *theory* in that kind of description and interpretation: theory's place is secure in Eisner's account – it is above question, as though to waver in one's confidence in it would be to commit some lese-majesty. What appears to elude Eisner in the making of the comparison with the humanities is the increasingly contested place of theory there, for he later goes on to assert the instrumental importance of theory, suggesting that 'one of the critical tasks in the preparation of qualitative researchers is practice in using theory to account for what they describe' (1991: 237). Not much reasoning is given for this exaltation of theory. The need for theory is taken to be so self-evident that assertion can stand quite confidently in the stead of reason. Glaser and Strauss are equally bold about theory, saying that 'Most important, it [grounded theory] works – provides us with relevant predictions, explanations, interpretations and applications' (1967: 1). No evidence is adduced to support the assertion that it 'works' or provides 'relevant predictions'. Confidence, it seems, is enough when it comes to asserting the value of theory.

One has to look a little deeper then – since explicit reasoning is often lacking – for the provenance of qualitative inquirers' romance with theory. Why, in other words, should these scholars – any scholars – want to develop theory in a qualitatively orientated study? One answer lies in theory's epistemological cachet, which is seemingly irresistible for academics, such that any serious inquiry is incomplete without it. Theory is taken to be at epistemology's apogee and is thus unavoidable for those who take themselves to be serious inquirers.

The argument about cachet, though, explains only a certain kind of superficial hallucination with the assumed benefits of theory. The provenance of qualitative researchers' attachment to theory comes, it seems to me, from three principal directions:

1. From what Mouzelis (1995) calls 'crypto-functionalism', evidenced for example in the assertion of Glaser and Strauss (1967: 1) that grounded theory 'provides us with relevant predictions, explanations, interpretations and applications'; the latter, I shall argue, is not what qualitative inquiry is about. To want to do this – to foreground the uniqueness of interpretation, at the same time as developing theory (in its 'generalizing' sense) – is to want to have one's cake and eat it;
2. From an assumption that it is only via the generality gifted by theory that social science, including education, will have anything constructive to offer policy. This may of course be a valid argument in instrumental terms, but it is not sufficient in itself to give value to theory. It depends in its instrumental sense on smoke and mirrors – on convincing policy makers that theory is that which separates the offer of the social scientist from the arbitrary and idiosyncratic 'interpretive screen' – as Vickers (1965: 69) describes it – developed by and used by the policy maker; 'theory' is the name for the external, independent guide which rises above the local, the parochial, the partisan;
3. From the assumption that theory is employed in the arts and humanities, wherein analysts' description and interpretation provide a model for the foregrounding of interpretative theory in social inquiry: if theory is appropriate there, the argument goes, it is appropriate here. Those who paint this picture, though, fail to address the contested status of theory in the humanities.

I shall examine each of these in the sections which follow.

1. Crypto-functionalism: theory is the culprit

At the root of the respect in which theory is held in qualitative inquiry is a confusion noted by Mouzelis (1995). He points out that there are essentially two kinds of theory used by social scientists and that the refusal to distinguish between the two (or, more likely, the neglect to make the distinction) 'has social scientists talking at cross purposes' (1995: 2). The two kinds of theory are: (a) theory as a set of statements telling us something new about the social world and which can be proved or disproved by empirical investigation; and (b) theory as tools for thinking. Mouzelis proceeds to note that the distinction is similar to that drawn by Althusser when the latter set out to distinguish between theory as a tool/means, which he termed 'Generalities II', and theory as a provisional end-product, 'Generalities III' (Althusser, 1979: 183-90). Nadel (1957) makes a similar distinction, as does Bourdieu (in Wacquant, 1989). While the distinction which Mouzelis draws is an important one when it comes to an explanation of the use of 'theory' in sociology, it should be noted that it is by no means the last word. While Althusser's distinction is crucial for understanding theory's meaning, that distinction has seldom, it seems to me, proved informative for sociologists, and almost any sociological text one picks up yields a different meaning for theory. Indeed, in a single volume on theory in that discipline, many and varied interpretations and uses appear. Martindale (1979: 18), for example, says that theory is 'any coherent group of general propositions used as explanatory principles for a class of phenomena'. Cicourel (1979) makes a distinction between 'weak' theory, which he says lies behind the inductive assumptions of field research, and 'stronger' theory. (The use of 'weak' and 'strong' is made as though these are some well-established descriptors of a tightly defined concept – theory – rather than vernacularly used adjectives for a common-sense notion, that notion being simply 'idea'.) Snizek (1979) studied 1434 articles from nine major sociological journals and decided that there were four general categories of theory: realist, quasi-realist, quasi-nominalist, and nominalist. The realist was focused on the study of group properties and the discovery of structural laws and was 'relatively nonempirical' (1979: 199) in research methods. With 'quasi' orientations the 'theoretical perspectives were essentially social psychological in nature' (1979: 198), while the nominalists had a 'psychological theoretical orientation' (ibid: 198). The matter is clearly complex and is made no less complex by Althusser's (1979) alternative set of definitions:

> I shall call *theory* any theoretical practice of a *scientific* character. I shall call 'theory' (in inverted commas) [sic] the determinate *theoretical system* of a real science (its basic concepts in their more or less contradictory unity at a given time): for example, the theory of universal attraction, wave mechanics, etc. . . . or again, the *'theory'* of historical materialism. In its 'theory' any determinate science reflects within the complex unity of its concepts (a unity which, I should add, is more or less problematic) the results, which will henceforth be the conditions and means, of its own theoretical practice. I shall call Theory (with a capital T), general theory, that is, the Theory of practice in general, itself elaborated on the basis of the Theory of existing theoretical practices (of the sciences), which transforms into 'knowledges' (scientific truths) the ideological product of existing 'empirical' practices (the concrete activity of men).
>
> (1979: 167, emphasis in original)

I have to confess to finding it impossible to understand what Althusser means here, particularly in the context of his other explanation of theory in Generalities II and III, and of his use of 'scientific'. This is clearly at variance with Popper's (1977) understanding of scientific theory, and also with Wright Mills's (1959). The latter would have called such an attempt 'grand theory' (given the inclusion of historical materialism as a scientific theory). What is clear, however, from Althusser's account is that there is some acknowledgement of the need to differentiate and categorize meanings, given the varied way that the word is used in sociology and political science.

Let's stick with the rather clearer explication Althusser gives in Generalities II and III. No one could argue about tools for thinking (Generalities II) though one could argue about why such tools have to be called 'theory', as does Bourdieu (in Wacquant, 1989). Calling most theory in social science 'gobbledygook', he says that his own 'theory' is merely the thinking tools which are temporary constructs which take shape to help his work. Used in this sense there is no reason, as Bourdieu himself implies, why one shouldn't simply call such tools 'thinking'. No reason, that is, unless one is looking for some additional insignia to mark one's seriousness as researcher or inquirer. 'Theory says ...', after all, sounds a lot better than 'I think that ...'.

While Bourdieu recognizes and addresses the important distinction between Generalities II and Generalities III, most qualitative inquirers ignore or elide it. They opt to discuss theory in its wide generalizing form, Generalities III, and here is where serious concerns emerge, for in doing this they appear to want to ride two horses at once. In doing qualitative research and accepting the tenets on which the validity of such work is premised, they want – in simultaneously seeking generalizing theory – to engage in two inconsistent activities. Borrowing Mouzelis's (1995: 7) words, they want to avoid 'unfashionable functionalist vocabulary ... while retaining its fundamental logic – with the result that crypto-functionalist elements and related distinctions are clandestinely reintro-duced into their writings'. The problems come in aspiration (and this is the case in qualitative inquiry in education) to Generalities III theory – with its intimations of regularity, generality and, as Hammersley (1992: 13) notes, 'universals'.

The dilemma of crypto-functionalism, then, centres on this notion of regularity, for regularity is surely not what the qualitative researcher is about. As Hans-Georg Gadamer (1960/1975: 6) put it, '...one has not grasped the nature of the human sciences if one measures them by the yardstick of an increasing knowledge of regularity'. This tension has been raised by some commentators – for example Roman (1992) describes what she calls the neo-positivist stance of naturalistic ethnography, and Stronach (1997) critiques the 'modernist pursuit' of a post-modern goal – but it is not raised enough. Hammersley (1992) provides a particularly intelligent and well-informed discussion of these tensions, these pro-blems and their consequences. Given the thoroughness and complexity of his examination, and given that he attempts a resolution of the pro-blems, I shall address his analysis in some detail, because for me the issues are far from resolved at the end of his analysis.

Hammersley notes, 'While ethnographers often express a commitment to theory, there has been relatively little discussion of the nature of the theory used in ethnographic work.' (1992: 34). He continues:

> If theories are probabilistic . . . then we cannot test them by searching for negative cases and reconstructing them when we discover such cases. Exceptions would not count against such theories, indeed they are to be expected. This seems to undercut the very possibility of the sort of theorizing that I outlined earlier and that I have argued elsewhere is a priority of the social sciences.
>
> (1992: 41)

He concedes the inconsistency in the qualitative project – of at once trying to hold to the tenets of constructionism (with its assumptions about particularistic meaning) while simultaneously seeking some universalistic theory. He notes,

> the 'theoretical descriptions' that ethnographers produce are little different from the descriptions and explanations employed by us all in everyday life. What distinctiveness they ought to have concerns not the *theoretical* character but the explicitness and coherence of the models employed, and the rigour of the data collection and analysis on which they are based.
>
> (1992: 22)

While Hammersley is frank in his confrontation of the problems which reside in a theory-seeking approach, it is difficult to escape the conclusion that he is ultimately seeking some kind of rescue mission for it. Note the discussion of *distinctiveness* in the passage just quoted: we should value the coherence, explicitness and rigour involved in the development of 'models'. This is an important sentence, for in it Hammersley, having accepted the dilemmas inhering in 'theory' dismisses 'theoretical character' as a topic of importance, substituting for it 'models', and these models will depend for their credibility on the quality of the fact finding and analysis used in their construction.

But in that sentence theory is made to walk into the mist, only to walk out again in different guise. The essential character of theory – its putative capture of the general or universal – cannot be dismissed by merely a change of clothes. It is not merely the speech-act 'theory' which is the problem – not the articulation of these particular syllables – but rather the pretension to capture a regularity, an essence, a generality, a universal, which will help us in explaining and predicting and so on. It's no use saying, 'let's forget about theory, it's the models that are important' for what else do models comprise (particularly if they are explicit and coherent) if it is not precisely the generalizing features of theory that make theory problematic? I shall return to this in a moment.

Hammersley concludes, 'descriptions cannot be theories . . . [but – and here comes theory again] all descriptions are theoretical in the sense that they involve concepts and are structured by theoretical assumptions' (1992: 28). The problem here is that one does not know why 'concepts' or 'assumptions' should be entitled to be adorned with the epistemological garland 'theoretical'. They are theoretical only in the sense that they conform to the kind of vernacular notions about theory which come from everyday generalization and 'practical syllogism'. As Russell puts it, 'human beings construct a set of generalizations, held together by *seemingly* theoretical postulates (such as 'an intention' and 'a belief') and inferences ('practical syllogisms'), and . . . this has a kind of protoscientific structure' (1992: 486, emphasis added). What seems to be happening here is that everyday beliefs, interpretations, generalizations and prejudices are being anointed as 'theoretical' (in its everyday sense) in order to confer on descriptions some theoretical character. Theory (with a definition change, from Generalities III to vernacular) is bent back on itself to support itself. Aside from the contestable legitimacy of this, there is simply no need to do it: description is description – it doesn't have to be theoretical (unless being 'theoretical' serves some separate purpose, and I'll come to this in the next section).

Despite his general acceptance of theory's problems, though, Hammersley (1992) proceeds with an appeal for the drawing-together which theory comprises by invoking criteria by which research and theory should be judged. 'Theory', in its regularities or Generalities III form, (albeit sometimes wrapped in the robes of 'models', as noted earlier) is clearly the likely escapee following his argument, since it is notions of regularity and generality which for him define theory.

Hammersley advances the argument in favour of regularity by developing criteria for judging research which will neutralize the objections to the development of – let's just call them 'regularizing heuristics'. These criteria will provide measures for the 'sufficiency of evidence' (1992: 70) offered by ethnographers. These criteria are *validity* and *relevance*. The former, validity, is to be assessed first by 'plausibility and credibility' (1992: 70), second by demanding more evidence where a costly decision is involved, and third by differentiating the nature of the claim being made by the researcher – whether to description, explanation or theory – and demanding different kinds of evidence depending on the claim.[1]

Now these are interesting criteria by which to address the serious dilemmas and inconsistencies in the qualitative researcher's project. The first one, plausibility and credibility, forms the cornerstone around which the others are built and it merits most attention: the suggestion is, to put it simply, that if *theory* is being aimed for rather than (merely) description we should demand more evidence, and if this is provided we should be satisfied that the claim to theory is justified. A claim has to be judged, in other words, on some detached reader-orientated assessment of the claim that is made. Some claims may be, in Hammersley's term, 'reasonably'

(1992: 70) accepted, while others will need more evidence to persuade the reader. There are immediate problems here, though – of misreporting, of naïvety, of interpretation, of misconduct.[2] However meticulously evidence appears to collected, analysed and interpreted, and however much data is presented for the inspection of the reader, qualitative method – depending, perfectly properly, on the validity of the ideographic – does not permit of the kind of reader assessment demanded by Hammersley. And quietude cannot be restored by appeals to the 'plausibility' or 'reasonability' of the research put on show.

Staring us straight in the face here is the question of how one makes checks as to the *reasonability* of claims on the basis of the data offered. We are talking, remember, about the use of 'reasonability' as a criterion for judging whether emergent theory can be straightforwardly accepted or whether the reader should demand more evidence from the 'theorist'.

An obvious bogey beckons from the qualitative archive on the question of the satisfactoriness of the reader's judgement. Margaret Mead's 'discoveries' about the Samoan islanders came to be believed on the basis of the apparent thoroughness and fastidiousness of her work and the persuasiveness of her arguments – on the back, in other words, of all the paraphernalia of supporting evidence that Hammersley suggests should be demanded. Such was the comprehensiveness of their acceptance, Mead's accounts and interpretations came to occupy a position equivalent to received knowledge. They came themselves to comprise what in other words was 'reasonable'.

But decades later, when Derek Freeman (1996) came to follow in Mead's footsteps, his conclusion was that the iconic anthropologist was duped and teased. Not only this, but Mead's conclusions had emerged after a surprisingly perfunctory piece of fieldwork: it had not been, after all, the detailed and thorough study that everyone had assumed. Freeman himself had become the adopted son to a Samoan family, learning Samoan in the process, and his conclusion from this immersion was that Mead's informants had been engaging in the favourite practice of *taufa'ase'e* or recreational lying. As one of his informants, Fa'apua'a Fa'amu told him, 'Samoan girls are terrific liars when it comes to joking. But Margaret accepted our trumped up stories as though they were true ... we just fibbed and fibbed to her' (Freeman, 1996: viii). It is interesting that Lincoln and Guba (1985: 296) introduce their discussion of the important 'credibility criterion' (similar to Hammersley's discussion) with the cautionary tale of Mead, but fail absolutely to resolve the problem of 'credibility' in this case (1985: 301).[3]

As Freeman puts it,

> Margaret Mead, the historical evidence demonstrates, was comprehensively hoaxed by her Samoan informants, and then, in her turn, by

convincing Franz Boas, Ruth Benedict and others of the 'genuineness' of her account of Samoa, she unwittingly misinformed and misled the entire anthropological establishment, as well as the intelligentsia at large, including such sharp-minded sceptics as Bertrand Russell and H.L. Mencken.

(1996: xiii)

If one thing is clear from this case, it is that what is plausible or reasonable, in the context of the methods and tenets of qualitative study, is far from simple to assess.

One also needs to look at misconduct. Recall that we are considering Hammersley's use of the criteria of plausibility, credibility and reasonability as measures for the acceptance of interpretation before that interpretation is taken to be a theory. It would surely be complacent to dismiss misconduct (or perhaps one should say over-enthusiasm or over-commitment) as an insignificant feature of social epistemology, particularly given the special status accorded to the integrity and validity of the individual researcher's own interpretations in qualitative inquiry. These interpretations are supposed to be valid in their own right – but if their wider validity is to depend on their *plausibility* we are placing a lot of responsibility in the hearts and minds of an assessing 'readerly' community, whose views of what is plausible will be predicated on the dominant view, the *Weltanschauung*, of the members of that community. It is salutary to note here that one of the most notorious incidents of misconduct ever in scientific history was perpetrated by a leading researcher in education, Cyril Burt, whose views were accepted, as much as anything, because of their plausibility among his contemporaries. Even Hearnshaw's (1979) sympathetic biography of Burt concedes that the man lied and fabricated evidence; he did this to suit facts about the heritability of intelligence which he 'knew' to be true – and his conclusions were ultimately embraced because others accepted them as plausible. The fact that Burt was a researcher in the quantitative rather than qualitative tradition provides no consolation here since no one could suggest that the particular paradigmatic assumptions under which one works offer any immunity from commitment, over-commitment or the tendency to reject alternative views – or that qualitative researchers have more inherent integrity than others. The fact that qualitative inquirers acknowledge, rather than deny, the necessity of interpretation makes them no less prey to the desire to see the data in terms of a particular interpretation – one shaped inevitably by their own predilections and prejudices – than their quantitative colleagues. The fact, in other words, of some putative *post-hoc* interpretation (as distinct from an *'ante-hoc'* hypothesis) does not inoculate one against the susceptibility to engage in deliberate (or at least semi-conscious) distortion.

Nor, and more important from the point of view of plausibility, can one's audience – as arbiters of plausibility – be in some way insulated from all their tacit expectations, insulated from prevailing academic, cultural and scientific orthodoxies, insulated from the things that are taken for granted without having to think, or what Bourdieu (in Bourdieu and Eagleton, 1994) calls *doxa*. Hammersley (2003) in a subsequent elaboration of his position suggests that 'Only knowledge claims which are likely to be accepted as plausible by most of a research community should be treated as if they are true', but one wonders what inoculates this community, or some satisfactory proportion of it, against employing in any assessment they make of plausibility the very prejudices and expectations that give shape to plausibility. It was partly this plausibility which made Burt's views acceptable to his intellectual community. Plausibility was the culprit, not the saviour.

Despite the potential for misconduct there has been strikingly little research by the educational academic community on ensuring its non-emergence. It is significant that the *Journal of the American Medical Association* could devote an entire issue to potential abuse, fraud and fabrication (see Rennie and Flanagin, 1998), yet there is little or no equivalence of this vigilance in education. While in the 15-year period to 1993, 132 papers were written about the use and abuse of peer review processes in medicine, only 4 existed in education (Speck, 1993).

On the reasonableness criterion for theory, a paraphrase of Stanley Fish (1994) is apposite: what is reasonable for you may not be reasonable for me, and may even seem unreasonable, that is, incompatible with the principles that ground my perception and judgement.

2. Theory as essential ingredient in social science's offer to policy

Generalizability, though disavowed in Hammersley's earlier discussion about theory, keeps raising its head. Later in his book, the reason for the resilience of generalizability becomes clear, as Hammersley outlines what he takes to be the goal of research. He says, 'the goal of any research is to provide information that is not only true, but which is also of relevance to issues of human concern' (1992: 85). There is, then, in this account an instrumental need for generalizability in social research which stands evidently distinct from whether such generalizability can be attained from, in this case, ethnographic – and, more widely, qualitative – research. He continues, 'Of considerable importance here is the question of how, as researchers and readers, we are able to generalize from findings about particular situations studied to conclusions that have such general relevance' (1992: 85). This can be done, he concludes, as long as the criteria he has outlined (that I have just discussed) are met. Later, he says that 'to be legitimate, ethnographic research must contribute to policy-making, in the broadest sense of that term' (1992: 123). Behind this assertion is what Stronach and MacLure (1997: 90) call the 'rationality of ... policy analysis' – which theory will underpin.[4]

But there's surely a move away here from the significance and importance of the ideographic in its own right. The motivation for this move seems to be a fear of the insignificance on its own of the particular. But why should we be so worried? A release from the notion that general principles are findable or useable does not portend a descent into unbridled subjectivity or nescience. As Fish notes, anti-foundationalism – the argument against the possibility of theory – is 'an argument for the situated subject, for the individual who is always constrained by the local or community standards and criteria of which his judgment is an extension' (1989: 323). From it comes an argument for accepting one's own and others' tacit knowledge and insider understanding. As Toulmin says, people

> demonstrate their rationality, not by ordering their concepts and beliefs in tidy formal structures, but by their preparedness to respond to novel situations with open minds – acknowledging the shortcomings of their former procedures and moving beyond them. Here again, the key notions are 'adaptation' and 'demand', rather than 'form' and 'validity'.
>
> (1972: vii)

The problem for a certain kind of theoretician is that 'adaptation' seems inadequate to the task of fabricating a useful, policy-informing social science. Consistent with the expectations of Althusser's 'Generalities III', research must – according to them – inform and be relevant. Research, theory and policy are intertwined here in a kind of symbiosis. None can survive without the others. The problem, I think, with this kind of reasoning is with what is taken to be the Other of theory. If theory, in the Generalities III sense, concerns the kind of generality, form and validity that can inform practice and policy, its Other is the contingent, the *ad hoc*, the situational, the ephemeral, the makeshift – and this, the intimation seems to be – is no use to anybody. The unmoored subject, uninformed by theory or evidence-based policy, will drift directionless and will offer nothing.

Are things really like that, though? Samuel Butler suggested in his *Notebooks* that 'Life is the art of drawing sufficient conclusions from insufficient premises', and this could perhaps be the motto of the qualitative researcher in education. There is really no need to fear the fall which a loosening of hold on theory (or rather what is supposed to be theory) might bring. Fish, from the context of literary and legal studies suggests that theory in the form of external and independent guides not only will never really be found (it might putatively be found), but it is also unnecessary to seek it because you will always be guided by the rules or rules of thumb that are the content of any settled practice, by the assumed definitions, distinctions, criteria of evidence, measures of adequacy, and such, which not only define the practice but structure the understanding of the agent who thinks of himself as a 'competent member'.

(1989: 325)

3. Theory in the humanities?

And the discussion of literary and legal studies brings us back to a key distinction inside the idea of theory and what theory can do. All of Fish's 'theory-talk' – the Generalities III talk, the generality talk, or what Howard Becker (1993: 218) calls 'science talk' – is theory on stilts. It is about local interpretation informing global interpretation. Qualitative inquiry can't do that, and part of its appeal when compared with other forms of inquiry is that it doesn't pretend to be able to. The part of its appeal which surely emerges for educators is its modesty of aspiration and pretension in that direction, with its dismissal of such pretend-science notions as reliability, validity, generalization, prediction. One of its attractions for educators is surely its humility – in taking from the local and illuminating and influencing the local, influencing one's own practice.[5] Any claim to generalizability is restricted to the illuminative from which others may – possibly – draw or engage with.

The position is similar in literary studies. As Knapp and Michaels in their celebrated paper 'Against Theory' put it,

> [Theory] is the name for all the ways people have tried to stand outside practice in order to govern practice from without. Our thesis has been that no one can reach a position outside practice, that theorists should stop trying, and that the theoretical enterprise should therefore come to an end.
>
> (1985a: 30)

Eisner, with his invocation of theory in the arts and humanities as a model for education seems often to return to the 'science talk' version of theory. He notes that 'one of the critical tasks in the preparation of qualitative researchers is practice in using theory to account for what they describe' (1991: 237). This is despite his awareness of the dilemma identified by Hammersley, noting that using theory 'is not easy, in part because of the generality of theory and the qualitative specificity of events'. Given this acknowledgement, it is surprising that he continues, 'Nevertheless, it is a task worth attempting'.

One senses in reading Eisner that he feels himself tugged in two directions, and this is quite predictable from Mouzelis's diagnosis of crypto-functionalism in so much theory-seeking and the riding-two-horses phenomenon that I have described emerging from it. Eisner suggests that 'it would be useful for students to have the opportunity to apply more than one theory to a situation in order to illustrate the different ways in which the situation can be interpreted' but proceeds to say that 'theories may simply be irrelevant or inadequate' (1991: 238–9). He notes that 'theory that can adequately provide a convincing explanation of the social or pedagogical scene in education may be scarcer than we believe' (1991: 239), but goes on to aver that teachers and students of education need 'to acquire the ability to use theory so that it can explain what perception has provided'.

What we have among this toing and froing is the proposition that although theory doesn't easily fit into the analytical frame of qualitative inquiry, it is however necessary. While theory will quite probably be misleading, it still will explain things for us – if only we look hard enough among alternative possibles for the *right* theory. There seems to be an elision in this line of reasoning between Generalities II and III theory: theory seems to be discussed in its 'thinking tools' form with an addendum that it will also do some explaining. There can be little denying that interpretation takes different shapes and forms depending on the knowledge, background, experience and predilections of the interpreter: it takes shape, in other words, depending on the 'hermeneutic brackets' (Hirsch, 1976: 5) provided by the individual interpreter. But this is a flat, even trivial observation: it cannot provide validation for theory's use in a Generalities III form. It cannot provide for any elevation of such hermeneutic brackets – the epistemic devices which arise by virtue of being human and having human experience – to a higher, informative form. It cannot, in other words, account for the pumping-up of thinking so that it becomes some kind of super-charged heuristic device. There are no such devices, for the 'tacit knowledge' (Polanyi, 1969) of interpretation is precisely that: tacit. As Fish (1989: 353) observes, 'Tacit knowledge is knowledge already known or dwelt in; it cannot be handed over in the form of rules or maxims and theories'.

In any case, when Eisner says that 'one of the critical tasks in the preparation of qualitative researchers is practice in using theory *to account for* what they describe' (1991: 237, emphasis added) he seems emphatically to be opting for the generalizing, explaining form of theory, not for theory as some kind of personal heuristic device. And the notion of a 'task' here seems to take us back to an instrumental justification for theory. Glaser and Strauss follow a very similar logical route when they say,

> We believe that the discovery of theory from data – which we call
> *grounded theory* – is a major task confronting sociology today, for, as we

shall try to show, such a theory fits empirical situations, and is understandable to sociologists and layman alike.

(1967: 1, emphasis in original)

The reader will notice the *non sequitur* between the clause saying that
there is a 'major task' in the discovery of theory, and the rest of the
sentence which goes on to assert that the major task exists because
theory 'fits empirical situations', and is understandable. The *non sequitur*
is made no less transparent by the 'for' (in the second line of the quotation); the 'for' is a sleight of hand – a logical legerdemain. 'For' in this
sentence is doing no work at all: one can't justify a 'task' on the grounds
given by Glaser and Strauss (namely that grounded theory fits empirical
situations and is understandable). It is like justifying the task of building a
bridge on the grounds that the metal of which the bridge is built is very
strong. The metal could indeed be very strong – it could be Kryptonite –
but even if it were it wouldn't justify the bridge, unless the bridge were
constructed merely for the purpose of demonstrating how strong the
metal was (and I personally know of no such bridges). Normally, bridges
are justified by the fact that place A needs to be connected easily with
place B and the bridge will do the connecting. Tasks are justified, in other
words, by the expected value of the intended outcomes – not by the
means, the intermediary processes involved in arriving at those outcomes. It is not at all clear from the reasoning of Glaser and Strauss what
product is gained with the invocation of theory, unless it is the less-than-
dazzlingly admirable one of justifying the discipline in which the work is
occurring.

But this is to digress. The point of looking at the *non sequitur* of Glaser
and Strauss (1967) was to address the poverty of reasoning around
theory. Some commentators have indeed examined the dilemmas inhering in this, as I have noted in the problems of 'crypto-functionalism', but
the consequence of their analysis is, strangely, not their own abandon-
ment of theory, but a search for alternative reasons for it. The results of
one version of this search come in argument from authority: theory is
used in the arts and humanities, *ergo* it must be worthwhile. (This is the
obverse of other social science theorists' wish for association with the
theory and epistemological habits of natural scientists.) But such assertions about the importance of theory to the arts and humanities are
undermined by the fierce debate about its place, standing and value
there. There, as in the social sciences (and discounting those who seek to
make theory any kind of structured thought), theory is an attempt to
understand the particular by reference to the general. This is the
meaning, as noted earlier, discussed by both Mouzelis and Hammersley.
And, as Knapp and Michaels (1985a: 13) likewise put it, theory in literary
criticism is 'the attempt to govern interpretations of particular texts by

appealing to an account of interpretation in general'. In this search for theory one finds, as in the project of some qualitative inquirers in education, the attempt to 'guarantee the ... validity of interpretations' (1985a: 13). Fish extends this by saying that theory attempts to substitute 'for the parochial perspective of some local or partisan point of view the perspective of a general rationality to which the individual subordinates his contextually conditioned opinions and beliefs' (1989: 319).

But Fish (1989) notes that no such guarantee is possible, for the problem (and it is a problem for literary theorists as much as for qualitative researchers in education) is about the separation of speech acts (as the data in any inquiry) and meaning, and no such separation is possible: the phenomena are indissoluble. The issue for the qualitative inquirer of a theoretical bent is about something which transcends the local interpretation; it is about whether inquirers can step aside from their beliefs and prejudices to deliver some detached pronouncement about meaning – some theory.

Should we, though (and this is a point that surely one ought not still need to make), be attempting to provide detachment? What is the point of detachment in a system of inquiry that foregrounds the significance of the local, particular or peculiar interpretation, with its own inflections, biases and prejudices. As Gadamer asked, 'Does understanding in the human sciences understand itself correctly when it relegates the whole of its own historicality to the position of prejudices from which we must free ourselves?' (1960/1975: 251). Our knowledge about the social world is as Foucault puts it, 'fragmentary, repetitive and discontinuous' (1980: 79). Regretting that knowledge has been 'buried and disguised in a functionalist coherence' (1980: 81), he says, in a statement which could, like Samuel Butler's, stand as a motto of the qualitative researcher, that we should 'entertain the claims to attention of local, discontinuous, disqualified, illegitimate knowledges against the claims of a unitary body of theory which would filter, hierarchize and order them in the name of some true knowledge' (1980: 83).

The American academic lawyer Brad Sherman, in talking about hermeneutics and the law, suggested that most nominally hermeneutic discussion offers 'an unhermeneutical approach to hermeneutics' (1988 395). My position here, to paraphrase him, is that the search for theory in qualitative research is characterized by an unqualitative approach to qualitative inquiry. The search for theory reveals a range of tacit assumptions and expectations which disclose that search to be part of another foundationalist – or at least neo-positivist – enterprise.

The contrast between the finders and the regularizers – the narrators and the theorists – in the humanities stretches back a long way, well beyond current debates. Indeed, the contrast is almost as old as thought itself, and the contrast when made is not advantageous to the regularizers. Collingwood, more than 50 years ago in his classic *The Idea of History* (1946/1994), in comparing the approaches to history of Herodotus and Thucydides concluded that the former contributed so much more because 'what chiefly interests Herodotus is the events themselves; what chiefly interests Thucydides is the laws according to which they happen' (1946/1994: 30). The problem with Thucydides, notes Collingwood, is that he 'is constantly being drawn away from the events to some lesson that lurks behind them' (1946/1994: 31). Favouring Herodotus' critical narrative questioning as a way of doing history, Collingwood notes, 'In reading Thucydides I ask myself, What is the matter with the man, that he writes like that?'. He answers that Thucydides forsook history for a kind of pretend psychology: 'It is not history at all, but natural science of a special kind. It does not narrate facts for the sake of narrating facts. Its chief purpose is to affirm laws' (1946/1994: 29). The problem is the same today: some people, unsatisfied with narrative in the humanities, seek the kind of fulfilment which for them can seemingly come only with the manufacture of regularizing theory.

Conclusion

Much of the problem of the use of 'theory' in qualitative research stems from the notion that it is needed. Why it is needed is not explained, or at least it is explained only in back-to-front terms. It is needed, in those back-to-front terms, in order that policy and practice can be influenced, and this reasoning in turn hinges on the epistemic prestige of theory – on its cash value, its credibility as an established way of corralling under-standing to enable explanation and prediction.

When one argues for the validity of qualitative inquiry one is arguing for a reinstatement of the validity of local interpretation and under-standing in a social world. Yet in 'theory' one recognizes a familiar melody line in social research – the search for reducing, generalizing and explanatory phenomena in place of the 'merely' contingent or narrative.

Those of a practical bent might ask why any of this is important. For if a preoccupation with theory exists, a critic of my position might ask, isn't this a relatively benign matter? Clearly, in theory's form as thinking or reflection (Althusser's Generalities II) there can be no charge against it. But this is why we must get our terms right, for the theory postulated by some qualitative inquirers rises above thinking. It is thinking on steroids: its ambitions and pretensions are great, its power to change practice – because of its acquired prestige – profound. In theory an instrument is being proffered which will supposedly enable, as Glaser and Strauss (1967: 1) put it, 'predictions, explanations, interpretations and applica-tions' (and I examine this claim further in Chapter 6). Theory is about, in other words, more than thinking, more than garden-variety noticing or everyday generalization. The claim advanced by those committed to theory is that theory provides us with something more secure epistemologically than everyday noticing. In place of local generalization and interpretation, something is being offered which works at a level above and beyond the epistemic devices with which we fashion judgements and decisions in our everyday lives. The parochial is transcended as theory is developed and promulgated. With such credentials theory can influence policy and practice.

But such broad influence can as likely be unproductive as benign. It is surely a simple recognition of the salience and validity of everyday epistemic devices that gives legitimacy to qualitative research, and to any local conclusions that might be drawn from it. Qualitative research is valid only in the sense that one's own judgement and interpretation are valid. Nothing, once one has accepted the validity of this assertion – not even the mention of theory – will confer an epistemic kitemark. All this matters, then, because a preoccupation with theory leads to educational inquiry taking routes which it would very possibly be better not taking. Linked with this, it matters because the scion of theory is a new kind of technical discussion, which leads to what Andreski calls, 'The over-emphasis on methodology and techniques, as well as adulation of formulae and scientific-sounding terms [which] exemplify the common tendency ... to displace value from the end to the means' (1972: 108–9).

It matters also because the distinction acquired by theory in other fields over the years has led to a kind of apotheosis, and this exaltation (once theory is, as Glaser and Strauss (1967) put it, 'discovered') can lead to a premature closure on interpretation, and even to a restriction on the very notion that interpretation has to be open. There is the assumption of a valency in theory and this supposed power is at the end of many a commentator's support of theory. Accepting the singularity–generality dilemma, they suggest nevertheless that social science can't progress unless it offers some kind of generalizable knowledge and the imprimatur of legitimacy inhering in theory to work which conforms to certain standards. But of course it is still – whether it is called 'theory', 'models' or 'Margaret' – about generality, and the dilemma persists, no matter how many tests are passed as to the quality of the work which leads to the generality.

Notes

1. Elsewhere, Hammersley (2003) interestingly elaborates on these issues and discusses them more in terms of the knowledge claims that are being made and the likely consequences of these claims.

2. This is not to suggest, of course, that the problem is with *mis*interpretation. A starting point in doing qualitative inquiry is in accepting the personal and idiosyncratic nature of interpretation. The problem is with the assumption that some correct interpretation is discernible which will underpin any 'theory' ultimately developed.
3. Paul Theroux's (1993) less scholarly but no less enlightening account of what the older Trobrianders thought of Malinowski puts in one's mind the possibility that another cultural icon may have been duped.
4. Pawson and Tilley (1997) and Pawson (2006) make arguments for what they call the 'realistic' identification of theory and its consequent use in policy.
5. as described in Helen Simons's (1980) nice phrase, 'the science of the singular'.

The use and abuse of 'theory': grounded theory

With David James

Sundance: Think ya used enough dynamite there, Butch?
From Butch Cassidy and the Sundance Kid

Butch Cassidy and the Sundance Kid hold up a train in which they know a great deal of banknotes are being transported. Having found the safe in which the money is locked away, Butch applies some dynamite to its door. He is more than successful, blowing up the safe and the entire railway carriage, and destroying the contents of the safe to boot.

We always seem to be seeking epistemological dynamite in our research. The purpose of this chapter is to use one kind of putative theory – grounded theory – as a case study in theory's use. The conclusion that I come to is that grounded theory (if indeed grounded theory is theory, and that's something I'll examine) destroys that which it seeks to unlock and explain.

I want to examine the intellectual origins of grounded theory, the reasons for its provenance, and the reasons for its continuing popularity in the applied social sciences. Especially, I wish to look at the claims of grounded theory to be theory, and why those who called it 'grounded theory' should want to apply the term 'theory' to the range of procedures and techniques associated with this construction of concepts.

This examination will be a critical one, for it seems to me that grounded theory provides excellent illustrations of some of the problems that have so far been addressed in this book: sloppy definition (or rather no definition) of what is meant by theory; the exploitation of the epistemological allure of theory in other areas; the discouragement of creativity and innovation among researchers; the damaging effects of what Becker (1993: 218) has called 'science talk' and what I have in the previous chapter referred to as 'crypto-functionalism'.

The origins of grounded theory

Grounded theory was developed and established nearly 40 years ago by Barney Glaser and Anselm Strauss. Their book *The Discovery of Grounded Theory* (1967) laid out a set of procedures for the supposed generation of theory from empirical data. Although I have my problems with it (and this chapter is dedicated to an explication of those problems) there can be little doubt that it has been a major – perhaps *the* major – contributor to the acceptance of the legitimacy of qualitative methods in applied social research. But the success of grounded theory in the 1960s and beyond – its success in helping to validate qualitative inquiry – depended on something of a sleight of hand in reasoning about inquiry. The use of the word 'theory' at that time helped to make legitimate certain kinds of inquiry that were looked down upon by those who considered themselves to be serious researchers. Hindsight enables one to see the debate of the time in context, and to move on.

Seen historically, grounded theory represented a resolution of different epistemological positions[1] and a solution to a broader problem about perceptions of the status of qualitatively based knowledge in the social sciences. It thus offered, if not quite a lifeline to the status of that knowledge, some firm rocks on which to stand in attempting to rescue it (see Alvesson and Sköldberg, 2000).

Four decades on, grounded theory continues to be used in a wide range of research settings, and is especially highly regarded as a method of social analysis in fields such as education and health studies[2]. Despite much critique, it continues to enjoy great kudos among educators, to the extent that its use can still seemingly validate the publication of a study's findings (see, for example, Harry et al., 2005). Strauss and Corbin (1997: vii) summarize the contemporary status of grounded theory when they say that grounded theory's methods are 'now among the most influential and widely used modes of carrying out qualitative research when generating theory is the researcher's principal aim'.

There can be little doubt that Strauss and Corbin are accurate when they make this large assertion. As Miller and Fredericks (1999) put it, the grounded theory approach has become the 'paradigm of choice' for qualitative researchers in education and other disciplines. And as Denzin (1994: 508) has noted, 'The grounded theory perspective is the most widely used qualitative interpretive framework in the social sciences today'.

Because it meets a need, grounded theory is bound to be popular. For while qualitative inquiry is absolutely valid, it is difficult to do. In education it may involve talking – as naturally as possible – with students, parents, teachers; it may entail taking part, watching and listening, in schools and other environments. But when all this is done, what comes next? Such ways of doing research can lead to a floating feeling, a lack of direction. What does one do with one's data? Surely, if one is a serious inquirer, one can't just talk about it. One must theorize, or at least that's what the experts say. So grounded theory offers a solution: a set of procedures, and a means of generating that all-important thing: theory. As such, it has become widely used.

In brief, existing criticism of grounded theory centres on three broad themes: first, that it over-simplifies complex meanings and inter-relationships in data; second, that it constrains analysis, putting the cart (procedure) before the horse (interpretation), and third that it depends upon inappropriate models of induction and asserts from them equally inappropriate claims to explanation and prediction. Let us look at some of the critical literature which exemplifies this debate.

Haig (1995), has queried grounded theory's reliance on a naïve model of scientific induction, inappropriate to the tenets of qualitative inquiry. Haig, together with others such as Miller and Fredericks (1999), points to what one might call the 'everydayness' of inductive reasoning. The thrust of these authors' argument is that this common, everyday induction is better described as 'inference to the best explanation' or what C.S. Peirce called 'abduction'. The important point is that it is the urge to theorize that drives the desire to be seen using something called 'induction'.

Robrecht (1995) notes that the elaboration of sampling procedures by Strauss and Corbin (which include instructions for techniques for open sampling, relational and variational sampling and discriminate sampling) diverts attention from the data towards techniques and procedures. As Robrecht puts it, these elaborations encourage researchers 'to *look for data* rather than *look at data*' (1995: 171, emphases in original). She recommends an alternative approach, that of Leonard Schatzman (1991), which seeks to extend the natural analytic process of everyday thinking by systematically examining different concepts that might be used to summarize events. The emphasis on that natural analytic process is a significant one and is a theme that will be rehearsed throughout this chapter and in the next.

A comprehensive list of criticisms is made by Dey (1999), who presents a host of ambiguities, confusions and unanswered questions. For example, he illustrates how tensions in the original formulation of the approach are revealed in the gulf that developed between the originators (see Glaser, 1992), such that the role of verification remains a 'puzzle' and the role of prior theory is unclear. Despite this critique, though, Dey maintains a surprising degree of optimism – even faith – in the approach. He sees grounded theory as capable of development and as offering a 'middle way' between ideographic and nomothetic theorizing. The validity of 'middle-way theorizing' will be addressed towards the end of the chapter.

Charmaz has over two decades been a developer of new forms of grounded theory (e.g. Charmaz, 1988, 2000) and her voice has been lucid in enabling its evolution. Some years ago, she offered a development of grounded theory which depended on an endorsement of five principles that kept faith with 'the form and logic' of the Glaser and Strauss approach. Those five principles were: the structuring of inquiry; the simultaneity of data collection and analysis; the generation of new theory rather than the verification of existing theory; the refinement and exhaustion of conceptual categories through theoretical sampling, and the direction to 'more abstract analytic levels' (1988: 125). More recently she has asserted that 'grounded theory can bridge traditional positivistic methods with interpretative methods' (Charmaz, 1995: 30). She rejects the claims to disinterestedness and objectivity present in earlier versions of grounded theory, noting that 'The myth of silent authorship is false but reassuring' (Charmaz and Mitchell, 1996: 299). She distinguishes between 'objectivist' and 'constructivist' grounded theory, aligning the former with 'awkward scientistic terms and clumsy categories' (Charmaz, 2000: 525). The result may be 'an overly complex architecture that obscures experience' (2000: 525). She offers a 'simplified, constructivist version of grounded theory' (2000: 514).

Valid as these critiques are, I challenge the need to call these forms of qualitative inquiry 'grounded theory' and suggest that in so doing – in continuing to want to call them 'grounded theory' with the corollary of the continued adherence to its precepts and techniques – there proceed two unwelcome sequelae. First, as I mentioned in Chapter 5, the claims of qualitative inquiry to be taken seriously in their own right (without the use of special method) are undermined, and second, unwelcome constraints on open, creative interpretation are imposed.

My arguments about the pretensions of grounded theory in education centre on a number of inter-related issues concerning the three key words in that seminal text, *The Discovery of Grounded Theory*: 'theory', 'discovery' and, underpinning both, the notion of 'ground'. I shall look at these in turn.

Theory

Why is grounded theory 'theory?'

'Theory' has not formed a major focus in existing critique about grounded theory. Yet the claim for grounded theory actually to be *theory* raises questions that have been central to this book: what it is to be theory, what is demanded and expected of theory, and why people expect their methods-for-making-sense to be called 'theory'.

In the preface to *The Discovery of Grounded Theory*, Glaser and Strauss justify the project of their book by noting ruefully that the interpretative sociologists of the Chicago tradition were associated with 'an unintegrated presentation of theory' (1967: vii). At the very outset of the book, then, something interesting emerges about the authors' views concerning knowledge and how it should be pursued. This can be summarized roughly as follows: qualitative research is valid, appropriate and necessary, but it does itself no favours by having no methodology to speak of, and by being unable to demonstrate how it develops good, integrated theory (or even any kind of theory). The latter – the development of theory – seems to be viewed as the *sine qua non* of serious inquiry.

Given the widespread use of grounded theory as a method of qualitative inquiry, it is important to recognize the character of the theory that Glaser, Strauss and their successors (for example, Charmaz, 1988, 1995, 2000) have consistently said they are seeking here. Theory is taken to be part of the canonical apparatus which allows us to make inferences and proffer explanations based on inductive processes.

Deep water is being traversed here. The issue of what theory might be in qualitative inquiry in is a tricky one (see Chapter 5, and Woods, 1992), since the word 'theory' has taken a wide variety of meanings, loose and tight, particularly in educational discourse, and this variety has of course been a major theme of this book so far. Given the plurality of view on this issue of theory, it is not surprising that Stanley Fish (1989), as I have noted in several places elsewhere in this book, rejects the meaningfulness of any of this discourse. He contends that such discourse about theory in the academy is not really about theory at all, but rather about what he calls *theory-talk*. He surely has a point and it is necessary here to try to draw on some of this definitional discussion, since – in the invocation of theory and the cachet it brings with it for inquiry – important issues about finding out, discovery, explanation and prediction are at stake. Are the theoretical claims of grounded theory valid? Why should grounded theorists want, in 'discovering' something, to call that which is discovered 'theory?'

Miller and Fredericks (1999: 539) offer some help here. They say that it is possible to see grounded theory in three main ways: (a) as an approach in 'the logic of discovery', (b) as being either 'accommodationist or predictivist'; (c) as a variant of 'inference to the best explanation'. This is a useful setting of scene, though I would prefer to simplify their taxonomy thus: the theory of grounded theory can, broadly speaking, be seen as being about (a) inspiration involving patterning or accommodation (see, for example, Thagard's, 1998, discussion of processes of discovery outlined in Chapter 3, or Kaplan, 1964, for a discussion of patterning); (b) generalization and induction. In its former, looser, sense it is principally about bringing ideas together, while in its latter form it adheres to positivist and functionalist expectations about explanation and prediction. The use of the word 'theory', as though it described one inductionist process, camouflages the confusion occurring here, and it enables further confusions to occur about the ends of qualitative inquiry.

The 'theoretical' notion in grounded theory, in other words, conflates and confuses two processes in inquiry. It conjoins the spark to inspiration (outlined in Chapters 2 and 3) with the predictive function of theory in the natural sciences and in functionalism. For describing what happens in qualitative research, the use of the term 'theory' only confuses what is going on. The former type – involving tacit patterning, interpretation and inspiration – is really a vernacular employment of the term 'theory', and is part of everyday reasoning and Schatzman's (1991: 304) 'common interpretive acts'. The latter is about generalization following systematic and extensive data collection, and the testing of the generalization for the purposes of verification or falsification.

Thus, to the question of Miller and Fredericks (1999), 'How does grounded theory explain?' I would answer, 'It doesn't', because grounded theory procedures are a scion of qualitative inquiry, and qualitative inquiry is about interpretation. Its credentials in the explanation department are limited. It is about – using Ricoeur's (1970) well known distinction – understanding before explanation. But on both counts, the former and the latter, theory as discovery and theory as part of an explanatory exercise, grounded theory fails to live up to its proponents' expectations. It fails because it promises too much – because it is unsatisfied with 'mere' understanding.

I explore the claims to 'discovery' later (under 'Discovery or Invention?'), but it is perhaps worth noting here some concern about the linking of theory and discovery when discovery is taken to mean creativity or finding-out. In grounded theory one sees signposts to investigatory avenues borrowed from natural scientific endeavour, but one should note here that natural scientists, whose notionally inductive-predictive theory is that commended by grounded theorists to the present day, hold far less firmly nowadays to the procedural guyropes they once cherished. Beck, a Nobel prize-winning physicist noted that 'The mechanics of discovery are not known ... I think that the creative process is so closely tied in with the emotional structure of an individual ... that ... it is a poor subject for generalization' (cited by Wright Mills, 1970: 69, and this was discussed in more detail in Chapters 2 and 3).

One must be careful, in other words, that in creating something called 'theory' (together with a set of procedural accompaniments for finding it) one does not inhibit rather than liberate discovery. Theory does not give birth to discovery: it patterns, systematizes and tidies cognitive leaps, having painstakingly employed the 'inference tickets' of Ryle (of which more later); it cannot act as a vehicle for creativity.

Theory in a loose, vernacular sense – to go back to 'I have a theory why my geraniums are dying' – is indeed about conjecture, and, if you like, about creativity. But this is far from what happens when theory is used scientifically – in natural or social science, a matter which Cicourel (1979) recognizes in his distinction between the 'weak theory' associated with the inductive assumptions of field research, and 'strong theory'. Charmaz (1995: 28) also implicitly recognizes a distinction of this kind in her acknowledgement that grounded theory represents what she calls 'middle range theories to explain behavior and processes'. The 'explain' is the problematic word here. 'Middle range', 'weak', 'protoscientific' or vernacular theories do not explain anything, since sophisticated 'inference ticket' procedures (described in the following section) are not present to enable it. Instead, they help us to understand. Understanding is a no less worthy ambition and there is a paradox in grounded theorists' continuing strivings for explanation.

Staying on theory as creativity for a moment, the problem comes for grounded theory (or indeed almost any theory in the social sciences) in claiming some status for one's *theory* ('middle range', 'weak' or 'protoscientific') as an instrument which works beyond the level of one's everyday patterning generalization and practical syllogism – beyond Polanyi's (1958) *personal knowledge* or the 'everyday knowledge' of Schutz and Luckmann (1974). For *theory* to be worth something, it must involve something more than these everyday patternings and tacit heuristic exercises, for such patternings and such exercises are what human beings do all the time *par excellence*. As Schatzman (1991: 304) notes, we are all the time using 'common interpretive acts' and unselfconsciously using these to help us order and comprehend the world. We all see links, discover patterns, make generalizations, create explanatory propositions – weak, vernacular or protoscientific theory, if you like – all the time, emerging out of our experience, and this is all 'empirical'. The problems come in distinguishing generalization from over-generalization, narrative from induction. I discussed Alasdair MacIntyre's (1985) objections to social science's pretensions to theory in Chapter 1, and it is worth reiterating that he suggests that social science's generalizations are not generalizations in any meaningful sense, that is to say, 'we cannot say of them in any precise way under what conditions they hold' (1985: 91). Devotees of grounded theory have yet to make a case that their kind of theory possesses characteristics of induction in the way that natural scientists' theories may.

The epistemological weapons of 'creative theory', in other words, have to offer more than natural everyday analytic skill, yet one cannot be confident that they will ever do such. Indeed, as Geertz (1975: 11) says, the marriage of subjectivism to formalism which such expectations for theory involve, often results in sterile debate about whether 'analyses . . .

in the form of taxonomies, paradigms, tables, trees, and other ingenuities
. . . are merely clever simulations'. What more, in other words, does any
of this kind of 'theorizing' give over and above our everyday thinking?
How does grounded theory stand above the patterning of our everyday
lives and everyday experience? One has to caution against the possibility
that, as Miller and Fredericks (1999: 548) put it, 'grounded theory is
basically a way of making an inductive argument dressed up in a new
label'.

Theory: riding two horses

Before looking in detail in the next section at claims to induction one
needs to examine a more general respect for theory in qualitative
research – a respect to which seekers of grounded theory appear to be
prey. Such an examination exposes for scrutiny a kind of reasoning
which leads to the belief that theory is essential to qualitative and ethnographic endeavour and I noted in Chapter 5 the provenance of this
reasoning in a blurring of the distinction we made earlier about
inspiration/patterning versus explanation/prediction. What certain of the
theorists of qualitative inquiry want to do is to ride two horses at once.
They want, to go back to Mouzelis's (1995: 7) account, to avoid 'unfashionable functionalist vocabulary . . . while retaining its fundamental
logic'.

The essential problem here, is in the conflating of the expectations of
one kind of theory with another. The problem is claiming that one set of
natural processes of understanding and patterning is congruent with the
claims to explanation found in natural science. The problem is with what
Mouzelis (1995) calls 'crypto-functionalism', and I explored this in detail
in Chapter 5. But one might add in parenthesis here that the odd thing
about grounded theorists' exposition is that there is nothing at all 'crypto'
or clandestine about the reintroduction of the functionalist elements. Far
from being in any way hidden, the functionalist elements are central:
they are written in big neon lights. Grounded theory is functionalism
incarnate. Far from being embarrassed about it, Glaser and Strauss make
much of grounded theory's reputed success in providing 'relevant predictions, explanations, interpretations and applications' (1967: 1). And
their successors make claims that are scarcely weaker.

Stirred in with all this 'science talk' – indeed, central to it for both for
Glaser and Strauss and for newer exponents such as Charmaz (1995) – is
the linking of theory with inductive reasoning. It is this to which I now
turn.

Theory and the inductive reasoning claim

As I have noted, proponents of grounded theory make much of the place of grounded theorizing in the repertoire of inductive inquiry (as distinct from what they call 'logically deduced' theory). What proponents of grounded theory are claiming here is that grounded theory, once established, will occupy a privileged epistemic place. The problem, they say, with work which depends on 'logically deduced' theory is that the cart comes before the horse: a previously contrived theory is confirmed with evidence. The spark to action in that way of going about things comes from *previously devised* theory – then researchers, untrained in the ways of inductive inquiry, go out and merely *verify* their theories through the collection of data. This, grounded theorists claim, is the wrong way round: the theory should follow the data collection. By contrast, and, they aver, consistent with the tenets of inductive reasoning, grounded theorists dispassionately gather the data and then pull the strand cleanly from it. The theory emerges from the data.

Their confidence about the legitimacy and usefulness of the separation of one kind of thinking and inquiry from another – inductive from deductive – is perhaps a product of the time in which pioneers Glaser and Strauss were writing, but the reliance on the importance of the inductive continues resolutely in more recent expositions (for example, Charmaz, 1988; Strauss and Corbin, 1998). With the continuing prominence given to this inductive notion, it is worth spending a moment or two on the genealogy of thinking about the 'correctness' of inquiry methods, for this separation of correct from incorrect, of inductive from deductive, was symptomatic of a more general tendency in the social sciences in the 1960s and 70s to assume that there was a Right Way of thinking and of inquiry. For example, many psychologists of the 1960s and 70s were, like Glaser and Strauss, confident about inductive method when they celebrated the psychological offer to education. The distinguished behavioural psychologist Stanley Bijou (1970: 65) confidently held up empirico-inductive inquiry (as distinct from the more suspect hypothetico-deductive inquiry) in telling the world 'What psychology has to offer education – now'. Inductive analysis was and is held up with pride, almost as a badge of office for the serious social analyst.

But, as I noted in Chapters 3 and 4, people tend to talk with far less certainty now about the relative benefits of one kind of method over another. Even back then, though, a third of a century ago, more reflective social scientists were wondering whether notions like induction were in fact at all useful in the human arena. Even then, for example, respected psychologist Sigmund Koch could say,

> In every period of our history we psychologists have looked to external
> sources in the scholarly culture – especially natural science and the

philosophy of science – for our sense of direction. And typically we have embraced policies long out of date in those very sources …

(1964: 4–5)

A realization has been dawning that the processes of discovery are not as discrete and separable as the use of terms like 'inductive theory' and 'logically induced' imply, something about which Popper (1989) wrote so forcefully. Popper asserted that science advances not by induction as such but by a process of 'conjectures and refutations'. It is imagination and creativity, not induction, that generates real scientific theories, Popper suggested, which is how Einstein could study the universe and change physics with little more than a pen and a piece of paper. As Popper put it, 'The belief that we use induction is simply a mistake. It is a kind of optical illusion'.

The prescient sociologist Wright Mills (1970), also writing, it should be noted, at the same time as Bijou and Glaser and Strauss, quotes a number of Nobel Prize-winning physicists on the fluid and unbounded nature of thinking, even in that 'hard' reductionist science. One of these says (in the gendered language of the time, for which, apologies) that 'There is no scientific method as such, but the vital feature of the scientist's procedure has been merely to do his utmost with his mind, *no holds barred*' (1970: 69, emphasis in original).

It is worth stressing the continuation of this theme in natural scientists' discussions of inductive method. The tone is one of self-effacement rather than certainty. The renowned biologist Peter Medawar (1982: 81) is specific in his doubt about the supposed benefits of induction, noting that 'the influence of inductivism … has in the main been mischievous' in its effects on social scientists. This is mainly because, he says, there is little real distinction in fact to be made between deductivism and inductivism. These words merely relate to 'postures we choose to be seen in when the curtain goes up and the public sees us' (1982: 88). Diffidence is the hallmark of the modern natural scientist when it comes to reflection on method.

But such diffidence, such tentativeness, about ways of finding out is not for grounded theorists: induction is good, and it is bound together with prediction in their thesis. And it is important to remember that faith in these tenets continues (see Strauss and Corbin, 1997, 1998). Induction is good, evidently, because it enables one to derive theory which will, in turn, enable one to order and to predict.

Let us unravel the implications of this a little further. It all depends on what is meant by 'predict' in our educational worlds, and whether the 'theory' that emerges can predict any better than our everyday judgments, or better indeed than any formula that will – by good luck – accurately predict. Ptolemy constructed an intricate calculus, increasingly refined with all sorts of bells and whistles ('epicycles' and 'equants'), for explaining and predicting the anomalous movement of the planets in what he assumed to be an earth-centred universe (see Russell, 1991). It was accurate enough – more accurate, indeed, than early Copernican calculations could manage – yet few would now be persuaded that the accuracy of his predictions added any veracity at all to his geocentric theory. Predictive accuracy does not make for explanatory veracity. On its own it's not enough: it doesn't provide what Ryle (1990) calls an *inference ticket*.

There is a difference between the noticing of an association and the confident issuing of an inference ticket. This difference is important, for we are invited to take grounded theory seriously precisely because *theory* – the jewel in epistemology's crown – is being established. We are talking, remember, about theory's power, according to Glaser and Strauss (1967), in enabling 'predictions, explanations, interpretations and applications' and the claim to explanation is no less muted in today's grounded theorists. We are not, in other words, talking about garden-variety noticing, or about everyday generalization.

The claim being advanced here is that grounded theory provides us with something more secure epistemologically than everyday noticing. It provides more, for example, than simply the modest 'protoscientific' theory of Russell (1992). In place of these weak contrivances, a power-tool is being proffered which works at a level above and beyond the fragile epistemic devices with which we fashion judgments and decisions in our everyday lives. The inferences provided by the theory are better than other inferences. It is worth taking a moment to consider this, since it is a profound and important assertion.

It rests implicitly for its legitimacy in associating itself with the generalizing power of other kinds of theory (the kinds described by MacIntyre, of which I gave an account in Chapter 3) without providing an account of the provenance of the legitimacy of 'grounded theory' itself. Where, in other words, are the 'inference tickets' coming from in the supposed process of induction involved in grounded theorizing? This is a crucial issue, given the claims of grounded theory's proponents.

As Ryle notes, natural scientists do have clear methods for establishing these inference tickets: 'Bacteriologists do discover causal connexions between bacteria and diseases … and so provide themselves with inference tickets which enable them to infer from diseases to bacteria' (1990: 117). But Ryle goes on to point out that these inference tickets – pointing to causality and its direction – depend for their validity on the quality of the associated fact finding and reasoning. Since Ryle's time an example in that very field, bacteriology, makes precisely his case, and this example – the discovery of the bacterium *Helicobacter pylori* – was examined in Chapter 3. The story of the discovery is a fascinating one in itself and a brief account of it is given on pp. 65–67, but the important point to note in the context of inference tickets is that when the association was observed between this bacterium and the presence of ulcers in patients with abdominal complaints, a wide range of additional work had to be undertaken to demonstrate that *H. pylori* was in fact the *cause* of the ulcer. It was perfectly possible, for example, that a weakening of the immune system brought on by the *prior* existence of an ulcer (the cause of which was uncertain) merely enabled adventitious colonization by *H. pylori*, rather than the ulcer itself being caused by *H. pylori*. The direction of causation, in other words, was still in doubt without the undertaking of considerable additional work to establish that direction – before the finger could be pointed at *H. pylori* as villain rather than merely free-loader. Ryle's point is that the mere notion of association and the mere notion of inference, coupled with a metaphor such as 'the rails of inference' adds almost a third dimension to what is really a narrative.

The association in itself, then, is insubstantial; the 'inference ticket' has to be painstakingly enabled by the additional work of a broad research community which replicates, tests alternative hypotheses and attempts to falsify. Only after these processes are complete do the grand ambitions of induction in natural science – namely, prediction and explanation – begin to be realizable.

The problem, says Ryle, is that functional differences between arguments and narratives are often obliterated in our everyday discourse. And here is the problem for grounded theory (or indeed any kind of theory in education). Interpretations of the kind made in grounded theory research offer, on their own, no inference tickets – they enable no prediction or explanation, or at least no better prediction or explanation than any of us would make on the basis of our many years of experience of being human.

What such interpretations offer is merely a narrative. But the point is not to be apologetic about narrative in social analysis. Narrative can be argued to offer more in the way of enlightenment than putative theory, while forsaking its epistemic pretensions. By saying it is merely a narrative, I am saying that it is not a narrative *and* something else: rather, it is a narrative and nothing else. There's no shame to be admitted in this. Nor does one assert that the ideographic constitutes an illegitimate kind of knowledge in educational inquiry. The particular and the narrative – the vignette, the portrait and the story – are valid and proper ways of doing educational inquiry. The legitimacy of this is at the root of Gadamer's hermeneutics.[3]

The mistake in much of the reasoning of those who propose grounded theory is to assume that qualitative inquiry can in any way share elements or end-points congruent with those of natural scientific inquiry. Not only is it to assume a continuing need for, to paraphrase

Rorty (1979), *commensuration* rather than *conversation*, it is to import with that assumption all the methodological algorithms – of which theory is only one – of commensuration. It is strange that some social scientists should continue to be so attracted by these methodological charms while their 'natural' scientific counterparts have become more reflective and less self-assured about the benefits of method. As I noted earlier, many of the latter question what uniquely is gained from induction and the extent to which it is separable from deduction, imagination, inspiration, insight or daydream in enabling shifts forward in what Ziman (1991) has uncomplicatedly called *Reliable Knowledge*. The result, of late, has been less arrogant conviction among natural scientists about methods of discovery or induction, albeit that the 'materials' on which they focus their inquiries permit generalization of a wholly different character from that possible in social inquiry.

Theory, grounded theory and qualitative inquiry

When one argues for the validity of qualitative inquiry one is arguing for a reinstatement of the validity of interpretation and understanding in a social world – and all educational worlds are inevitably social. That understanding is built out of what we, as people, make of others' – teachers', parents', children's – utterances, gestures and actions. They are built, then, out of what Oakeshott called

> an inheritance of feelings, emotions, images, visions, thoughts, beliefs, ideas, understandings, intellectual and practical enterprises, languages, relationships, organizations, canons and maxims of conduct, procedures, rituals, skills, works of art, books, musical compositions, tools, artefacts and utensils – in short, what Dilthey called a *geistige Welt*.
>
> (1967a: 157)

Interpretations are built, in other words, out of what it is to be human. A method will not substitute for the essentials of this humanity; it will not enable one to substitute some formula for divining meaning which is not provided by the inheritance spoken of by Oakeshott. And why should one expect any method to provide such a surrogate? Whence emerged the urge to move beyond everyday understanding and discover some methodological proxy? The answer lies at least partly in the notion of *theory* in 'grounded theory', for in the search for such theory one recognizes a familiar tune in social research. It is the search for explanatory phenomena that become accessible via a neutral observation language wherein the observer rises above the merely contingent and interpretable.

Followers of positivism, so reviled by the new theorists of the social sciences, could at least be said to have established methodological ground-rules which were true to what they assumed to be positivism's tenets. Grounded theorists, by contrast, want it both ways. They want the comfortable feeling that comes from a denial of the arrogance of foundationalism and essentialism – and this is understandable enough. But they want this insignia of intellectual adulthood while clinging on to an epistemological security blanket – one woven from the associated notions that (a) some clearer distillation of truth can be established about the particulars and generalities of social behaviour; and (b) that this can be established using the cogs and levers of structured inquiry. Far from the notion that understanding is irreducible, their project is to step aside from the ineffable and rise above it to emerge with theory.

The significance of this extends beyond the status and acceptability of grounded theory. It stretches to the nature of educational inquiry itself, and its place in shaping educational discourse and the educational enterprise. For grounded theory is merely an *example* – it is not an exception to the rule – of a reflex response to those foundationalist impulses.

Ground

Whence 'emergence?' Commitment or distance?

> One must remember that because *emergence* is the foundation of our approach to theory building, a researcher cannot enter an investigation with a list of preconceived concepts, a guiding theoretical framework, or a well thought out design. Concepts and design must be allowed to emerge from the data.
>
> (Strauss and Corbin, 1998: 34, emphasis in original)

How are grounded theorists to quarantine themselves, as social selves, from the data they are analysing and reanalysing to enable 'theory' to emerge? And how can they transcend this and move outside it to stand on neutral 'ground?' When Strauss and Corbin (1998: 99) say, 'We know that we never can be completely free of our biases [so we must] ... acknowledge that these influence our thinking and then look for ways in which to break through or move beyond them', how is this distance, this 'beyond', this 'ground', to be achieved? And why should one want to move to some uninflected beyond?

How is the grounded theorist to emerge with anything that is not merely reportage if that theorist is not using his or her own person to emerge with the 'theory?' The question is not really 'How is distance to be found?' but rather 'What use is distance even if it can be found?' The credibility of much that is at the root of qualitative inquiry is at stake here: the issues concern the legitimacy of the immediate, and the immediately made social construction. Everything in such inquiry balances on the meanings that we as people read into the social encounters we make in life.

To think about these meanings and their relevance for the 'moving beyond' claims of grounded theory, a reverse Schank and Abelson test is helpful. The Schank and Abelson test is one used by the cognoscenti of artificial intelligence to determine whether a machine is responding intelligently. A complex sentence such as 'A woman went into a restaurant and ordered a hamburger; when the hamburger came she was very pleased with it; and as she left the restaurant she gave the waiter a large tip before paying her bill' would baffle a computer which was then posed with the question, 'Did the woman eat a hamburger?' [4] That is to say, it would baffle the computer unless the machine were to be fed a ludicrously long set of instructions incorporating vast amounts of knowledge – or unless, and this is the important bit, the computer had some means of hermeneutically 'bracketing' (as Hirsch, 1976: 5, puts it) the information so that it was meaningful. It would baffle the computer unless the computer was, in other words, to all intents and purposes human – in the sense that it contained all the sense apparatuses, accumulated knowledge and modes of response that make humans human.

Now consider the test in reverse. Consider human grounded theorists, rather than a computer, being asked to take the hamburger question as a Schank and Abelson test. Could they fail it? Or to put the case more starkly, consider the grounded theorist presented with the sentence (perhaps from a transcript): 'The child approached the teacher with her book; the teacher shouted, 'No!' and pushed the child outside the door'. Could the grounded theorist, presented with the question, 'Did the teacher act reasonably?' fail to answer the question? Not even with a superhuman feat of energy could grounded theorists detach themselves from their backgrounds, from their own sets of hermeneutic brackets, from all the knowledge, biases and prejudices they have about human behaviour, to deny interpretation and fail to answer the question in one way or another.

It should not, of course, be necessary to make this point, since one would assume that it is the position of the qualitative researcher: a starting point of such researchers is surely that meaning is constructed by the interpreter. The interrelationship between interpreter and interpretation is indissoluble; there is no ground, no hidden truth residing somewhere in the data ready to inscribe itself, just as there is no Lockean *tabula rasa* in the researcher waiting to be engraved. But – and it's a major 'but' – this is not the starting point of Glaser and Strauss and their successors. For while they say that one should not start a piece of research with preconceived theories, they proceed to say that '... it is presumptuous to assume that one begins to know the relevant categories and hypotheses until the 'first days in the field,' at least, are over' (1967: 34). Subsequently, Glaser (in his differences with Strauss) described the naïve emptiness with which a researcher should enter the research scene as 'abstract wonderment' (1992: 22).

Yes, 'abstract wonderment'. If the assumption of foreknowledge is taken to be presumptuous, it is nothing to the presumptuousness of assuming the empty, directionless, uninflected mind of 'abstract wonderment.' For the latter – a mind which will fail any Schank and Abelson test – is a contradiction in terms. Nor is it as presumptuous as 'we believe that grounded theory will be more successful than theories logically deduced from *a priori* assumptions' (Glaser and Strauss, 1967: 6). The problem is that *a priori* assumptions are uneliminable, and this fact – far from being a source of anguish – is what the qualitative researcher should expect: *a priori* assumptions are what make study (a) worthwhile, and (b) possible.

Those disgraced 'theories logically deduced from *a priori* assumptions' are no more or no less sinister than the already existing hermeneutic brackets in the researcher's head – the stuff of which interpretation is made. These also comprise '*a priori* assumptions' albeit that someone hasn't taken the trouble to write them down in order to verify them. For why is the researcher there at all? There must be some assumption that the chosen topic is a worthy field for study. As Gadamer (1960/1975: 251) puts it, 'the meaning exists at the beginning of any ... research as well as at the end: as the choice of the theme to be investigated, the awakening of the desire to investigate, as the gaining of the new problematic'. There can be little doubt that some process of verification – albeit implicit rather than explicit – is going on.

Theory, grounded theory and gift-wrapped meaning

> It is impossible to say just what I mean!
> But as if a magic lantern threw the nerves in patterns on a screen:
> Would it have been worth while
> If one, settling a pillow or throwing off a shawl,
> And turning toward the window, should say:
>   'That is not it at all,
>   That is not what I meant, at all'.
>
> Eliot (1969)

There is a central problem in the search for grounded theory. It is that there is no untethered spirit existing in the minds of researchers which will enable them neutrally and inertly to lay some cognitive framework over the data they collect to allow them to draw 'theory' dispassionately from this data, this ground. These researchers are human beings who walk, talk to friends, tend their gardens, watch TV, read books, go to lectures. They have histories of friendships, relationships, of household life of one kind or another. They understand guile, happiness, sadness, envy, deceit, irony. Their heads are full of notions – notions about equality, justice, freedom, education, the future, hope, fraternity, charity, feeding the cat and parking the car. These are precisely the things that comprise and give structure to their mental lives. They are what makes the drawing of themes from the data possible. They are not things which can be put to one side temporarily for the purpose of discovering 'theory'. As Fish (1994: 295) puts it, it is simply 'zany' to assume that you can 'in some way step back from, rise above, get to the side of your beliefs and convictions' in such a way that you will be able to survey the data unencumbered by the grip of those beliefs and that mental structure. What narcotic will enable the relaxation that will permit this? More importantly, what will be left when the narcotic has worked? For these things are the fabric of mental life and to imagine a mode of being devoid of them is to imagine nothingness.

To be fair to grounded theorists, they are not unique in their imaginings of epiphany coming *ex nihilo*. Such imaginings lie also at the root of the seemingly irrepressible search for ever-better theory and ever-better method in qualitative research. It is a desire to have it both ways, to take on board the fortuitousness and uncertainty of a Gadamerian hermeneutics while cleaving to the attractive idea that there is some determinate and explicable social universe – some ground – waiting to be scrolled out.

The collateral assumption to scrolling out, of course, is that the scrolls, once scrolled out, can be deciphered. The hieroglyphics written on them can be transcribed and painstakingly translated using the tools of grounded theory. Beneath the code is a rich meaning ready for another to understand. The concealed assumptions lurking here in all of grounded theory's processes and machinery are about language acting as a barrier to understanding. It is almost as though language is seen as a kind of inert conduit for some real, underlying meaning: the conduit has to be split open for meaning to escape. Indeed, the splitting-open is made explicit in the word 'fractured', which is used by grounded theorists – for example by Strauss (1987: 55), who says that 'coding ... fractures the data, thus freeing the researcher from description and forcing interpretation to higher levels of abstraction'. Researchers, with the tools of comparative analysis furnished by grounded theory, will break the cipher – they will be freed from description and mere narrative to discover the theory. But grounded theorists and other qualitative researchers are surely first and foremost human listeners – listeners who interpret more or less well on the basis of their experience of being human – on the quality of their shared knowledge, shared history and shared understandings. Listeners should surely be, in Wittgenstein's words, 'haunted by explanations' (cited in Kenny, 1994: 221) if they have any sensibility about the frailty of knowledge which an understanding of qualitative inquiry brings them.

As anyone who has worked with a transcription of someone else's interview tape would confirm, capturing others' meaning will depend on all kinds of unarticulated and half-articulated signs – the gaze that is a second too long, the gesture, the tone, the intonation, the word used in a special way, the language games. If these 'fugitive data' are indeed pro-cessed without conscious deliberation, as cognitive science confirms is probable (see, for example, Schooler and Melcher, 1995; Claxton, 1997), how likely are they to be accessible via the incomparably clumsier textual weapons of grounded theory? Indeed, in the very notion of 'thick description' and its distinction from 'thin description' – a distinction bor-rowed from Gilbert Ryle by Geertz (1975) – lies the recognition that such weapons will not be successful in divining meaning. As Geertz goes on to point out, in interpreting meanings one cannot be a 'cipher clerk' (1975: 9).

Even if one could, in other words, 'fracture' the data, clean it up, map it to its barest neural components, one would be no closer to a definitive understanding. Even if, as T.S. Eliot (1969) put it in *The Love Song of J. Alfred Prufrock* 'a magic lantern threw the nerves in patterns on a screen', we should still be able to demur from some imposed interpretation. There is, in other words, no 'ground' when interpretation is being spoken of. Fish (1989: 343) notes that 'candidates for the status or position of "ground" have included God, the material or "brute act" world, rationality in general and logic in particular, a neutral-observation lan-guage, the set of eternal values, and the free and independent self'. The problem with grounded theory is, to paraphrase Fish, that it is implicated in everything it claims to transcend.

Discovery

Discovery – or invention?

One ought to consider the significance of the word *discovery* in con-sidering the theory of grounded theory. The choice of the word 'discovery' says much about the epistemic project Glaser and Strauss imagined themselves to be leading, and they led this project with no trace of false modesty. Indeed, Strauss and Corbin began a more recent book (1998: 1) with a long quotation from Galileo, which they suffixed with the words 'we, like Galileo, believe that we have an effective method of discovery'. One needs to look in more detail at this claim to discovery, particularly when the claim is made solid, rather than metaphorical, with this astonishing self-comparison.

Discovery is a process of uncovering, revealing, disclosing that which is there. The assumption in the use of 'discovery' is therefore that meaning is laid open for all to see following the employment of some method of finding. Discovery is in no way synonymous with 'tentatively suggesting'. The idea that a 'theory' can be 'discovered' therefore puts that theory a long way away from interpretation. In the opposition of the interpretative to the normative and the illuminative to the definitive, grounded theory – proudly boasting a pedigree from qualitative inquiry's stable – surely aspires to interpretation and illumination. The mere use of 'discovery', however, divulges expectations closer to the normative and the definitive – to a correspondence view of knowledge.

The fact that the word 'discovery' is used in preference to 'invention' (or 'construction', or even 'generation') is revealing. 'Discovery' involves the disclosure of well hidden but already existing phenomena; it concerns things that exist, albeit that they're hard to find. By contrast, *invention* refers to things that exist only in an infinite universe of possibly existing things. Thus, the moons of Jupiter, the molecular structure of DNA and the tomb of Tutankhamen are discovered. On the other hand, the spinning-jenny, diesel engines, iambic pentameters and the telephone are invented.

When the word 'discovery' is used, the presumption is therefore of the revelation of a solid, disclosable thing – an entity, transcending interpretation. The quite explicit assumption of grounded theorists is that the paraphernalia and machinery of inquiry can reveal this entity with 'analytic tools' (Strauss and Corbin, 1998: 87). Invention, by contrast, is a creative process in which one of myriad possible constructions is made out of the stuff – concrete or mental – available.

Let's put 'invention' in the place of 'discovery' in *The Discovery of Grounded Theory* so that it becomes *The Invention of Grounded Theory*. The reason it doesn't work so well is because 'invention' implies one unique construction among a plethora of possible constructions. Inventions are mutable and fragile, not static and solid. In fact, inventors are sure that their inventions will change and improve: Alexander Graham Bell, one imagines, did not assume that his telephone would be the last word in electronic communication. He did not claim to have *discovered* the telephone. Diffidence must surely be the *sine qua non* of the inventor. 'Discovery', on the other hand, implies little diffidence in one's ontological assumptions.

Discovery implies a clean lineage from thing to thought and an uncomplicated correspondence between the two. The thought is merely a doppelganger for the thing. But in fact this correspondence can never really exist when it comes to the things of the mind. The historian Simon Schama (1996: 7) makes this point in discussing the discovery of 'wild' America: 'The presumption was that the wilderness was out there, somewhere, in the western heart of America, awaiting discovery, and that it would be the antidote for the poisons of industrial society'. But, of course, that wilderness was a fabrication, a dream spun of wishes; it was an invention dressed up as a discovery, or as Schama puts it, 'the healing wilderness was as much the product of culture's craving and culture's framing as any other imagined garden' (1996: 7). The point is that notions, dreams, even grounded theories, are products of cultured minds. Unlike the moons of Jupiter, they are not discovered.

Researchers can, then, be justifiably inductive and analytical about what is assumed unproblematically to exist, what is already 'there', in the way that they cannot be analytical about that which is only possibly there and that which changes its shape depending on the knowledge, disposition and dreams of the listener or viewer. All the technical procedure and analytic tools of grounded theory therefore admirably fit the bill for 'discovery' – but discovery is far from what happens in the process of divining meaning, and this surely ought to be a starting point for the qualitative researcher.

The choice of the word 'discovery', then, reveals much about the way that the proponents of grounded theory think about knowledge. But even more is revealed by the way that they knot together 'discovery' with the idea of 'ground'. Together, 'discovery' and 'ground' reveal the notion of capturing a truth somewhere out there, which is of course to say, nowhere near the seeker.

Developments in grounded theory: what do they offer?

Some three decades have passed since the inception of grounded theory and while many continue to promote the methods in forms similar to the original (e.g. Strauss and Corbin, 1997, 1998), others, as I noted earlier, have offered significant developments. In these developments, though, as I shall try to indicate, there are persisting issues to be resolved. How do the tools of grounded theory, even in these new forms, make what occurs superior to everyday interpretation? How might the looser and more tentative forms of interpretation that go with 'common interpretive acts' be inhibited or demoted if the methodological proxies of 'theoretical' analysis persist? And what does a continuing insistence on the procedural signposts of grounded theory encourage researchers to ignore?

Let us look at a recent use of grounded theory and speculate on how it might have differed from another analysis of the same subject not benefiting from grounded theory. Clarke (1998), an ex-student of Strauss, undertakes an analysis of the American reproductive sciences which, she reports, emerges out of grounded theory analysis. She notes, in a general description of grounded theory, that 'the data are coded, and codes are densified and ultimately integrated into an analysis' (1998: 278). However, her very brief description of the method occurs at the end of an appendix in a book of over 400 pages. In fact, although a generous attribution to grounded theory is made, it is impossible to see how the detailed analysis – depending on interviews, documentary data and ' "insider" histories – accounts of events and discoveries, biographies and autobiographies, status reports and so on written by reproductive researchers' (1998: 277) in any way develops out of the specifics of grounded theory. One has to speculate (speculate, since no evidence of the use of codes or densification is offered) how the inductive process has differed from, for example, that which occurred in other first-rate analyses which have not employed grounded theory, such as the classic *Labeling the Mentally Retarded*, written by Jane Mercer (1973) which likewise used unstructured interviews, community survey and official records to draw conclusions about the social nature of learning disability. The speculation leads one to believe that little can have been added by Clarke's use of grounded theory.

Indeed, as Becker (1996) points out, Mercer's classic about labelling occurred in the context of other iconic texts that also used a range of methods and analytical strategies. Becker gives as examples *Black Metropolis* (Drake and Cayton, 1945) and *Boys in White* (Becker et al., 1961) which drew upon and used data of broad provenance – interview, statistical, observational. These are studies where people have, as Geertz (1995: 20) puts it, worked *'ad hoc* and *ad interim'*. In more recent, but related, work – looking at the over-representation of students of certain ethnicities in special education programmes – it is difficult (to put it at its most hopeful) to see the benefits of the grounded theoretical analysis of Harry et al. (2005) over the non-grounded analysis of, say, Tomlinson (1982) or Benjamin (2003).

If one is freed from methodological constraint one is in turn freed to depend more on one's own experience, more on Dilthey's *geistige Welt* – on all the things of the mind in the world. Those things are available to us because we are all members of a species that commonly inhabits and shares the same universe and the experiences it offers, sharing understandings and sharing meaning making. Their availability comes neither by dint of grounded theory nor any other prescription of method which leads to 'theory'. In fact, looking back on iconic studies and how grounded theory *followed* (not preceded) them, the point is reinforced that much of the original impetus for the formulaic guidance of grounded theory came from the desire to gain the respect and trust of the 'scientific' social scientists in the 1960s – to be able to talk about procedures, reliability, validity and so on. As Robrecht (1995: 170) puts it of *Boys in White* (for which Strauss, incidentally, was one of the research team), 'The lack of explicit methodological procedures served as a focal point for criticism from the general scientific community ... The challenge to those interested in qualitative methods, then, was to provide a more rigorous explanation of these methods'. As Sanders (1995: 92) put it, the aim seems often to continue to counter positivist critique 'through more-rigorous-than-thou instructions about how information should be acquired and pressed into an analytic mold'. But there should surely be no need any longer to point to proxy indicators of a research programme's validity. To want to do this, to want to summon up methods and instruments as if these were the insignia of some higher authority which offered an imprimatur of legitimacy, by implication relegates the more direct understandings and interpretations of qualitative researchers. What is the message being conveyed to the dissertation committees, granting agencies and tenure review boards if the putative shibboleths of positivism and functionalism are so doggedly grasped?

Steps in more helpful directions have been made in the 30 years since *The Discovery* was published. Lincoln and Guba (1985), for example, draw the constant comparative method from grounded theory with enthusiastic recommendations as to its value as a means for processing data, but with equally clear warnings as to the hollowness of the putative ends, namely prediction and explanation. The constant comparative method seems sometimes to form the essence of method in qualitative inquiry: Pawson (2006: 74–6), for instance, describes for his 'realist synthesis' a process of constant comparison that involves refining a preliminary hypothesis by 'juxtaposing, adjudicating, reconciling, consolidating and situating the evidence'.

As I see it, the mere existence of the term 'grounded theory', with its key assumptions of 'ground', 'theory' and 'discovery' lures any newer forms of qualitative inquiry which cleave to its assumptions back into the same problematic territory. Earlier in this chapter, I briefly described Charmaz's *constructivist* grounded theory. But what might be gained by seeking a revised grounded theory of this kind? Charmaz (2000: 525) says, 'In short, constructing constructivism means seeking meanings' but it is unclear – in distinguishing this from other forms of seeking meaning – why this has to be called 'grounded theory'. She proceeds, 'My version of grounded theory fosters the researcher's viewing the data afresh, again and again' (2000: 526). Again, one needs to ask how this differs from the induction or abduction of our everyday sense, how it differs from using the tacit and spoken tools of normal sense making, of 'common interpretive acts' – of review, rehearsal, of talking about it with friends, of employing practical syllogism, recognition, evaluation, coming to a conclusion. What Charmaz is doing in her constructivist grounded theory sounds very much like the process of hard work and inspiration that combines to enable interpretation and new insights in any field, in the natural or social sciences, in the arts or humanities. One wonders what the grounded theoretical ingredients in Charmaz's new form of grounded theory contribute in addition to this. Moreover, one wonders whether they may in fact *inhibit* rather than *enable* 'common interpretive acts' as Schatzman (1991) indicates was indeed the case with many of his students who notionally employed grounded theory.

The trouble is that the simple understanding moves aside for a proxy – admittedly a self-consciously mutable and personal one with more recent manifestations of grounded theory – but this proxy is made to stand superior to our other forms of understanding. It is the imposition of an *enhanced* understanding that is troubling, and it occurs not just in grounded theory, not just in ethnography, but throughout the social sciences so willingly drawn upon by educators. Some time ago, Vernon (1964: vii) made the same point about psychologists' methods and suggested that 'the unsophisticated methods that we ordinarily use in understanding people in daily life' are likely to produce knowledge every bit as accurate and reliable as that coming from psychological tools, however sophisticated.

What Charmaz seems to be arguing for is a rediscovery of the symbolic interactionism that grounded theory sought to transcend. In so doing, she endorses a wholly appropriate and interpretivist form of constructivism. What is puzzling is her apparent need to tether this to grounded theory as a methodological label. While Charmaz's form of constructivist grounded theory moves grounded theory far from its inception point in the ideas of Glaser and Strauss, it still – in wanting to call itself grounded theory – adheres to grounded theory's core principles. That is to say, it adheres to the notion of 'ground' (the idea there is something beyond and underpinning) and the notion of 'theory', that one can perform some supervening process which will interpret interpretation.

Grounded theory misses the best

Grounded theory was necessary in the 1960s, when social scientific inquiry was needing to demonstrate its scientific credentials. Theory, at the pinnacle of the pile of scientific credentials, needed to be foregrounded – and Glaser and Strauss achieved this feat, managing to get the word 'theory' even into the title of their book. To those who called 'Where is your epistemic collateral? Where is your theory?' they provided difficult-to-refute answers. They made a major contribution to making qualitative inquiry legitimate. The question, though, at the beginning of the twenty-first century has to be, to paraphrase Knapp and Michaels (1985a: 26): since there is nothing left for theory to *do*, what is there left for theory to *be*?

But the most important practical issue, particularly for educators and educational researchers, is neither whether the algorithms of grounded theory are justified, nor whether they enable the induction, explanation and prediction that Glaser and Strauss (and others more recently) have claimed for them. The most important issue is rather about what is missed or dismissed if one continues to use grounded theory, and continues thereby to promote the theoretical precepts embodied in its name. Grounded theory, with its procedural machinery, relegates the clear accounts of researchers themselves, whether these be students, teachers or other professionals. Examples of such clear narrative can be found in James Patrick's classic *A Glasgow Gang Observed* (1973), or in the 'fictional' narrative of classroom life given by Sconiers and Rosiek (2000). Here, narrative is told simply and clearly with no pretence that by some methodological alchemy it will be transformed to something more secure in its epistemic status. In none of these looser narratives will be found the sort of elevation of a methodological prescription that one finds in grounded theory. More typical is an insistence that knowledge is everywhere, that all such knowledge is valid and that we should feel unconstrained it its collection, use and analysis. A preoccupation with method (and not just in grounded theory) makes for mirages of some kind of reliable knowing, and this in the end makes us almost more concerned with the method than the message.

Notes

1. As Charmaz has put it, grounded theory combined Glaser's 'positivistic methodological training in quantitative research from Columbia University' with Strauss's Chicago school 'pragmatist philosophical study of process, action and meaning' (2000: 512).
2. For example, Babchuk (1997) identifies a plethora of grounded theory investigations in education. These range over a vista of topics from the study of costs and benefits associated with participation in adult basic education programs (Mezirow et al., 1975), to academic change (Conrad, 1978), to middle-school students' perceptions of factors helping the learning of science (Spector and Gibson, 1991), to reference group socialization of secondary-school teachers (Gehrke, 1981), to teachers' perspectives on effective school leadership (Blase, 1987). Many more are identified by Babchuk. Clearly, grounded theory is viewed as a most accessible and appropriate – perhaps *the* most accessible and appropriate – way of doing qualitative research in education.
3. As Gadamer (1960/1975: 311) notes, in arguing for the legitimacy of experience, the dignity of science depends on the 'fundamental repeatability' of experience. In answering Bacon's opposition to 'empty dialectical casuistry' (1960/1975: 313), he suggests that in studies of what it is to be human – in the 'human sciences' – 'the only scientific thing is *to recognise what is*' (1960/1975:

466, emphasis in original). No method can help us achieve this recognition.
4. This is a paraphrase of the use of the Schank and Abelson test used by John
   Searle (1982).

Less theory

> Immaturity is the inability to use one's own understanding without the
> guidance of another ... The motto of enlightenment is therefore: Sapere
> aude! Have courage to use your own understanding! ...
>
> (Kant, 1784:1)

Fewer rules, more thinking

A message of the last chapter, and of the book so far, has concerned the
inhibition to creativity that the imperative to theorize may create. It has
been about restricting expectations on the supposed capacity for generalizing, for extrapolating, for predicting and for organizing thinking
that theory is meant to confer. And it has been about the need, or
otherwise, for rules surrounding the construction of 'theory'. Connected
to this, in this chapter I take up the theme introduced at the close of
Chapter 2: the possibility of fewer rules and less theory; of more bricolage
and more *ad hocery*. I try to indicate how abstention from structure and
imposed rules can free inquiry to make for research that is just as
searching as other kinds of more structured, more 'theoretically-located',
inquiry.

Rules and laws are necessary in many spheres of life and are essential
in the conduct of certain techniques in research. They also exist in the
rules of thumb and ways of doing that come as part of the discourses of
any settled practice. There is no need to deny or to eschew these. But
when it comes to the organizing principles putatively behind research, or
the supposedly theoretical ends that are being striven for, it is less clear to
me how rules help produce more interesting or more useful research.
Indeed, the argument of the last chapter is that rules play no part in the
better or cleaner extraction of what is supposed to be 'theory' from 'data'.

The only part they play is in maintaining the pretence that putative theory can be 'discovered' and that special methods have to be involved in the 'discovery'. It is worth repeating here Feyerabend's advice: '*anarchism*, while perhaps not the most attractive *political* philosophy, is certainly excellent medicine for *epistemology*' (1993: 9, emphases in original).

Feyerabend makes an important point in juxtaposing political philosophy and epistemology, for there are those who discuss the consequences of this kind of relaxation as though it were equivalent to political anarchy in the seriousness of its unwelcome consequences. Fish expounds on the issue and makes it clear that an absence of the kind of rules that some seek even in social and everyday discourse will not be as calamitous as they fear. In talking of the philosopher Israel Scheffler's fears about the consequences of being persuaded by the writings of Thomas Kuhn, he notes that Scheffler (and many others) fear that those consequences

> are disastrous and amount to the loss of everything we associate with rational inquiry: public and shared standards ... checks against irresponsibility, etc. But this follows only if anti-foundationalism is an argument for unbridled subjectivity, for the absence of constraints on the individual; whereas, in fact, it is an argument for the situated subject, for the individual who is always constrained by the local or community standards and criteria of which his judgment is an extension ... Thus anti-foundationalism cannot possibly have the consequences Scheffler fears; for, rather than unmooring the subject, it reveals the subject to be always and already tethered to the contextual setting that constitutes him and enables his 'rational' acts.
>
> (1989: 322–3)

The purpose of this chapter is to examine the sorts of parameters that can or should surround inquiry in education if one lets go of the idea of 'theory' in the many forms that that word has taken in educational research. When is structure needed, and for what purposes? And how can we enquire and research without the scaffold and structure that theory is supposed to confer? To answer these questions one first needs to reiterate some of the definitional issues, for the point that I have been making through much of this book is that theory as it is understood by the research community in education seems to be needed partly because it takes so many genial forms. If it is constituted by so many good things, who can gainsay its value? This is theory as Hydra, wherein a new theory manifestation is available for every potential purpose. I have looked at why educators (and social scientists more generally) should want to call every kind of thinking and reasoning 'theory' and have suggested that it is often down to theory's epistemological allure: theory has the Midas touch, offering specialness to what may seem to be mundane and importance to what seems trivial.

This is not, emphatically, to say that much educational research is mundane or trivial. Rather, theory is often the agent in the anticipation and perception of mundanity and triviality (for example, of certain kinds of action research). In the relationship that is fabricated between theory and non-theory, certain kinds of inquiry are made to seem trivial by their conspicuous simplicity, transparency and practical value. The construction of theory is a response to an impulse to make abstract, to generalize, to seek explanation at another level. If there is this imperative to seek such generalizing entities then that which is not in some way contributing to that enterprise – the simple, the 'untheorized' – is made to seem inferior.

I can put the possibility of creativity more theatrically by recalling the scene from *Butch Cassidy and the Sundance Kid* – the one where the physically unremarkable Butch is faced by the gigantic ogre, Harvey. The bloodthirsty crowd is baying . . .

> Butch: No, no, not yet, not until me and Harvey get the rules straightened out.
>
> Harvey: Rules – in a knife fight? No rules!
> At the confirmation of 'No rules', Butch kicks Harvey in the groin and the giant crumples into a heap on the ground:
>
> Butch: Well if there ain't gonna be any rules, let's get the fight started. Someone count 'One-two-three-go'.

The less complex the rules, the more the potential for innovative solution. Fish puts the case for the absence of directed rules and their development in practice:

> The student studies not rules but cases, pieces of practice, and what he or she acquires are not abstractions but something like 'know-how' or 'the ropes,' the ability to identify (not upon reflection, but immediately) a crucial issue, to ask a relevant question, and to propose an appropriate answer from a range of appropriate answers. Somewhere along the way the student will also begin to formulate rules or, more properly, general principles, but will be able to produce and understand them only because he or she is deeply inside – indeed, is a part of – the context in which they become intelligible.
>
> (1989: 126)

Will no one rid me of this turbulent priest?

A discussion in this chapter of the consequences of theory, in whatever form, leads me to raise the issue of the concluding comments Carr (2006) makes in his recent article on life without theory. As he ends the article he reflects on what he can permit himself to suggest as a corollary from his argument about the absence of theory from teacher education. He winds up the paper on a guarded note, saying that he has made a 'theoretical argument' (2006: 156) that the educational theory project should be abandoned, with the paradoxical caveat that nothing follows from this 'theoretical argument'. This is important for me, since if he is right, there is no point to the current chapter.

There are two issues. One is that his paper has been principally about 'educational theory' set in the historical context of its development towards personal theory and is thus in a particular place, a little to one side of any wider debate about theory and its consequences. It is certainly the case, as he argues, that such personal theory is inseparable from practice and thus cannot be said to have any consequences *for* practice. This leads, though, to a second issue about the context of theory more generally, and here he is talking about it as a form of argument separated from practice. The position is entirely different here, for here 'theory' (in one of its many costumes) is denoting argument – argument for a purpose, and with consequences – as distinct from the 'muttered rehearsal' (Ryle, 1949: 296), the silent soliloquy, involved in personal theory.

My position is that all thinking activity, including all argument, should not be conflated to 'theory'. Carr's argument is not a 'theoretical argument'. It is an argument – no more and no less. It is a discourse based on reason. There is no reason to call it 'theoretical', except insofar as there is a vernacular meaning for 'theoretical' in 'abstract'. In continuing to talk about theory – to call his argument 'theoretical' – he is surely jumping at shadows. (He is not alone among post-foundational proponents in this perseveration about 'theory', as Knapp and Michaels, 1985a, point out.) The problem with a discourse that has become over-familiar with using the words 'theory' and 'theoretical' is that it somehow seems unable to purge itself of the word. (One sympathizes with Henry II in *Murder in the Cathedral* with his 'Will no one rid me of this turbulent priest?'). The solution Carr comes to in justifying the project of his article is to say that 'this does not negate the possibility of it [the 'theoretical argument'] having the kind of practical influence that any theoretical discourse may have as a mode of rhetorical persuasion'. But there is no need for this transmutation from 'theoretical argument' to 'rhetorical persuasion'. The problem is with the insertion of the 'theoretical' before the 'argument', and one wonders what has induced the impulse behind it. An argument is a form of reason occurring as part of a practice, as part of all of the discourses that occur within a practice. As Fish (1989: 323) suggests, one cannot pretend – in the idea of 'theory' or 'theoretical argument' – to have distance from these discourses 'because it is only within them that [one] can think about alternative courses of action or, indeed, think at all'. In other words, what Carr has done is to have thought, intelligently and perspicuously, about practice, and, as it happens, about the topic of theory.[1] And this has consequences. There is no need to engage in any tergiversation about the argument or its consequences, for that argument is not a form of reason above and separate from one's study, one's professional experience, one's understanding, one's immersion in the literature, and so on. It is part of one's practice. To imagine that it is otherwise is to engage in what Fish calls 'theory hope' (1989: 322–4) – an assumption that such thinking is 'theorizing', or a form of reasoning above and beyond that which occurs as part of the practices and discourses in which one is engaged as a thinking professional.[2] And these have consequences that I feel it is legitimate to discuss unapologetically in this chapter.

Falling prey to theory hope

As I come to this stage in the book I wonder whether the metaphors of Hydra and Midas in my commentary on theory so far have been too kind. Perhaps more accurate as an analogy is theory as virus. Like the virus, theory takes many forms, mutates regularly, is infectious, resilient and hard to pin down. And like the virus, if my argument is valid, it feeds off and damages its host. The problem here is that the multitude of theory forms and theory talk allows expectations about certain kinds of theory and hopes about its power to infuse into all of those theory forms, all of that theory talk. And the hope about theory's power means that all of the false expectations infect every theory form – every innocuous reflection, every conjecture, every use of literature – in such a way that the theory-saturated environment in educational research becomes distorted as it seeks to follow the contours of what it assumes to be good inquiry.

The problems with 'theory hope' are serious and concern more than the mere assumption that there is some kind of discourse that stands superior to practice. First, it transforms the tentative into the secure: with theory comes a slipperiness on one's grip that knowledge is provisional or tentative, for 'theory hope' is accompanied by narratives of explanation and epistemic security. Wanting theory is like wanting to hold Mummy's hand in the dark. In this respect, theory in education, as I noted in Chapter 2, is as far from ideas about Popperian falsification as it could be. Theory in education is treated as if it is to be cherished, not falsified: far from being the intellectual construction to be relentlessly assailed, it is the proud fortress for one's thinking. And second, it constrains a capacity to look at something straightforwardly. The urge to make abstract curtails any straightforward satisfaction with the individual situation as described – its details, its idiosyncrasies, its context and its history. This has had unfortunate effects on certain kinds of research and inquiry, which are taken to be inferior to others.

What, then, are the genial forms that theory takes, for it is not those forms that themselves are the cause of the set of problems when it comes to 'theory'. I do not wish in any way to minimize the importance of those forms. The issue is that confusion reigns when 'theory' is applies to any or all of those forms – and once the theory genie is released from the bottle all kinds of associated expectations, all kinds of theory hopes, arise about the conduct of the ensuing inquiry and the conclusions that can be drawn from it. The forms in which theory is used, and some possible alternatives to their use, are summarized in Table 7.1.

Table 7.1. Verbal hygiene in thinking about theory

'Theory' as used		Possible alternatives to 'theory'
Theory contrasted with fact	*Call it ...*	conjecture
Theory, or theorizing, as thinking	*Call it ...*	thinking
Personal theory or practical theory	*Call it ...*	reflection; reflective practice
Theory as a body of knowledge	*Call it ...*	a body of knowledge
Theory as a clearly developed argument	*Call it ...*	a clearly developed argument
Theory as craft knowledge	*Call it ...*	craft knowledge

Omitted from Table 7.1 are grand theory and scientific theory. I discussed in Chapters 2 and 3 the views of those who suggest that theory as it is used in the natural sciences is surrounded by parameters and checks that are not matched in the social sciences and education. And 'grand theory' is a term used mockingly by Wright Mills (1959: 23) to describe the expectation among social scientists that their disciplines should attempt to build systematic theory of 'the nature of man and society'; he saw this effort as an obstacle to progress in the human sciences. I take it as given that grand theory is not what is generally wanted in educational research and that those who promote theory in contemporary discourse are not attempting to promote grand theory. (There are, though, those who feel that it is important – see Turner, 2004.)

But we do want conjecture, thinking, dialogue, argument, and collected bodies of evidence and understanding. One of the points made in Chapter 3 is that if all of inquiry, all types of thinking, are reduced and flattened out to be described as 'theory' there is an impoverishment brought to the exercise of inquiry. It is worth repeating Frank Smith's (1992) categorization of thinking words into those concerned with 'forward' thinking (such as *expect, imagine, foresee*), those concerned with 'current' thinking (e.g. *argue, analyse, examine*), and those that refer to 'past' thinking (e.g. *deduce, review, reflect*). One can, with one's knowledge of educational discourse and one's reading of its literature substitute the word 'theorize' for any of these words. For example,

'I expect that the sample of girls will perform better in reading than the sample of boys'.
becomes
'I theorize that the sample of girls will perform better in reading than the sample of boys'.

'I argue that the promotion of inclusive education in Turkey is unthinkingly mirroring that in the West'.
becomes
'I theorize that the promotion of inclusive education in Turkey is unthinkingly mirroring that in the West'.

'We have reflected on these findings and emerge with three conclusions'.
becomes
'Our theorization on these findings leads to three conclusions'.

The reason that these substitutions apparently work is not because the word 'theory' in these instances is doing anything useful. Rather, it is because familiarity with the employment of the word 'theory' in educational discourse makes the sentences seem meaningful. Theory has become a synonym for all of this other, more precisely described conceptual activity. Does this matter? Why should it matter if one form of account, one form of vocabulary is used rather than another? My reasoning so far in this book leads me to assert that it matters because for the educator 'theory' is part of a technical vocabulary: we have to know what we are talking about when we use the word. Overuse of 'theory' dilutes and homogenizes the way that inquiry is thought about, discussed and undertaken. Nuances are steamrollered, subtleties flattened, richnesses attenuated. Not only this, but the caution and provisionality inhering in ideas such as 'expect', 'imagine', 'argue' and 'reflect' evaporate. Because of theory's supposed epistemological muscle, an unwarranted confidence and solidity is imparted to one's beginnings, one's findings and one's interpretations with its use.

What kind of thinking? Or, 'What have the Greeks ever done for us?'

> All right, but apart from the sanitation, the medicine, education, wine, public order, irrigation, roads, a fresh water system, and public health, what have the Romans ever done for us?
>
> Monty Python's *Life of Brian*

To extend Frank Smith's taxonomy, I have compiled some constructs about thinking in Table 7.2. Clearly not a serious or exhaustive commentary on Greek philosophy, it is given, rather, to reinforce the point about the gradations in shade and colour that one can give to ideas about thinking, and the blotting-out of these gradations that occurs when they are all reduced to 'theory'.

Table 7.2. What have the Greeks ever done for us? Forms of thinking

Greek term	Meaning	Comment
Aisthêsis	perception or observation	This is not knowledge but something on which knowledge can be built, or from which it can be induced.
Apodeixis	demonstration or proof	For example, by means of syllogism.
Doxa	common opinion	Perhaps similar to latter-day 'received wisdom', to 'ideology', to Foucault's 'discourse' or Giddens's (1996: 69) 'practical consciousness. Bourdieu (in Bourdieu and Eagleton, 1994) talks of *doxa* to mean what is understood via cultural and scientific orthodoxy, and so on.
Eikon	changing likeness	Since the world is only the changing likeness (eikon) of an unchanging model (paradeigma), its description can only be provisional and likely (eikos), not a final and immutable representation of reality.
Eikos	what is likely, or probable	When induction (or epagôgê) is used, we can talk confidently about what is probable.
Empeiria	a *knack* or skill acquired through practice	The person having *empeiria* might have certain skills, but would not be able to explain why what was being done should work. *Empeiria*, a technical knack, can be contrasted with *episteme*, knowledge (but see Chapters 3, 4 and 5 where I use Ryle's discussion about the distinction between 'know-how' and 'know-that' to ask whether any distinction is actually valid in relation to teaching).
Epagôgê	Induction	Proceeding from particulars up to a universal (as distinct from *de*duction or *sullogismos*, which is an argument in which something different from the suppositions results from them).
Epistêmê	knowledge	Knowledge requires that reasons are given as to why something is the case.
Heuriskein	to discover	Archimedes jumped out of the bath shouting, 'Heureka', meaning 'I've found it'. The 'I've found it!' of Heureka (or Eureka) is related to today's meaning of heuristics in 'rules of thumb'. (Note that Archimedes did not leap from his bath, shouting, 'I have a theory!'). Similar to Kohler's (1925) apes' 'Ah Ha!'.

Greek term	Meaning	Comment
Logos	divine reason, argument	*Logos* exists beyond any particular sense perception. Later, through Aristotle, *logos* becomes associated with language and 'logic'.
Metanoia	change of mind	From the prefix 'meta' meaning 'beyond' (as in 'metaphysics') and 'noia' meaning 'the mind'. So, going beyond the mind. A change of mind, particularly in the context of 'repentance'. Metamorphosis. Also, in rhetoric, finding a better way of expressing something.
Paradeigma	unchanging model	An unchanging model, to which one's knowledge of the world, via experience, can provide an approximation. Used by Kuhn for the notion of *paradigm* – in other words a fixed set of assumptions (about the way inquiry should be conducted).
Phronêsis	practical intelligence	Rather like *empeiria* and *technê* – in today's terms, practical reasoning, craft knowledge, or tacit knowing – the ability to see the right thing to do in the circumstances.
Rhetoric	appropriateness of discourse	Helps people to work out what is likely (eikos). Because the rhetorical situation is centrally bound up with the nature of those who listen to or read discourse, *audience* itself becomes integral to the understanding of rhetoric. Rhetoric is therefore never about discourse in the abstract; it is always concerned with directing one's words with particular intentions towards certain audiences.
Technê	craft/craftsmanship	A craft or skill, distinguished from *epistêmê* by the absence of underlying principles of understanding.

In the brief sketch outlined in Table 7.2 can be seen a storehouse of different ideas that are discussed in contemporary educational research.[3] The point I am trying to get over from using it is the richness of ideas for thinking about inquiry. Words are our tools for thinking, and the invasion of 'theory' into all them reduces the variety of those tools, depleting our resources for thinking. Once established, its influence is corrosive, diminishing our capacity to think about inquiry. Prominently in Table 7.2 there is the idea of tentative, provisional knowledge present in *eikos*. This is often called 'personal theory' or 'practical theory' in today's discourse about inquiry, as I have noted elsewhere in this book. But for reasons I have discussed, the use of 'theory' for such tentative practical generalizations seems wholly inappropriate.

Related to *eikos*, there is the idea of changing one's view, or finding a better way of expressing things, present in *metanoia*. There is tacit knowing and craft knowledge present in *empeiria* and *phronesis*. All of these ideas – *eikos, metanoia, empeiria* and *phronesis* – describe processes of change in thinking and knowledge as practice develops. Movement in one's position is key. The idea of *phronesis* is developed interestingly by Elliott (2006: 182) in his discussion of democratic rationality in educational research and what he calls 'the marriage between phronesis and technê, and the banishment of episteme'.

And one can see how ideas such as paradigm have changed. From the Greek *paradeigma*, meaning unchanging model, came Kuhn's use of the word 'paradigm' in *The Structure of Scientific Revolutions* (1970) to mean the unvarying set of practices and understandings that come from the influence of custom, convention, existing knowledge, existing procedures and existing interpretations in physics. Kuhn's message is that once these ligatures surround inquiry it is impossible to move beyond certain understandings when new findings and new interpretations make the old suppositions untenable. A new paradigm has to be adopted and employed. It is important to emphasize that Kuhn was writing about physics (see Fuller, 2002, for a discussion), since the widespread adoption of the notion of paradigm has allowed significant adaptations in its meaning in the social sciences. Here, 'paradigm' has come to mean sets of ontological and epistemological presuppositions, while the important 'unvarying' meaning has taken a back seat.

Chunking and heuristics: the best in the circumstances

A little inaccuracy sometimes saves a ton of explanation. (H.H. Munro (Saki))

A crucial idea that comes out of Table 7.2, and one that is important for the rest of this chapter, is that of *Heuriskein*, known by the more familiar 'Eureka!' of Archimedes, and the development of the idea of 'heuristic'. The idea is of discovery[4] rather than absolute knowledge. As Pólya puts it,

> Heuristic, or heuretic, or 'ars inveniendi' was the name of a certain branch of study, not very clearly circumscribed, belonging to logic, or to philosophy, or to psychology, often outlined, seldom presented in detail . . . The aim of heuristic is to study the methods and rules of discovery and invention.
>
> (1945/2004: 112)

He likens it to scaffolding for our thinking, a metaphor, of course, used also by Vygotsky about language and thinking. As the idea has been developed more recently in information science, a heuristic is a rule of thumb that leads to conclusions and predictions that may not be correct all of the time, but are good enough most of the time (see Newell et al., 1957; Tversky and Kahneman, 1974). It is a temporary model developed out of experience and takes as one of its starting points the fact that we are unable in most circumstances to gather enough information about all of the relevant variables to warrant the drawing of watertight conclusions. Such situations are common in the human sciences, and possibly ubiquitous in the research contexts of education. We therefore make judgements about what is important, and we develop pathways to action based on these judgements. The heuristic is a route that allows one to proceed in circumstances such as this. Though it may produce errors in making decisions, these will be errors of a different character from those that emerge from putative theory, in education or elsewhere, for there is no assumption that these heuristics will not be imperfect. We will proceed on a tentative basis, as though we may be wrong.

The psychologist George Miller (1956), in a groundbreaking paper, gave clues about the nature of the everyday heuristic. He called the process of organizing undertaken by human beings – a process that one could liken to a tacit development of heuristic – 'chunking'. He noted that there are limitations to the amount of raw data that we can hold in our heads: limitations on reception, processing and remembering. 'By organizing the stimulus input simultaneously into several dimensions and successively into a sequence of chunks, we manage to break (or at least stretch) this informational bottleneck' (1956: 96). The process of chunking goes on both deliberately and tacitly, occurring most commonly through the use of language at its different levels. Thus, at the most primitive level, the chunking is of phonemes into words, at once assimilating and organizing very large amounts of data into more manageable chunks. At another level up, those words may be chunked into common syntactic constructions and beyond this into ideas. Miller notes that a great deal of learning has gone into the formation of these chunks and categories. Categorization is at the heart of the process for Bruner et al. (1972: 16), who note that 'To categorize is to render discriminably different things equivalent, to group the objects and events and people around us into classes, and to respond to them in terms of their class membership rather than their uniqueness'. As I noted in Chapter 5, Simon (1983) links this tacit process of incremental chunking with what is called 'intuition'.

Miller's chunking sounds very similar to the 'bracketing' of Edmund Husserl. In his *Ideas: A General Introduction to Pure Phenomenology* (1913/ 1983) Husserl introduced the term 'phenomenological reduction', a method of reflection involving 'bracketing existence'. Interestingly, Husserl's phenomenology finds its descendents in the sociologies of Alfred Schutz (1962) and Berger and Luckmann (1979) – in the view, in other words, that individual thinking is not simply the product of social facts or social forces but itself shapes and creates knowledge of the world. Understanding is the product of interaction with others and it is constructed from below, not imposed from above. Berger and Luckmann make claims about 'the foundations of knowledge in everyday life' which are constructed out of 'subjective processes (and meanings) by which the intersubjective commonsense world is constructed' (1979: 20). They suggest that understanding is built out of diverse thinking tools occurring across the cultural spectrum, from language, reminiscence, folk tales, proverbs and professional vocabularies.[5] Such building-blocks are drawn on and put together variously in the different circumstances in which we confront everyday life, so that the world is always one of 'multiple realities' (1979: 21). They quote Pascal in his *Pensées*: 'The truth on this side of the Pyrenees, error on the other'. The consequence is summed up by Schutz (1964: 93): 'the knowledge of the man who acts and thinks within the world of his daily life is not homogeneous; it is (1) incoherent, (2) only partially clear, and (3) not at all free from contradictions'. The phenomenological tradition is clear that methods for studying such intersubjectively constructed worlds have to take form in ways that do not mirror the assumptions residing in folk models of theory-first science.

Though from an entirely different intellectual tradition, the literary critic E.D. Hirsch (1976: 18) emerges with similar conclusions. He too picks up the 'bracketing' of Husserl. Describing the everyday understandings that we come to as 'local hermeneutics', he suggests that these provide provisional, tentative models for interpretation and analysis. In this regard, he distinguishes local hermeneutics from 'general hermeneutics', the latter laying claim to principles that hold true all of the time.[6] Local hermeneutics, by contrast, are about what is probable, rather than what is universal:

> Every example of local hermeneutics known to me ... exists in the realm of what Bacon called 'middle axioms', which is to say the realm of probabilities rather than universals. Local hermeneutics consists of rules of thumb rather than rules. As a system of middle axioms, local hermeneutics can indeed provide models and methods that are reliable most of the time.
>
> (1976: 18)

Thus, 'middle axioms' and local hermeneutics exist in everyday notions such as the rule of thumb and the knack. Talking of the rule of thumb and distinguishing it from the rule, pure-and-simple, Fish (1989: 317) notes that the conditions of its use 'vary with the contextual circumstances of an ongoing practice; as those circumstances change, the very meaning of the rule (the instructions it is understood to give) changes too'.

These are informal, changeable devices for interpretation, analysis and action. Their trademark lies in their malleability as distinct from the rigidity that inevitably comes to be characterized by the kind of theory that I have described in the rest of this book. Such models for interpretation are paralleled in the Piagetian *schema* and the Kellyan *construct* (see Bannister and Fransella, 1971), themselves inheritors of a constructivist position.

Hirsch proceeds to call for an eclectic bringing-together of ideas summarized in what he calls 'corrigible schemata' of different provenance – from psychology, art history, philosophy of science, and epistemology:

> It is very remarkable how widespread is the pattern I have been discussing ... no doubt an hypothesis is not just the same as Husserl's 'intentional object', which in turn is not exactly the same as Piaget's 'schema', Dilthey's 'whole', or Heidegger's 'pre-understanding'. Yet important features of all these proposals are quite identical in their character and function, and also in their connection with what we call meaning.
>
> (1976: 35)

Hirsch's synthesis collates many ideas that stress the provisional and corrigible 'thinking tool'. His work is commendable in its interdisciplinarity though there are several cognate ideas, all of which have been mentioned in the preceding chapters, which can be added. There are notions such as the common interpretive act (Schatzman, 1991), bounded rationality (Simon, 1982), Bourdieu's 'thinking tool' (in Wacquant, 1989: 50), or Althusser's Generalities II (Althusser, 1979: 183–90) – all of which describe much the same kind of process: a fluid understanding that explicitly or tacitly recognizes the complexity of the intersubjectively constructed worlds in which we live. They describe our processes of garnering and organizing information to analyse and deal with those worlds in the most propitious ways. Like the heuristic, such ways may not provide watertight guarantees of success in dealing with a particular problem, but are unpretentious in their assumptions of fallibility and provisionality.

Sacks (1989: 365–75) suggests that proverbs fall into the same broad category. Proverbs – and I would say idioms as well – draw upon collected experience to express a general kind of proposition. Such a proposition will hold most of the time but not always – the examples Sacks gives being, 'You're stacking the deck'; 'He's hitting below the belt'; 'Plus ça change, plus c'est la même chose'. Importantly, Sacks makes the point that such devices have an automatically understood character: one does not *expect* them to obtain all of the time and in all circumstances. In an entertaining discussion, he gives the example of a report from a newspaper in which diplomats and government officials are talking about Premier Khrushchev's demise. One diplomat ventures, 'Better the devil you know, than the one you don't know'. Sacks makes the point that no one would seriously ask, 'What's the evidence for that?' The saying is expressing a popularly held generalization, but one that it would be preposterous to treat in the same way as the kind of proposition that a natural scientist might make.

Allied to proverbs are analogies. Tavor Bannet (1997: 655) interestingly relates Wittgenstein's and Derrida's discussions of what happens during analogy. For Wittgenstein, she says, analogy is not just the juxtaposition of objects of comparison, any more than it is merely illustrative. In its use both in science and the humanities, analogy for Wittgenstein 'is a traditional method of reasoning from the known to the unknown, and from the visible to the speculative' by carrying familiar terms and images across into unfamiliar territory. In a similar vein, Derrida describes analogy as a form of translation: 'a way of transporting something from place to place, from old to new, from original to copy, and from one (con)text to another' (Tavor Bannet, 1997: 655). What is being spoken about here seems to be the process of bringing together, of juxtaposing, seeing similarities and making generalizations across context.

Rorty makes the point that the emergence of this kind of generalization marks the similarity between the sciences and the humanities, not the differences. The sciences and the humanities, Rorty argues, use different forms of the same phenomenon – being hermeneutical in different ways:

> On my view, being 'interpretive' or 'hermeneutical' is not having a special method but simply casting about for a vocabulary which might help. When Galileo came up with his mathemetized vocabulary, he was successfully concluding an inquiry which was, in the only sense I can give the term, hermeneutical ... I think that it would do no harm to adopt the term 'hermeneutics' for the sort of by-guess-and-by-God hunt for new terminology which characterizes the initial stages of any new line of inquiry.
>
> (1982: 199–200)

It is the 'by-guess-and-by-God hunt' that is significant. This sounds rather like Pólya's (1945/2004: 172) suggestion that one needs is to have 'brains and good luck' and to 'sit tight and wait till you get a bright idea'. It is similar to the Ah Ha! – that process of intuition attributed by Simon (1983) to tacit processes of incremental chunking. In education, the significance of the intuitive has been explored perspicuously by Atkinson and Claxton (2000).

Watertight guarantees of success in the employment of heuristic or the reliance on intuition are unattainable, or at least if they were ever attainable they would be useless, as Douglas Adams made clear in *The Hitch-hiker's Guide to the Galaxy* (1979). A supercomputer is built for the specific purpose of revealing the answer to the question of Life, the Universe and Everything. After seven and a half million years it comes up with the answer: 42.

'Forty-two!' yelled Loonquawl. 'Is that all you've got to show for seven and a half million years' work?'

'I checked it very thoroughly', said the computer, 'and that quite definitely is the answer. I think the problem, to be quite honest with you, is that you've never actually known what the question is'.

It's as well to have boundaries on the questions that are asked, for the usefulness of the generalizations that are drawn will relate to the ambit of those questions. More importantly, it's as well to understand the constraints on the possibility of generalization and what may follow from it. Returning to Schön's observations on the dangers of abstraction made in Chapter 1, one needs to be careful about attempts to make abstract, to synthesize, to find principles, and predict on the basis of the synthesis. While the thinking processes of natural scientists, social scientists and those in the humanities may, in reality, be not so very different as Rorty (1982), Latour and Woolgar (1979), Lynch (1985) and many others suggest, there are clear differences in the quality of the generalizations – the quality of the so called 'theory' – that can be drawn in each arena.

Corrigibility and metanoia

The point of this discussion on heuristics and allied phenomena has been to demonstrate – and validate – the existence of the tacit and explicit forms of problem solving occurring as part of the practice of our work and everyday lives. Such forms of problem solving have been and are to an extent relegated by the notion of theory, by virtue of potential reference to a discourse outside and above those practices. A point I have tried to make is that unpretentious problem solving – the 'common interpretive acts' of Schatzman (1991), the thinking tools of Bourdieu (1992), or heuristics – whatever one wants to call them – alongside a methodological 'bricolage'[7] can sit unapologetically inside a pragmatist or post-foundational position. There is no need to worry that they constitute some reinvention of theory by another name, for there is no assumption that they exist outside practice or exist superior to such practice. They are not, in other words, part of 'theory hope'. They are part of, and emerge from, our practice and our business of everyday being. They emerge from our work, our interactions with others, our reading, our discussions. They grow with our action, our practice and our experience. They are characterized by revision and informal experiment, by flexibility and corrigibility – in other words by *metanoia* rather than by framework and rule, or by theory.

From Procrustean bed to thinking tool. Theories as faces in the clouds

> Our brightest blazes of gladness are commonly kindled by unexpected sparks.
>
> Samuel Johnson

To ask how such forms of problem solving might be capitalized upon would be to miss the point of the discussion in the foregoing chapters, for it can be done in any way. The key distinction between such an approach and a putatively theoretical one is its tentativeness, its assumptions of fallibility and its corrigibility. The assumption is that the work and the intuitions, the investigative tricks and the analytical methods of anybody working in any settled practice – actuaries, doctors, engineers, mathematicians, nurses, physicists, reporters, teachers, zookeepers – are to all intents and purposes similar. The principal difference in what emerges lies in the nature and generalizability of the conclusions that they might draw from their conjectures and inquiries and the caution and provisionality that has to be attached to these, as I discussed in Chapter 3.

None of this is to vindicate lyrical assumptions about mysterious, unarticulable and inexplicable practice. It is not to perpetuate a 'secret garden' view of education, in which enigmatic, idiosyncratic, unknowable processes guide the teacher in ways that no onlooker, no researcher (nor any teacher) could possibly understand. Such assumptions, as Furlong (2000) points out, would be untenable. On the contrary, it is to place the educator's development and inquiry about that development visibly within the educator's practice and to ensure adequate standards of explanation and communication about these. Hammersley puts it this way:

> It is not the case, of course, that the judgments made by scientists are simply intuitive, in the sense of being idiosyncratic claims to knowledge that have to be accepted or rejected at face value. There is a requirement in science that judgments be explained to others to the extent that this can be done, and corroborated wherever possible by other research. And what cannot be sufficiently explained, assessed or corroborated cannot be accepted as knowledge. In my view this must be applied in educational research as much as in any other scientific field of inquiry. But there is no way in which to guarantee the validity of judgments by proceduralisation. Indeed, seeking to proceduralise the practice of research and the assessment of its findings is counterproductive: it involves distortion of the tacit knowledge that we cannot but rely upon.
>
> (2005a: 1)

Indeed, dialogue could be seen as necessary and integral part of inquiry, as Hammersley (2005c) makes clear in explaining that for Gadamer 'inquiry is above all a dialogue with others'. Instead of assuming that the educator's development can be guided by some distal theory, it is to assert that it is guided by practice and experience. It is to reiterate the point that research about teaching occurs within that practice, using for example Stenhouse's (1975) model of 'research-based teaching' or models of action research as described, for example, by Winter (1987), Torrance (2004), Elliott (2004) and others. The role of the researcher is to engage with that action and that practice (albeit that one should always remember Ernest Hemingway's advice: 'Never mistake motion for action').

How do we do this? There are no recipes, but simply straightforward advice. Pólya (1945/2004), for example, suggests that problem solving in research or elsewhere involves some basic ingredients:

1. Understanding the problem;
2. Seeing how elements within the problem are connected, seeing how the unknown is linked to the known, and making a plan;
3. Carrying out the plan;
4. Looking back at the completed solution, reviewing and discussing it.

He goes on to describe a 'short history of heuristic', running through a number of 'tricks' such as the use of analogy. This sounds not dissimilar to the process of action research just described. There is nothing magical about this, or about that.

In a similar vein, Becker (1998) talks explicitly and unapologetically of the 'tricks' of the researcher. Citing Geertz's searches for ever-newer and ever-better forms of discourse to keep up with what is going on in the world, he makes the point that convention, social and scientific, is the enemy of inquiry. We need, he says,

> ways of expanding the reach of our thinking, of seeing what else we could be thinking and asking, of increasing the ability of our ideas to deal with the diversity of what goes on in the world. Most of the tricks I describe are devoted to that purpose.
>
> (1998: 7)

For Becker, a trick – of which he gives many examples in his book – is, in short, a device for solving a problem and offering ways around existing discourses of explanation. He divides his tricks into those of *imagery*, *sampling*, *concepts* and *logic*. They are surely part of Lévi-Strauss's bricolage, where the first practical step is retrospective: bricoleurs will

> turn back to an already existent set made up of tools and materials, to consider or reconsider what it contains and, finally and above all, to engage in a sort of dialogue with it and, before choosing between them, to index the possible answers which the whole set can offer to his problem.
>
> (1962/1966: 19)

Other kinds of tricks might include the thought experiments that have such an impressive pedigree and have had such extraordinary consequences in physical science, or the kinds of dialogue that Plato used for Socratic dialogues, with positions being contested and defended. Or the dialogue could be a simple narrative of explanation or argument. Look at what the physicist-cum-mathematician-cum-psychologist Douglas Hofstadter (2000: 434) does to explicate some abstruse points about his subject. Instead of writing an impenetrable essay, he invents a discussion between Achilles and the tortoise:

Tortoise: When you discuss a word or a phrase, you conventionally put it in quotes ... This is called the USE-MENTION distinction.

Achilles: Oh?

Tortoise: Let me explain. Suppose I were to say to you,
Philosophers make lots of money.
Here, I would be USING the word to manufacture an image in your mind of a twinkle-eyed sage with bulging moneybags. But when I put this word – or any word – in quotes, I subtract out its meaning and connotation, and am left only with some marks on paper, or some sounds. That is called 'MENTION'. Nothing about the word matters, other than its typographical aspects – any meaning it might have is ignored.

Achilles: It reminds me of using a violin as a fly swatter. Or should I say 'mentioning'? Nothing about the violin matters, other than its solidity – any meaning or function it might have is being ignored. Come to think of it, I guess the fly is being treated that way, too.

Tortoise: Those are sensible, if slightly unorthodox, extensions of the use-mention distinction. But now, I want you to think about preceding something by its own quotation.

Achilles: All right. Would this be correct?

'HUBBA' HUBBA

Tortoise: Good. Try another.

Achilles: All right.

'"PLOP" IS NOT THE TITLE OF ANY BOOK, SO FAR AS I KNOW'

"PLOP" IS NOT THE TITLE OF ANY BOOK, SO FAR AS I KNOW.

Tortoise: Now this example can be modified into quite an interesting specimen, simply by dropping 'Plop'.

Achilles: Really? Let me see what you mean. It becomes

'IS NOT THE TITLE OF ANY BOOK, SO FAR AS I KNOW'

IS NOT THE TITLE OF ANY BOOK, SO FAR AS I KNOW.

Tortoise: You see, you have made a sentence.

The subject is unimportant; here a fictional text is used to offer an argument or explanation about something otherwise difficult to explain.[8] The point of giving this example here is to demonstrate how far original and imaginative forms of discourse in scholarship and inquiry outside the social sciences have come. Would such allegory be dared in education today? The nearest I can think of is in Harold Benjamin's highly influential discussion of the 'saber-toothed curriculum' (Peddiwell, 1939), where fiction and humour were used to make an argument about the nature of the curriculum. One hopes that a culture of performativity and fears of charges of levity and lack of scientific rigour do not increasingly inhibit such original, such powerful, such creative discourse.

Dialogue is just one example and I don't want to over-state its importance, but its use emphasizes some of the interpretational issues that were raised in Chapter 6. As a further instance I can give an example from one of my own research projects, for the children's charity Barnardos, when it struck me that I should let the dialogue do its own work rather than managing it and 'theorizing' it in ways that a grounded theorist would. I thus presented a complete interview, with nothing omitted save personal details, as almost a whole chapter, with minimal commentary. It lost nothing from this lack of interpretation. In fact the narrative gains immediacy from the absence of treatment, and the problems of interpretation that arise with grounded theory, or other forms of interpretative techniques (discussed in Chapter 6), do not arise to the same extent. Here is the first page of the interview transcript – the interview is between the project's researcher, Julie Webb (JW), and headteacher David Walker (DW):

JW: *Could you tell me about how the inclusion initiative came about originally?*

DW: Yes. It's quite a long story really, I think, because there's two things that happened. If you like, there's the outer events and for me personally there were some inner things that were going on as well. In 1991, I'd been [head teacher] at the school three years, and in that time we increased the occupancy, we built the school up from a position where it had been in some difficulties, and it was doing well. So we agreed that at that point we would just look around and see what was on the horizon in special educational needs. And we looked at a lot of things, not just at inclusion. We looked at things like conductive education, special therapies, all sorts of stuff. One of the things that I went to, and Steve Connor went to, was the first Inclusion Conference, which was held in Cardiff... they invited the Canadians over, George Flynn, Marsha Forest, John O'Brien and Judith Snow. And Barnardos committed resources to staff going, so there were quite a lot of Barnardos staff there. There were something like ten Barnardos staff there.

Some of the things that George Flynn was saying about the outcomes for people who'd been in special education: jobless-ness, alcoholism, potential for crime, vulnerability ... all those things hit me very powerfully at a time when I was personally feeling quite vulnerable. And also I think that the sense of – there was an alternative to the special school. And it affected me a lot.

And I think the other important element was that Steve Connor had gone as well. So I wasn't going to something and then coming away on my own – I actually had somebody I could talk things through with. Steve and I *did* talk it through, an awful lot. I think Steve is extraordinarily good at thinking strategically. You know, he can get hold of something and he can have a sense of how you could move towards it. He's better at that than I am. But where I think I can help is that I can operationalize that. Kind of, 'OK, if that's the direction we're going down, this is what we need to do'. And so between us I think we actually formed a very good alliance. And it was quickly apparent – it was shortly after that that Vivian was appointed as deputy and we had a clear ally in Vivian. And Peggy had taken over as administrator around that time and Peggy was also an ally. So as the senior management team we were quite strong.

JW: *So would you say that those issues, of outcomes for segregated schooling, were something that you hadn't really devoted much time to before? Was there not much research available in this country or ... ?*

DW: My own background before being at PMS was children who have emotional and behavioural difficulties. And I suppose at some level I'd always been concerned with *those* children that there was very little follow-up after school as to what happened to them. I think perhaps, I don't know, I was busy *doing* the job, and, in a way, not knowing about what happens afterwards is kind of – useful. You don't have to think about it. And once it had been articulated for me by George Flynn, I think there were two things: one was it felt right when he said, you know, 'These are the outcomes'. I thought, yes, at some level I knew this, and I think the second thing was, once you know some-thing, once *I* know something I can't ignore it, can't leave it alone ...

So I think at that point it was clear for me – it sort of emerged over the discussions I had with Steve – in effect I was being faced with two choices: one was to leave and go and do something else somewhere else, or two was to take this school through the process – either I was going to leave the school or the school was going to leave me. And I suppose I began to – it wasn't an immediate thing – if you put something far enough in the future it doesn't feel like it's too desperate here and now, does it – so notions about including children and so on were talked about at that point about five years down the line and we were quite clear in our own minds it would take about five years to do this. And we held to that in fact. But by doing that we gave ourselves time, I think, to say, 'Well, OK, so are there some small things that we can do now?' And I think that was actually, well for me it was quite important.

(Thomas et al. 1998: 83–5)

What else might one do? Going back even further and looking back on my own PhD research, I remember that I spent a great deal of time trying to 'theorize' what I was doing, and trying to 'locate' my work in theory. The literature, my colleagues, my fellow students and my supervisors all exhorted me to find theoretical angles and theoretical location. As I explained in Chapter 1, I had serious confusions about what any of this theory talk meant, and this confusion about theory has led to my subsequent interest, and ultimately to this book. But at the time the confusions assumed proportions of major significance: I wanted to gain my doctorate, after all, and if I'm honest the disinterested pursuit of knowledge was less important than this goal. I wasn't, to quote Oscar Wilde, 'young enough to know everything' and I felt far too unconfident about my inchoate doubts and confusions about theory to challenge received wisdom and risk failure.

I therefore set off on those doctoral studies toeing the line: I sought to locate my work in theory. My topic was the new (at the time) phenomenon of extra adults in classrooms: support teachers, instead of withdrawing children from the classroom, had taken to working inside it alongside the classteacher; numbers of teaching assistants were beginning to grow; parents were being encouraged to work in the classroom. I wanted to see what all of this meant, how the classroom teacher felt about it, and how the incoming adults felt about what they were doing and what they could be doing.

How could I theorize about this? I first sought to discuss the subject in the context of social psychology. What had social psychologists to say about all of this – about someone who was familiar with working on their own being confronted with onlookers? It led me to 'theory' about role: role confusion, role ambiguity and role clarity figured large in my thinking. This wasn't enough, though, since I wanted to be *really* sure of gaining my doctorate and I wasn't certain that the body of knowledge about 'role' was sufficient to constitute theory. So for good measure I sought to interpret the notion of role in the context of more over-arching and respectable theories – theories that were unambiguously theories and that no one could deny were theories. I employed attribution theory and construct theory, and I used various techniques (such as 'network analysis' and 'construct mapping') in the process.

Did any of this help in my understanding of the phenomenon of extra people in the classroom? The short answer is 'no'. The long answer is that it distorted what I did and how I thought about it. It pleased the examiners, who pronounced it an excellent piece of work, especially I guess because of the super-abundance of theorization of one kind or another. But as I felt it, I was being led down paths along which I didn't want to walk. As I have looked back on the work, I realize that the parts I refer to again and again are the untheorized bits, and particularly the Appendix, where I gave the undigested report of my diary working as a support teacher in a secondary school.[9] I have been surprised that others, when they have read the book that followed from the doctorate (Thomas, 1992), also seem to have gained most from that Appendix. Disappointing though this is, after my seven years' work theorizing, I can understand how this raw narrative offers more insights than my 'theorization'. I give now a sample of that untheorized diary:

---

3 May

I make my way to Xanthe's class again, a little late, having been talking to the head of support. I haven't spoken in detail to Xanthe yet about the team teaching idea. Last week's meeting with her was too tense to broach the topic. When I come in this week the situation seems rather similar. Xanthe is taking the class from the front and the children are messing around as they were last week. Xanthe holds up a small glass tank with a funnel upside down over something (a small plant, I think) and compares it with another similar set of objects. The children have to compare the two sets and say how they are different:

Child: There's more water in that one.

Child: One's all dirty – yeugh.
         The session is to show that carbon dioxide is taken up by plants:

Child: That dirt's carbon dioxide!
         Explanations are again punctuated with inconsequential intrusions:

Child: Anyone got a rubber!
         These become so intrusive that Xanthe eventually loses her temper and raises her voice. This has some effect on the children, who temporarily quieten down. She capitalizes on this by saying,

Teacher: Right we'll have two minutes of complete silence – not a word.
The children respond to this: they are now clear about the rules
and what is expected of them. Again I feel redundant – not
only redundant, but worse that I am compounding the
situation by my presence, and perhaps that Pauline, the
teaching assistant, is in a similar position. She must feel some
degree of inhibition about doing what comes naturally to her to
quell the sorts of problems that she is experiencing. Again,
there is no way that I feel I can intervene in the immediate
situation without making things worse ...

Eventually the explanation is complete and the children are
told what they have to do with their own glass containers. A
few begin to do it. Some conspicuously, or not so
conspicuously, don't. I make my way to a boy who has not
associated himself with any group, and has begun no work. He
is drawing pictures of cars. He says that he cannot start as he
hasn't got his book. 'Miss' is engaged elsewhere and ought not
to be disturbed to get the book. Would she have it anyway?
This boy seems quite happy in the knowledge that he will not
have to do, nor will he be pestered to do the work in hand. His
answers about the experiment are monosyllabic and I am left
wondering, again, where I should begin given the nature of the
work and the children's difficulties understanding it.

The noise level rises and children generally seem to be only
very peripherally concerned with the task in hand. They have to
draw the two sets of apparatus, and say how they look different
... About half of the children have drawn something; the others
are making no attempt to start, are chatting, walking round the
class or occasionally shouting something out. There doesn't
seem to be anyone particularly in need of help, though certain
of the children clearly are demanding more of the teacher's
attention, and they are getting it. Asking them what they
understand of the task in hand, the answers are very similar to
last week's, limited to procedural comments, or a rehashing of
the answers made earlier: the water's dirty; there's more water
in this one. My responses can also only be procedural, given the
appropriateness or otherwise of the task for this group. They are
nowhere near understanding what is going on, neither do they
care. My comments are of the variety: do you know what to do?
How are they different? Have you drawn anything yet? The
children's responses last for only as long as I am present. I feel
more acutely the inappropriateness of this kind of support and
the support which the teaching assistant is providing.

(Thomas, 1992: 209–11)

Sadly, my attempts to theorize on this have proved less lasting and less
useful to me than the diary itself (and I won't bother to include examples

of the 'theorization' here). If I were modest, I would say that this was because of my own shortcomings as a theorist during my doctoral work, but I don't really, deep down believe this to be the case. Indeed, my immodesty has been confirmed by my subsequent experience of examining postgraduate and doctoral work, where I see a search for theory inexorably leading to many of the same kinds of distortions of good ideas that occurred in my own case.

Some might say that avenues of theoretical analysis provide leading-off points, platforms from which to jump, and this is the sense meant by Foucault (1980: 81) when he suggests that established theories can be played with, theatricalized and caricatured. He seems to be saying that they should be treated merely as starting points in a kind of brainstorming exercise. One can certainly do this in a more or less deliberate way, but one must be aware in so doing that one is using such constructs merely as Bourdieu's 'thinking tools'. One should be wary of using them as lenses or moulds for thinking. (See Bourdieu, in Wacquant, 1989: 50).

One more example: this one also from my own PhD. This one is given to show how I used a theory – George Kelly's (1955/1991) personal construct theory – for framing my analysis, but in fact the model I adopted ultimately veered so far from that which the theory would have dictated that it would surely be rejected by proponents and followers of construct theory (for there are, indeed, 'followers'). The thing was, that I *felt* that theory should be used to frame the analysis – because of all the expectations that I have already discussed – but this theory ultimately produced such a restricting die into which I had to pour my thinking that I was forced to change it substantially. While I am convinced now of the absolute correctness of my decision, at the time I was haunted by fears of how this would be seen by my supervisors and my examiners. How dare I damage the theory?

For this element of my research I had undertaken eight semi-structured interviews with support teachers. These were initially to be analysed using the framework of personal construct theory to reveal the 'bipolar' nature of the constructs held by these teachers. But it occurred to me before very long that 'bipolarity', an idea central and essential to construct theory, was unnecessary. What I was trying to do, after all, was find out the ways that support teachers thought about their work – the problems and the opportunities; they may have construed things in particular ways, but why should these construals be 'bipolar'?

I decided to use Jones's (1985) cognitive mapping as a way of interpreting my findings and presenting that interpretation. Jones's method enables the drawing-out of bipolar constructs and further enables the revelation of another aspect of construct theory, which is about the ordinal relation between constructs. This is as part of the 'organization corollary' – as Kelly (1955/1991: 5) puts it, 'Each person characteristically evolves for his convenience in anticipating events, a construction system embracing ordinal relationships between constructs'. So there are superordinate and subordinate constructs. Jones's mapping system reveals constructs in which the subordinate and superordinate constructs are linked.

I decided that the theoretical corset was becoming too tight. I boldly asserted, 'The adaptation I use will make no pretence at drawing such distinctions [i.e. between subordinate, superordinate constructs, etc.]. The "constructs" elicited will be related to the interpretive schemata isolated earlier, and interrelationships will be marked if they are evident'. However, given my fears about potential charges of misuse and abuse to the theory, I hedged my bets by proceeding with 'The personal nature of the respondents' own construct systems will then be discussed in the light of this analysis, drawing out the bipolar nature of these personal constructs where this is evident and any superordinate and subordinate features'. I did this, but it added nothing to the analysis.

To illustrate the process and my adaptation of it I reproduce here the explanation of my adaptation, followed by an example of one of those cognitive maps and my commentary on it:

> For the purposes of the mapping, key statements are summarised and boxed for clarity. Each box is numbered as an identification code for reference in the subsequent commentary. Numbers and the shape of the map are arbitrary in Jones's system; here, the numbers retain the temporal flow and logic (which may be of interest) by representing the sequence of the utterances. Where statements are interrelated they are joined by lines. A continuous arrowed line indicates a connotative relationship whereby the utterance at the end of the arrow appears to subsume or explain in some way the related utterance. Dotted lines represent tentative links between ideas. Shaded boxes represent the clearest elicitation of personal constructs and the labels in upper-case accompanying them represent what Jones calls second-order categorisations, which are schemata grounded in those of the interviewee, but framed in the context of the research already undertaken.
>
> This is a head of support in a secondary school. Here, the perception of threat is ascribed to personal features of the teacher: confidence (1) or discipline problems (2) causing in this teacher's mind the perception of threat. The construct appears in this respondent's mind to be linked with personality: it might be called 'high self-regard versus low self-regard' on the part of the teachers with whom she works. She linked threat, at least in the sequence of her account, with territory: the specific territorial marking shown by (3) subsumes a range of expectations concerned with the proper role of the 'remedial teacher' and fear about having someone else present.
>
> Organisation, construed apparently as 'formal teaching versus mixed ability teaching', restricts the role she is able to fulfil (6, 7, 10). She feels like a 'spare part' in some classes.
>
> Although it is not as crucial as it was for the previous respondent, communication ('good communication versus poor communication') is

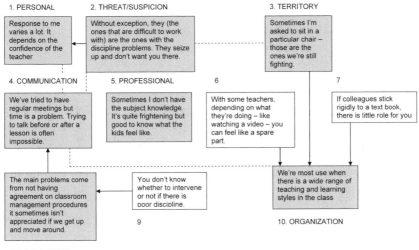

important in the construct system of this interviewee. Subsumed under it is the notion of role clarity; in (4) and (8) are clear statements that good communication will be about establishing procedures. In turn, role will be positively shaped by a greater emphasis on this communication. In this interview, then, there are both dispositional and situational attributions.

I have said that construct theory was distorted out of recognition by my adaptations of it. However, it provided me with ideas – or tools for thinking in Foucault's and Bourdieu's terms. But, like faces in the clouds, these are temporary images that lead the mind this way or that. They cannot – or at least they have not provided for me – prescriptions for the course and design of my research or the interpretation of its findings. Had I allowed them to do so, as in certain places I did, my work would have been (and was) the poorer for it.

* * *

Remembering Igor Stravinsky's comment that 'Too many pieces of music finish too long after the end', I think I should be closing. I can't end better than Wilfred Carr, who says,

> those who were engaged in the twentieth-century educational theory debate have been climbing a ladder that we are now in a position to throw away. And, if this is so, then all that now remains to be done is to accept, without regret or nostalgia, that the educational theory project has run its course and that the time has now come for us to bring it to a dignified end.
>
> (2006:150)

Carr is talking here of an *educational* theory debate, that is to say – if I read him correctly – one rather more restricted than the one at which I have been trying to look in this book. If one could draw a Venn diagram of theory use and theory talk, and one could put all ideas about theory into one circle, and all ideas about personal knowledge into another, and one then overlapped the circles by a sliver, Carr's conception of educational theory as it is currently conceived would be in the intersection. For me, the debate is far broader. Wherever one places the debate, whether it can come to an end, dignified or otherwise, is a moot point. It is perhaps a little too optimistic to think that it can, for we have all, to repeat Schön's (1987) comment, 'been socialized to ... believe that the only thing that really counts ... is *theory*, and the higher and the more abstract and the more general the theory, the higher the status it is'. The best hope is perhaps for a more reflective, more hesitant approach to theory – or in the word beloved of American educators, one that is more 'nuanced'. To be critical and self-critical is the key, even in one's approach to theory.

Notes

1. The fact that it is *about* theory, of course, does not make it 'theoretical' (except in the most superficial sense), and this is not, I assume, what Carr means when he talks of a 'theoretical argument'.
2. As Knapp and Michaels (1985b: 145) suggest, to think there is a distinction between having beliefs and 'really knowing' is to be a theorist. Carr accepts that there is no 'real knowing', so in the terms of Knapp and Michaels he is not one. But this does not diminish the validity or force of his argument.
3. For a more discursive account, particularly of the relationship of *technê* and *epistêmê* see Parry (2003).
4. ... but emphatically not discovery of 'theory', for reasons given in Chapter 6.
5. This is similar to Oakeshott's (1989: 65) 'historic languages ... customs, conventions, procedures and practices, canons, maxims and principles of conduct'.
6. Only if the claims of general hermeneutics were accurate (i.e. to principles that hold true all of the time, which of course is impossible in education) would it have earned the right to call itself 'theory', Hirsch (1976) says.
7. Interestingly Lévi-Strauss's discussion of bricolage comes in his book *The Savage Mind* (1962/1966), which in its original, French form, *La Pensée Sauvage*, offers a pun in the alternative meaning, namely *wild pansies*. Lévi-Strauss suggested the English title be *Pansies for Thought*.
8. ... namely, a sort of word mirroring of Gödel's self-referential construction.
9. I can imagine that many, picking up this book (and not, inexplicably, having read it from the front cover to the present point), seeing that I say that my thoughts for the diary were 'untheorized', would say, 'But you were theorizing all the time you were writing the diary'. I wasn't: I was thinking, not theorizing. See the rest of the book.

References

Adams, D. (1979) *The Hitch-hiker's Guide to the Galaxy*. Basingstoke: Pan.

Adams, J. (1912) *The Evolution of Educational Theory*. London: Macmillan.

Adams, J. (1927) *Educational Theories*. London: Ernest Benn.

Althusser, L. (1979) *For Marx*. London: Verso.

Alvesson, M. and Sköldberg, K. (2000) *Reflexive Methodology: New Vistas for Qualitative Research*. London: Sage.

Anderson, L.W. and Pellicer, L.O. (1990) Synthesis of research on compensatory and remedial education, *Educational Leadership*, 48(1): 10–16.

Andreski, S. (1972) *Social Sciences as Sorcery*. London: André Deutsch.

Atkinson, T. and Claxton, G. (2000) *The Intuitive Practitioner*. Maidenhead: Open University Press.

Ayer, A.J. (1985) *Ludwig Wittgenstein*. London: Penguin.

Babchuk, W.A. (1997) Glaser or Strauss? Grounded theory and adult education. Paper presented to the Midwest Research-to-Practice Conference in Adult, Continuing and Community Education. Michigan State University, East Lansing, Michigan, 15–17 October.

Ball, S.J. (1993) Self doubt and soft data: social and technical trajectories in ethnographic fieldwork, in: M. Hammersley (ed.) *Educational Research: Current Issues*. London: Paul Chapman.

Ball, S.J. (1995) Intellectuals or technicians? The urgent role of theory in educational studies. *British Journal of Educational Studies*, 33: 255–71.

Bannister, D. and Fransella, F. (1971) *Inquiring Man: The Psychology of Personal Constructs*. Beckenham: Croom Helm.

Barnes, B. (1990). Thomas Kuhn, in Q. Skinner (ed.) *The Return of Grand Theory in the Human Sciences*. Cambridge: Canto.

Barrett, W. (1978) *The Illusion of Technique*. New York: Anchor Doubleday.

Barrow, J. (1997) *The values of science*. Oxford: The Amnesty Lectures.

Bassey (2001) A solution to the problem of generalization in educational research: fuzzy prediction. *Oxford Review of Education*, 27(1): 5–22.

Bateson, G. (1972/2000) *Steps to an Ecology of Mind*. Chicago: University of Chicago Press.

Becker, H.S. (1993) Theory: the necessary evil, in D.J. Flinders and G.E. Mills (eds) *Theory and Concepts in Qualitative Research: Perspectives from the Field.* New York: Teachers College Press.

Becker, H.S. (1996) The epistemology of qualitative research, in R. Jessor, A. Colby and R. Schweder (eds) *Essays on Ethnography and Human Development.* Chicago: University of Chicago Press.

Becker, H.S. (1998) *Tricks of the Trade.* Chicago: University of Chicago Press.

Becker, H.S., Geer, B., Hughes, E.C. and Strauss, A.L. (1961) *Boys in White: Student Culture in Medical School .* Chicago: University of Chicago Press.

Benjamin, S. (2003) *The Micropolitics of Inclusive Education.* Maidenhead: Open University Press.

Berger, P.L. and Luckmann, T. (1979) *The Social Construction of Reality: A Treatise in the Sociology of Knowledge.* Harmondsworth: Penguin.

Berlin, I. (1969) *Four Essays on Liberty.* Oxford: Oxford University Press.

Berlin, I. (1979) *Against the Current.* London: The Hogarth Press.

Berlin, I. (1996) *The Sense of Reality.* London: Chatto & Windus.

Bijou, S.W. (1970) What psychology has to offer education – now, *Journal of Applied Behavior Analysis*, 3: 65–71.

Blase, J.J. (1987) Dimensions of effective school leadership: the teacher's perspective, *American Educational Research Journal*, 24(4), 589–610,

Blaser, M.J. (ed.) (1989) *Campylobacter Pylori in Gastritis and Peptic Ulcer Disease.* New York: Igaku-Shoin.

Bourdieu, P. (1992) Thinking about limits, *Theory, Culture and Society*, 9: 37–49.

Bourdieu, P. and Eagleton, T. (1994) Doxa and common life: an interview, in S. Zizek (ed.) *Mapping Ideology.* London: Verso.

Bouveresse, J. (1995): *Wittgenstein Reads Freud: The Myth of the Unconscious.* Princeton, NJ: Princeton University Press.

Bower, T.G.R. (1982) *Development in Infancy* (2nd edn). San Francisco: W.H. Freeman.

Brooker, P. (1991) Postmodern postpoetry, in A. Easthope and J. Thompson (eds) *Contemporary Poetry Meets Modern Theory.* Hemel Hempstead: Harvester Wheatsheaf.

Brown, A.L. and Campione, J.C. (1986) Psychological theory and the study of learning disabilities, *American Psychologist*, 41: 1059–68.

Bruner, J. (1986) *Actual Minds: Possible Worlds.* Boston, MA: Harvard University Press.

Bruner, J., Goodnow, J.J. and Austin, G. A. (1972) Categories and cognition, in J.P. Spradley (ed.) *Culture and Cognition.* New York: Chandler.

Bruner, J. and Postman, L. (1949) On the perception of incongruity: a paradigm, *Journal of Personality*, 18: 206–23.

Bryant, P.E. (1984) Piaget, teachers and psychologists, *Oxford Review of Education*, 10(3): 251–9.

Bryant, P.E. and Kopytynska, H. (1976) Spontaneous measurement by young children, *Nature*, 260: 773.

Bryman, A. and Cramer, D. (1994) *Quantitative Data Analysis for Social Scientists.* London: Routledge.

Butz, W.P. and Torrey, B.B. (2006) Some frontiers in social science, *Science*, 312 (5782): 1898–1900.

Canguilhem, G. (1994) The various models, in F. Delaporte (ed.) *A Vital Rationalist: Selected Writings from Georges Canguilhem*. New York: Zone Books.

Carr, W. (1987) What is an educational practice?, *Journal of Philosophy of Education*, 22(2): 163–75.

Carr, W. (1995) *For Education: Towards Critical Educational Enquiry*. Buckingham: Open University Press.

Carr, W. (2006) Education without theory, *British Journal of Educational Studies*, 54(2): 136–59.

Carr, W. and Kemmis, S. (1986) *Becoming Critical: Education, Knowledge and Action Research*. London: Falmer.

Chambers, J.H. (1992) *Empiricist Research on Teaching: A Philosophical and Practical Critique of Its Scientific Pretensions*. Dordrecht: Kluwer Academic.

Charmaz, K. (1988) The grounded theory method: an explication and interpretation, in R.M. Emerson (ed.) *Contemporary Field Research: A Collection of Readings*. Prospect Heights, IL: Waveland Press.

Charmaz, K. (1995) Grounded theory, in J.A. Smith, R. Harré and L. Van Langenhove (eds) *Rethinking Methods in Psychology*. London: Sage.

Charmaz, K. (2000) Grounded theory: objectivist and constructivist methods, in N.K. Denzin and Y.E. Lincoln (eds) *Handbook of Qualitative Research* (2nd edn). Thousand Oaks, CA: Sage.

Charmaz, K. and Mitchell, R. (1996) The myth of silent authorship, *Symbolic Interaction*, 19: 285–302.

Checkland, P.B. (1972) Towards a systems based methodology for real-world problem solving, *Journal of Systems Engineering*, 3(2) .

Checkland, P.B. (1981) *Systems Thinking, Systems Practice*. Chichester: Wiley.

Chomsky, N. (1980) *Rules and Representations*. Oxford: Blackwell.

Cicourel, A.V. (1979) Field research: the need for stronger theory and more control over the data base, in W.E. Snizek, E.R. Fuhrman and M.K. Miller (eds) *Contemporary Issues in Theory and Research: A Metasociological Perspective*. London: Aldwych.

Clarke, A. (1998) *Disciplining Reproduction: Modernity, American Life Sciences and the Problems of Sex*. Berkeley, CA: University of California Press.

Claxton, G. (1997) *Hare Brain Tortoise Mind: Why Intelligence Increases When You Think Less*. London: Fourth Estate.

Cohen, L. and Manion, L. (2000) *Research Methods in Education (5th edn)*. London: Routledge.

Collingwood, R.G. (1946/1994) *The Idea of History*. Oxford, Oxford University Press.

Conrad, C.F. (1978) A grounded theory of academic change, *Sociology of Education*, 51:101–12.

Cover, T.L. and Blaser, M.J. (1992) Helicobacter pylori and gastroduodenal disease, *Annual Review of Medicine*, 43: 133–45.

Crews, F. (1997) *The Memory Wars: Freud's Legacy in Dispute*. London: Granta.

Crosby, A.W. (1993) *Ecological Imperialism: The Biological Expansion of Europe*. Cambridge: Canto.

Dawkins, R. (1982). *The Extended Phenotype*. Oxford: Oxford University Press.

De Bruyn Ouboter, R. (1997) Heike Kamerlingh Onnes's discovery of superconductivity, *Scientific American*, 276(3): 84–9.

Deleuze, G. (1993) Rhizome versus trees, in C.V. Boundas (ed.) *The Deleuze Reader*. New York: Columbia University Press.

Dennett, D.C. (1993) *Consciousness Explained*. London: Penguin.

Denzin, N.K. (1994) The art and politics of interpretation, In N.K. Denzin and Y.S. Lincoln (eds) *Handbook of Qualitative Research*. Thousand Oaks, CA: Sage.

Derrida, J. (1978) *Writing and Difference*. London: Routledge & Kegan Paul.

Deutsch, K.W., Platt, J. and Senghaas, D. (1971) Conditions favoring major advances in social science, *Science*, 171(3970): 450–9.

Dewey, J. (1920) *Reconstruction in Philosophy*. New York: Holt.

Dewey, J. (1966) *Selected Educational Writings*. London: Heinemann.

Dey, I. (1999) *Grounding Grounded Theory: Guidelines for Qualitative Inquiry*. London: Academic Press.

Dilthey, W. (1883/1989) *Selected Works: Introduction to the Human Sciences Vol 1*. Princeton, NJ: Princeton University Press.

Donaldson, M. (1978) *Children's Minds*. London: Fontana.

Douglas, M. (1975) *Implicit Meanings*. London: Routledge.

Drake, St.C. and Cayton, H. (1945) *Black Metropolis*. New York: Harcourt, Brace and Co.

Dyson, F. (1997) *Imagined Worlds*. Cambridge, MA: Harvard University Press.

Eagleton, T. (1991) *Ideology*. London: Verso.

Eagleton, T. (2004) *After Theory*. London: Penguin.

Eisner, E. (1991) *The Enlightened Eye: Qualitative Inquiry and the Enhancement of Educational Practice*. New York: Macmillan.

Eliot, T.S. (1969) *The Complete Poems and Plays of T.S. Eliot*. London: Faber & Faber.

Elkind, D. (1967) Piaget's conservation problems, *Child Development*, *38*: 15–27.

Elliott, J. (2004) Making evidence-based practice educational, in G. Thomas and R. Pring (eds) *Evidence-based Practice in Education*. Maidenhead: Open University Press.

Elliott, J. (2006) Educational research as a form of democratic rationality, *Journal of Philosophy of Education*, 40(2): 169–85.

Feyerabend, P. (1993) *Against Method* (3rd edn). London: Verso/New Left Books.

Finn, G. (1992). Piaget, psychology and education, *Scottish Educational Review*, 24(2): 125–31.

Fish, S. (1989) *Doing What Comes Naturally*. Oxford: Clarendon Press.

Fish, S. (1994) *There's No Such Thing as Free Speech*. Oxford: Oxford University Press.

Foucault, M. (1980) Two lectures in C. Gordon (ed.) *Power/Knowledge: Selected Interviews and Other Writings 1972—1977 – Michel Foucault*. London: Harvester Wheatsheaf.

Foucault, M. (1981). Questions of method: an interview with Michel Foucault, *Ideology and Consciousness*, 8(Spring): 3–14.

Foucault, M. (1985) *Discipline and Punish: The Birth of the Prison*. Harmondsworth: Penguin.

Fouts, R.S. and Fouts, D.H. (1993) Chimpanzees' use of sign language, in P. Cavalieri and P. Singer (eds) *The Great Ape Project: Equality beyond Humanity*. London: Fourth Estate.

Freeman, D. (1996) *Margaret Mead and the Heretic: The Making and Unmaking of an Anthropological Myth*. Victoria: Penguin Books.

Fuller, S. (2002) *Thomas Kuhn: A Philosophical History for Our Times*. Chicago: Chicago University Press.

Fuller, S. (2003) *Kuhn vs Popper*. Cambridge: Icon Books.

Furlong, J. (2000) Intuition and the crisis in teacher professionalism, in T. Atkinson and G. Claxton (eds) *The Intuitive Practitioner*. Maidenhead: Open University Press.

Gadamer, H.-G. (1960/1975) *Truth and Method*. London: Sheed and Ward.

Garrison, J.W. (1988) The impossibility of atheoretical educational science, *Journal of Educational Thought*, 22(1): 21–6.

Geertz, C. (1975) *The Interpretation of Cultures*. London: Hutchinson.

Geertz, C. (1995) *After the fact: Two Countries, Four Decades, One Anthropologist*. Cambridge, MA: Harvard University Press.

Gehrke, N.J. (1981) A grounded theory study of beginning teachers' role personalization through reference group relations, *Journal of Teacher Education*, 32(6): 34–8.

Gelman, R. (1982) Accessing one-to-one correspondence: still another paper about conservation, *British Journal of Psychology*, 73: 209–21.

Giddens, A. (1990) Jürgen Habermas, in Q. Skinner (ed.) *The Return of Grand Theory in the Human Sciences*. Cambridge: Canto.

Giddens, A. (1991) *Modernity and Self-identity: Self and Society in the Late Modern Age*. Cambridge: Polity Press.

Giddens, A. (1994) *Beyond Left and Right: The Future of Radical Politics*. Cambridge: Polity Press.

Giddens, A. (1996) *In Defence of Sociology*. Cambridge: Polity Press.

Giroux, H.A. (1988) Postmodernism and the discourse of educational criticism, *Journal of Education*, 170(3): 5–30.

Gitlin, A., Siegel, M. and Boru, K. (1989) The politics of method: from leftist ethnography to educative research, *Qualitative Studies in Education*, 2(3): 237–53.

Glaser, B.G. (1992) *Basics of Grounded Theory Analysis*. Mill Valley, CA: Sociology Press.

Glaser, B.G. and Strauss, A.L. (1967) *The Discovery of Grounded Theory: Strategies for Qualitative Research*. New York: Aldine.

Glenn, S.A. (1993) Onset of theory of mind: methodological considerations, *Early Child Development and Care*, 86: 39–51.

Grayling, A.C. (1997) Intellectual or academic, *Prospect*, Jan.: 15.

Green, A. (1994) Postmodernism and state education, *Journal of Education Policy*, 9(1): 67–83.

Gruber, H.E. and Voneche, J.J. (eds) (1977) *The Essential Piaget*. London: Routledge and Kegan Paul.

Haack, S. (2003) *Defending Science – Within Reason: Between Scientism and Cynicism*. Amherst, NY: Prometheus Books.

Haack, S. (2005) Disentangling *Daubert*: an epistemological study in theory and practice. *Journal of Philosophy, Science and Law*, 5, May. Available at: www.psljournal.com/archives/all/haackpaper.html

Habermas, J. (1973) *Theory and Practice*. Boston, MA: Beacon Press.

Habermas, J. (1990) *The Philosophical Discourse of Modernity: Twelve Lectures*. Cambridge: Polity Press.

Habermas, J. (1991) *Communication and the Evolution of Society.* Cambridge: Polity Press.

Habermas, J. (1992) The dialectics of rationalisation in P. Dews (ed.) *Autonomy and Solidarity: Interviews with Jürgen Habermas* (revised edn). London: Verso.

Haig, B.D. (1995) Grounded theory as scientific method. *Philosophy of Education, 1995: Current issues* (pp. 281–290). Urbana: University of Illinois Press.

Haldane, J.B.S. (1965) The duty of doubt, in A.F. Scott (ed.) *Topics and Opinions.* London: Macmillan.

Hall, C.S. and Lindzey, G. (1978) *Theories of Personality* (3rd edn). New York: Wiley.

Hammersley, M. (1985) From ethnography to theory: a programme and paradigm in the sociology of education, *Sociology,* 19(2): 244–59

Hammersley, M. (1992) *What's Wrong with Ethnography?* London: Routledge.

Hammersley, M. (2001) On Michael Bassey's concept of the fuzzy generalization, *Oxford Review of Education,* 27(2): 219–25.

Hammersley, M. (2003) Too good to be false? The ethics of belief and its implications for the evidence-based character of educational research, policymaking and practice. Paper presented at the British Educational Research Association Annual Conference, Heriot-Watt University, Edinburgh, 11–13 September.

Hammersley, M. (2005a) Assessing quality in qualitative research. Presentation to ESRC TLRP seminar series: Quality in Educational Research, University of Oxford, 7 July.

Hammersley, M. (2005b) A brief response about dissent, the 'duty of doubt', etc, *International Journal of Research and Method in Education,* 28(2): 105–7.

Hammersley, M. (2005c) Countering the 'new orthodoxy' in educational research, *British Educational Research Journal,* 31(2): 139–55.

Harry, B., Sturges, K.M. and Klinger, J.K. (2005) Mapping the process: an exemplar of process and challenge in grounded theory analysis, *Educational Researcher,* 34(2): 3–13.

Hearnshaw, L.S. (1979) *Cyril Burt: Psychologist.* London: Hodder and Stoughton.

Hill, D., McLaren, P., Cole, M. and Rikowski, G. (1999) *Postmodernism in Educational Theory.* London: The Tufnell Press.

Hirsch, E.D. (1976) *The Aims of Interpretation.* Chicago: University of Chicago Press.

Hirst, P.H. (1966) Educational theory, in J.W. Tibble (ed.) *The Study of Education.* London: Routledge and Kegan Paul.

Hirst, P.H. (1993) Educational theory, in M. Hammersley (ed.) *Educational Research: Current Issues.* London: Paul Chapman.

Hoffman, B. (1973) *Albert Einstein.* London: Hart-Davis MacGibbon.

Hoffman, P. (1989) *Archimedes' Revenge.* London: W.W. Norton.

Hofstadter, D.R. (2000) *Gödel, Escher, Bach: An Eternal Golden Braid.* London: Penguin.

Holton, G. (1995) The controversy over the end of science, *Scientific American,* 273(4); 168.

Hoy, D. (1990) Jacques Derrida, in Q. Skinner (Ed.) *The Return of Grand Theory in the Human Sciences.* Cambridge: Canto.

Hughes, M. (1975) Egocentrisms in preschool children. Unpublished PhD dissertation, University of Edinburgh.

Hume, D. (1748/1910) *An Enquiry Concerning Human Understanding.* New York: P.F. Collier & Son.

Husserl, E. (1913/1983) *Ideas Pertaining to a Pure Phenomenology and to a Phenomenological Philosophy: General Introduction to a Pure Phenomenology.* Dordrecht: Kluwer.

Ignatieff, M. (1997) 'Where are they now?, *Prospect,* 22 August.

Illich, I. (1979) *Deschooling Society.* London: Pelican.

Illich, I. and Sanders, L. (1988) ABC: *The Alphabetization of the Popular Mind.* London: Penguin.

Jeffares, A.N. (ed.) (1962) *W.B. Yeats Selected Poetry.* London: Macmillan.

Jenkins, R. (1992) *Pierre Bourdieu.* London: Routledge.

Jones, S. (1985) The analysis of in-depth interviews, in R. Walker (ed.) *Applied Qualitative Research.* Aldershot: Gower.

Kant, I. (1784) An answer to the question: 'What is enlightenment?' Available at http://philosophy.eserver.org/kant/what-is-enlightenment.txt

Kaplan, A. (1964) *The conduct of inquiry.* San Francisco: Chandler Publishing.

Karmiloff-Smith, A. and Inhelder, B. (1974) If you want to get ahead, get a theory, *Cognition,* 3(3): 195–212.

Kavanagh, D. (1987) *Thatcherism and British Politics: The End of Consensus?* Oxford: Oxford University Press.

Kelly G.A. (1955/1991) *The psychology of personal constructs. Vol. II.* London: Routledge.

Kenny, A. (ed.) (1994) *The Wittgenstein Reader.* Oxford: Basil Blackwell.

Kerlinger, F.N. (1970) *Foundations of Behavioural Research.* New York: Holt, Rinehart and Winston.

Knapp, S. and Michaels, W.B. (1985a) Against theory, in W.J.T. Mitchell (ed.) *Against Theory: Literary Studies and the New Pragmatism.* Chicago: University of Chicago Press.

Knapp, S. and Michaels, W.B. (1985b) A reply to Richard Rorty: What is pragmatism?, in W.J.T. Mitchell (ed.) *Against Theory: Literary Studies and the New Pragmatism.* Chicago, University of Chicago Press.

Knapp, S. and Michaels, W.P. (1987) Against theory 2: hermeneutics and deconstruction, *Critical Inquiry,* 14: 49–68.

Koch, S. (1964) Psychology and emerging conceptions of knowledge as unitary, in T.W. Wann (ed.) *Behaviorism and Phenomenology.* Chicago: University of Chicago Press.

Köhler, W. (1925) *The Mentality of Apes.* New York: Harcourt.

Kuhn, T. (1970) *The Structure of Scientific Revolutions* (2nd edn). Chicago: University of Chicago Press.

LaBoskey, V.K. (1993) A conceptual framework for reflection in preservice teacher education, in J. Calderhead and P. Gates (eds) *Conceptualizing Reflection in Teacher Development.* London: The Falmer Press.

Latour, B. and Woolgar, S. (1979) *Laboratory Life: The Social Construction of Scientific Fact.* Beverly Hills, CA: Sage.

Lawson, A.E. (1992). What do tests of 'formal' reasoning actually measure?, *Journal of Research in Science Teaching,* 29(9): 965–83.

LeCompte, M.D. (1994). Defining reality: applying double description and chaos theory to the practice of practice, *Educational Theory,* 44(3): 277–98.

Lévi-Strauss, C. (1962/1966) *The Savage Mind*. Chicago: The University of Chicago Press.

Levitas R. (ed.) (1986) *The Ideology of the New Right*. Cambridge: Polity Press.

Lewin, K. (1951) *Field Theory in Social Science: Selected Theoretical Papers*. New York: Harper and Row.

Lincoln, Y.S. and Guba E.G. (1985) *Naturalistic Inquiry*. Beverly Hills, CA: Sage.

Lindblom, C.E. (1979) Still muddling, not yet through, *Public Administration Review*, 39: 517–26.

Lynch, M. (1985) *Art and artifact in laboratory science*. London: Routledge.

McGarrigle, J. and Donaldson, M. (1974) Conservation accidents, *Cognition*, 3: 341–50.

MacIntyre, A. (1985) *After Virtue: A Study in Moral Theory*. London: Duckworth.

MacIntyre, D. (1993) Theory, theorizing and reflection in initial teacher education, in J. Calderhead and P. Gates (eds) *Conceptualizing Reflection in Teacher Development*. London: The Falmer Press.

McIntyre, D. (1995) Initial teacher education as practical theorising: a response to Paul Hirst, *British Journal of Educational Studies*, 43(4): 365–83.

Magee, B. (1982). *Men of Ideas*. Oxford: Oxford University Press.

Martindale, D. (1979) Ideologies, paradigms and theories, in: W.E. Snizek, E.R. Fuhrman and M.K. Miller (eds) *Contemporary Issues in Theory and Research: a Metasociological Perspective*. London: Aldwych Press.

Medawar, P.B. (1974) *The Hope of Progress*. London: Wildwood House.

Medawar, P.B. (1982) *Pluto's Republic*. Oxford: Oxford University Press.

Medawar, P.B. and Medawar, J.S. (1977) *The Life Science*. London: Wildwood House.

Meiklejohn, A. (1966). Knowledge and intelligence, in R.D. Archambault (ed.) *Dewey on Education*. New York: Random House.

Mercer, J. (1973) *Labeling the Mentally Retarded*. Berkeley, CA: University of California Press.

Mezirow, J., Darkenwald, G.G. and Knox, A. (1975) *Last Gamble on Education*. Washington, DC: Adult Education Association of the USA.

Miller, G.A. (1956) The magical number seven, plus or minus two: some limits on our capacity for processing information, *Psychological Review*, 63: 81–97.

Miller, S. and Fredericks M. (1999) How does grounded theory explain?, *Qualitative Inquiry*, 9: 538–51.

Millson, P. and Singh, S. (eds) (1996) *Fermat's Last Theorem*. London: BBC.

Mitchell, W.J.T. (ed.) (1985) *Against Theory: Literary Studies and the New Pragmatism*. Chicago: The University of Chicago Press.

Monmaney, T. (1993) Marshall's hunch, *New Yorker*, 20 September.

Mouly, G.J. (1978). *Educational Research: The Art and Science of Investigation*. Boston, MA: Allyn and Bacon.

Mouzelis, N. (1995) *Sociological Theory: What Went Wrong?* London: Routledge.

Nadel, S.F. (1957) *The Theory of Social Structure*. London: Cohen and West.

Namier, L.B. (1955). *Personalities and Powers*. London: Macmillan.

Naughton, J. (1981). Theory and practice in systems research, *Journal of Applied Systems Analysis*, 8: 61–70.

Newcomer, P.L. and Hammill, D.D. (1975) 'ITPA and academic achievement, *Reading Teacher*, 28: 731–42.

Newell, A., Shaw, J.C. and Simon, H.A. (1957) *Programming the logic theory machine.* Proceedings of the 1957 Western Joint Computer Conference, pp. 230–40.

Newman, J. and Clarke, J. (1994) Going about our business: the managerialisation of public services, in J. Clarke, A. Cochrane and E. MacLaughlin (eds) *Managing Social Policy.* London: Sage.

Nisbett, R.E. (ed.) (1993). *Rules for Reasoning.* Hillsdale, NJ: Lawrence Erlbaum Associates.

Nisbett, R.E. and Wilson, T.D. (1977) Telling more than we can know: verbal reports on mental processes, *Psychological Review,* 84: 231–59.

Nozick, R. (1993) *The Nature of Rationality.* Princeton, NJ: Princeton University Press.

O'Connor, D.J. (1957) *An Introduction to the Philosophy of Education.* London: Routledge and Kegan Paul.

O'Neill, O. (2002) *A Question of Trust.* London: BBC Publications.

Oakeshott, M. (1962) *Rationalism in Politics.* London: Methuen.

Oakeshott, M. (1967a) Learning and teaching, in R.S. Peters (ed.) *The Concept of Education.* London: Routledge and Kegan Paul.

Oakeshott, M. (1967b) *Rationalism in Politics and Other Essays.* London: Methuen.

Oakeshott, M. (1972) Education, the engagement and its frustration, In R.F. Dearden et al (eds) *Education and the Development of Reason.* London: Routledge and Kegan Paul.

Oakeshott, M. (1989). Education: the engagement and the frustration, in T. Fuller (ed.) *The Voice of Liberal Learning: Michael Oakeshott on Education.* London: Yale University Press.

Oancea, A. (2005) Criticisms of educational research: key topics and levels of analysis, *British Educational Research Journal,* 31(2): 157–83.

Parry, R. (2003) *Episteme* and *Techne: The Stanford Encyclopedia of Philosophy.* Available at http://plato.stanford.edu/archives/sum2003/entries/episteme-techne/

Patrick, J. (1973) *A Glasgow Gang Observed.* London: Eyre Methuen.

Pawson, R. (2006) *Evidence-based Policy: A Realist Perspective.* London: Sage.

Pawson, R. and Tilley, N. (1997) *Realistic Evaluation.* London: Sage.

Peddiwell, J.A. (1939) *The Sabre-tooth Curriculum.* New York: McGraw-Hill.

Peierls, R.E. (1960) Wolfgang Ernst Pauli: 1900–1958. *Biographical Memoirs of Fellows of the Royal Society,* Vol. 5, 174–92. Available at http://links.jstor.org/sici?sici=0080–4606%28196002%295%3C174%3AWEP1%3E2.0.CO%3B2–L

Penrose, R. (1994) *Shadows of the Mind.* Oxford: Oxford University Press.

Pepin, B. (2006) Personal communication.

Philp, M. (1990) Michel Foucault, in Q. Skinner (ed.) *The Return of Grand Theory in the Human Sciences.* Cambridge: Canto.

Piaget, J. (1973) *The Child and Reality: Problems of Genetic Psychology.* London: Frederick Muller.

Piattelli-Palmarini, M. (ed.) (1980) *Language and Learning: The Debate between Jean Piaget and Noam Chomsky.* Cambridge, MA: Harvard University Press.

Polanyi, M. (1958) *Personal Knowledge: Towards a Post-critical Philosophy.* London: Routledge and Kegan Paul.

Polanyi, M. (1969) *Knowing and Being: Essays by Michael Polanyi.* London: Routledge and Kegan Paul.

Pólya, G. (1945/2004) *How to Solve It*. Princeton, NJ: Princeton Science Library.

Popper, K.R. (1953/1974) Science: conjectures and refutations. Paper presented at the British Council conference, Developments and Trends in Contemporary British philosophy, Peterhouse College, Cambridge

Popper, K.R. (1966) *The Open Society and Its Enemies*. London: Routledge and Kegan Paul.

Popper, K.R. (1968) *The Logic of Scientific Discovery*. London: Hutchison.

Popper, K.R. (1977) On hypotheses, in P.N. Johnson-Laird and P.C. Wason (eds) *Thinking: Readings in Cognitive Science*. Cambridge: Cambridge University Press.

Popper, K.R. (1989) *Conjectures and Refutations* (5th edn). London: Routledge.

Pring, R. (2000) *Philosophy of Educational Research*. London: Continuum.

Quine, W.V. (1963) *From a Logical Point of View*. New York: Harper and Row.

Rajagopalan, K. (1998) On the theoretical trappings of the thesis of anti-theory; or; why the idea of theory may not, after all, be all that bad: a response to Gary Thomas, *Harvard Educational Review*, 68(3): 335–52.

Rennie, D. and Flanagin, A. (1998) Congress on biomedical peer review: history, ethics and plans for the future, *Journal of the American Medical Association*, 280: 213–14.

Ricoeur, P. (1970) *Freud and Philosophy: An Essay on Interpretation*. New Haven, CT: Yale University Press.

Roberts, R.M. (1989) *Serendipity: Accidental Discoveries in Science*. New York: Wiley.

Robrecht, L. (1995) Grounded theory: Evolving methods, *Qualitative Health Research* 5: 169–77.

Roman, L. (1992) The political significance of narrating ethnography, in: M. LeCompte, W. Millroy and J. Goetz (eds.) *The Handbook of Qualitative Research in Education*. San Diego, CA: Academic Press.

Rorty, R. (1979) *Philosophy and the Mirror of Nature*. Princeton, NJ: Princeton University Press.

Rorty, R. (1982) *Consequences of Pragmatism (Essays: 1972—1980)*. Minneapolis, MN: University of Minnesota Press.

Rorty, R. (1991) *Essays on Heidegger and Others: Philosophical Papers, Vol II*. Cambridge: Cambridge University Press.

Rorty, R. (1998) *Advancing our Country: Leftist Thought in 20th-century America*. Cambridge, MA: Harvard University Press.

Russell, B. (1956) Galileo and scientific method, in A.F. Scott (ed.) *Topics and Opinions*. London: Macmillan.

Russell, C.A. (1991) The spread of Copernicanism in Northern Europe, in D. Goodman and C.A. Russell (eds) *The Rise of Scientific Europe 1500–1800*. London: Hodder & Stoughton.

Russell, C.A. (ed.) (1996) *Science in Europe 1500–1800: Vol. 1 A Primary Sources Anthology*. Milton Keynes: Open University Press.

Russell, J. (1992) The theory theory: so good they named it twice?, *Cognitive Development*, 7: 285–319.

Ryle, G. (1949) *The Concept of Mind*. London: Hutchinson.

Ryle, G. (1990) *The Concept of Mind*. London: Penguin.

Sacks, H. (1989) Lecture thirteen: On proverbs, In G. Jefferson (ed.) *Harvey Sacks: Lectures 1964–1965*. Dordrecht: Kluwer.

Saint-Just, L. (1976) De la nature, in A. Liénard (ed.) *Saint-Just: Théorie-politique: Textes établis et commentés par Alain Liénard*. Paris: Seuil.

Sanders, C. (1995) Stranger than fiction: insights and pitfalls in post-modern ethnography, in N.K. Denzin (ed.) *Studies in symbolic interaction* 17. Greenwich, CT: JAI.

Schama, S. (1996) *Landscape and Memory*. London: Fontana Press.

Schatzman, L. (1991) Dimensional analysis: notes on an alternative approach to the grounding of theory in qualitative research, in D.R. Maines (ed.) *Social Organisation and Social Process: Essays in Honor of Anselm Strauss*. New York: Aldine.

Scheffler, I. (1967) Philosophical models of teaching, in: R.S. Peters, (ed.) *The Concept of Education*. London: Routledge and Kegan Paul.

Schön, D.A. (1987) Educating the reflective practitioner. Paper presented to the Annual Meeting of the American Educational Research Association, Washington, DC.

Schön, D.A. (1991) *The Reflective Practitioner: How Professionals Think in Action*. Aldershot: Avebury.

Schooler, J.W. and Melcher, J. (1995) The ineffability of insight, in S.M. Smith, T.B. Ward and R.A. Finke (eds) *The Creative Cognition Approach*. Cambridge, MA: MIT Press.

Schunn, C.D. and Klahr, D. (1995) A 4–space model of scientific discovery, in J.D. Moore and J.F. Lehman (eds) *Proceedings of the Seventeenth Annual Conference of the Cognitive Science Society*. Mahwah, NJ: Erlbaum.

Schutz, A. (1962) Collected *Papers Vol. I: The Problem of Social Reality*. The Hague: Martinus Nijhoff.

Schutz, A. (1964) The stranger: an essay in social psychology, in *Collected Papers. Vol. II. Studies in Social Theory*. The Hague: Martinus Nijhoff.

Schutz, A. and Luckmann, T. (1974) *The Structures of the Life World*. London: Heinemann.

Sconiers, Z.D. and Rosiek, J.L. (2000) Historical perspective as an important element of teachers' knowledge: a sonata-form case study of equity issues in a chemistry classroom, *Harvard Educational Review*, 70(3): 370–404.

Searle, J.R. (1982) Minds, brains and programs, in D.R. Hofstadter and D.C. Dennett (eds) *The Mind's I: Fantasies and Reflections on Self and Soul*. London: Penguin.

Selden, R. and Widdowson, P. (1993). *A Reader's Guide to Contemporary Literary Theory*. Hemel Hempstead: Harvester Wheatsheaf.

Sherman, B. (1988) Hermeneutics in law, *Modern Law Review*, 51: 395–415.

Siegel, H. (1997) *Rationality Redeemed*. London: Routledge.

Simon, H.A. (1982) *Models of Bounded Rationality: Behavioral Economics and Business Organization*, Vol. 2. Cambridge, MA: MIT Press.

Simon, H.A. (1983) *Reason in Human Affairs*. Oxford: Basil Blackwell.

Simons, H. (1980) *Towards a Science of the Singular*. Norwich: CARE, UEA.

Skinner, Q. (ed.) (1990) *The Return of Grand Theory in the Human Sciences*. Cambridge: Canto.

Smith, F. (1992) *To Think: In Language Learning and Education*. London: Routledge.

Smith, G.B. (1995) *Nietzsche, Heidegger, and the Transition to Postmodernity*. Chicago: University of Chicago Press.

Snizek, W.E. (1979) Toward a clarification of the interrelationship between theory and research: its form and implications, in W.E. Snizek, E.R. Fuhrman and M.K. Miller (eds) *Contemporary Issues in Theory and Research: A Metasociological Perspective*. London: Aldwych Press.

Speck, B. W. (1993) *Publication Peer Review: An Annotated Bibliography*. Westport, CT: Greenwood Press.

Spector, B.A. and Gibson, C.W. (1991) A qualitative study of middle school students' perceptions of factors facilitating the learning of science: Grounded theory and existing theory. *Journal of Research in Science Teaching*, 28(6): 467–84.

Stenhouse, L. (1975) *An Introduction to Curriculum Research and Development*. London: Heinemann.

Storr, A. (1997) *Feet of Clay: A Study of Gurus*. London: HarperCollins.

Strauss, A. (1987) *Qualitative Analysis for Social Scientists*. Cambridge: Cambridge University Press.

Strauss, A. and Corbin, J. (eds) (1997) *Grounded Theory in Practice*. Thousand Oaks, CA: Sage.

Strauss, A. and Corbin, J. (1998) *Basics of Qualitative Research: Techniques and Procedures for Developing Grounded Theory*. Thousand Oaks, CA: Sage.

Stronach, I. (1997) Research method in the postmodern (book review), *Sociological Research Online*, 2: 160–1.

Stronach, I. and MacLure, M. (1997) *Educational Research Undone: The Postmodern Embrace*. Buckingham: Open University Press.

Suppes, P. (1974) The place of theory in educational research, *Educational Researcher*, 3(6): 3–10.

Susser, M. (1967) Causes of peptic ulcer: a selective epidemiological review, *Journal of Chronic Diseases*, 20: 435–56.

Suzuki, D. (1995). Ulcer wars. Horizon transcript, Programme Number: LSFA543K. London: BBC

Tavor Bannet, E. (1997) Analogy as translation: Wittgenstein, Derrida, and the law of language, *New Literary History* 28(4): 655–72.

Thagard, P. (1998) Ulcers and bacteria I: Discovery and acceptance. *Studies in History and Philosophy of Science. Part C: Studies in History and Philosophy of Biology and Biomedical Sciences*, 29: 107–36.

Theroux, P. (1993) *The Happy Isles of Oceania: Paddling the Pacific*. London: Penguin.

Thomas, G. (1992) *Effective Classroom Teamwork: Support or Intrusion*. London: Routledge.

Thomas, G. (1997) What's the use of theory?, *Harvard Educational Review*, 67(1): 75–105.

Thomas, G. (2002) Theory's spell: on qualitative inquiry and educational research, *British Educational Research Journal*, 28(3): 419–34.

Thomas, G. and Pring, R. (2004) *Evidence-based Practice in Education*. Maidenhead: Open University Press.

Thomas, G., Walker, D. and Webb. J. (1998) *The Making of the Inclusive School*. London: Routledge.

Thomson, A. (1996) *Critical Reasoning: A Practical Introduction*. London: Routledge.

Thouless, R.H. (1968) *Straight and Crooked Thinking*. London: Pan.

Tibble, J.W. (ed.) (1966) *The Study of Education*. London: Routledge and Kegan Paul.

Toffler, A. (1985) *The Adaptive Corporation*. Aldershot: Gower.

Tolstoy, L.N. (1954) *Anna Karenin*. London: Penguin.

Tomlinson, S. (1982) *A Sociology of Special Education*. London: Routledge and Kegan Paul.

Torrance, H. (2004) Using action research to generate knowledge about educational practice, in G. Thomas and R. Pring (eds) *Evidence-based Practice in Education*. Maidenhead: Open University Press.

Toulmin, S. (1972) *Human Understanding. Vol I*. Oxford: Clarendon Press.

Turner, D.A. (2004) *Theory of Education*. London: Continuum.

Turney, J. (2004) Review of defending science: within reason: between scientism and cynicism, *Times Higher Educational Supplement*, 23 April.

Tversky, A. and Kahneman, D. (1974) Judgment under uncertainty: heuristics and biases, *Science* 185(4157): 1124–31.

Van Goor, R., Heyting, F., and Vreeke, G.-J. (2004) Beyond foundations: signs of the new normativity in philosophy of education, *Educational Theory*, 54(2): 173–92.

Vauclair, J. (1996) *Animal Cognition*. Cambridge, MA: Harvard University Press.

Vernon, P.E. (1964) *Personality Assessment: A Critical Survey*. London: Methuen.

Vickers, G. (1965) *The Art of Judgment: A Study of Policy Making*. London: Chapman and Hall.

Wacquant, L.D. (1989) Towards a reflexive sociology: a workshop with Pierre Bourdieu. *Sociological Theory*, 7: 26–63.

Warburton, N. (1996) *Thinking from A to Z*. London: Routledge.

Wason, P. and Johnson-Laird, N.J. (1972) *Psychology of Reasoning: Structure and Content*. London: B.T. Batsford.

White-Miles, H.L. (1993). Language and the orang-utan: the old 'person', in P. Cavalieri and P. Singer (eds) *The Great Ape Project: Equality beyond Humanity*. London: Fourth Estate.

Winter, R. (1987) *Action Research and the Nature of Social Inquiry: Professional Innovation and Educational Work*. Aldershot: Gower.

Wood, J.M., Nezworski, T., Lilienfeld, S.O. and Garb, H.N. (2003) *What's Wrong with the Rorschach? Science Confronts the Controversial Inkblot Test*. San Francisco: John Wiley.

Woods, P. (1992) Symbolic interactionism: theory and method, in M.D. LeCompte, W.L. Millroy and J. Preissle (eds) *The Handbook of Qualitative Research in Education*. New York: Academic Press.

Wright Mills, C. (1959/1970) *The Sociological Imagination*. New York: Holt.

Yeats W.B. (1970) The writings of William Blake, in J.P. Frayne (ed.) *Uncollected Prose by W.B. Yeats, Vol I: First Reviews of Articles 1886–1896*. London: Macmillan.

Yeats, W.B. (1980) *Yeats: Selected Criticism and Prose*. London: Pan.

Ziman, J. (1991) *Reliable Knowledge*. Cambridge: Canto.

Index

RIGOUR AND COMPLEXITY IN EDUCATIONAL RESEARCH

Joe Kincheloe and Kathleen Berry

- What does it mean to engage in rigorous research?
- What does a researcher need to know to produce such research?
- What is specifically involved in multiple method bricolage research?

In an era where talk abounds about scientific rigour and evidence-based research in education, this groundbreaking book presents a new and compelling examination of these concepts. Arguing that much of what is promoted as 'rigorous inquiry' is reductionistic and ultimately misleading, the authors present an alternative to such approaches to educational inquiry.

Rigour and Complexity in Educational Research provides readers with an understanding of the complexities of educational research, and of the interrelationships between multiple methods, theoretical perspectives, philosophical orientations, social positionalities, modes of power, and narrative strategies.

The authors use the French term *'bricolage'* to signify the use of a variety of research tools and ways of seeing. The book then constructs a new conception of rigour in research that is culturally sensitive and socially transformative, and shows researchers how to use multiple methods. After developing this approach, the authors devise a practical process of initiating researchers into the *bricolage*, and provide concrete examples and guidelines for using this innovative approach.

This book is important reading for academics, researchers and students undertaking education and social science courses.

Contents: *Introduction: The power of the bricolage: Expanding research methods - Redefining rigor and complexity in research - Questions of disciplinarity/interdisciplinarity in a changing world - Redefining and interpreting the object of study - Structures of bricolage and complexity - Feedback looping for increasing complexity - Bricolage is many a new thing understood - References.*

208pp
978-0-335-21400-6 (Paperback)   978-0-335-21401-3 (Hardback)

BECOMING A RESEARCHER

A Companion to the Research Process

Mairead Dunne, John Pryor and Paul Yates

This innovative book combines what most books separate: research as practical activity and research as intellectual engagement. It clarifies and makes explicit the methodological issues that underlie the journey from initial research idea to the finished report and beyond.

The text moves the researcher logically through the research process and provides insights into methodology through an in-depth discussion of methods. It presents the research process as an engagement with text. This theme moves through the construction of text in the form of data and the deconstruction of text in analysis. Finally the focus moves to the reconstruction of text through the representation of the research in the report. Following through each of these stages in turn, the chapters consider either a practical issue or a group of methods and interrogate the associated methodological concerns. In addition, the book also addresses the rarely explored issues of the researcher as writer and researcher identity as core elements of the research process.

The book provides a range of insights and original perspectives. These successfully combine practical guidance with the invitation to consider the problematic nature of research as social practice. It is an ideal reference for those embarking on research for the first time and provides a new methodological agenda for established researchers.

Contents: *Introduction - Part 1 Distinguishing data: Constructing text - The logic of enquiry - Talking with people: Interviewing - Knowing with numbers: Questionnaires - Being There: Observation - Part 2 Dicing with data: Deconstructing text - Breaking down data: Routes to interpretation - Worrying at words: Discourse analysis - Pulverizing policy: Deconstructing documents - Part 3 Data with destiny: Reconstructing text - Writing research: Authoring text - The Selfish text: Research and identity - Methods and methodology.*

208pp

978-0-335-21394-8 (Paperback)   978-0-335-21395-5 (Hardback)